OVER THE TOP

HOW ONE MOVE CHANGED A CLIMBER'S LIFE

RUSSELL FRALICK

DISCOVERY HOUSE
PUBLISHERS®

Over the Top: How One Move Changed a Climber's Life

© 2013 by Russell Fralick

Discovery House is affiliated with RBC Ministries,
Grand Rapids, Michigan.

Scripture taken from the NEW AMERICAN STANDARD BIBLE®. Copyright © 1960, 1962, 1963, 1968, 1971, 1972, 1973, 1975, 1977 by The Lockman Foundation. Used by permission. (www.Lockman.org)

ISBN: 978-1-57293-751-2

Interior design by Michelle Espinoza

Printed in the United States of America

First printing in 2013

*For Sophia Elizabeth and Hannah Grace. The Christian walk
is the hardest climb in the world, but the view from the top
is the best there is. May your zeal for Him always exceed my own,
and may you both see vistas far beyond my own dreams.*

*And for Debbi . . . Always my favourite climbing partner,
always looking ever upward. I will try to keep up.*

CONTENTS

A WORD ABOUT ENGLISH: BRITISH AND AMERICAN

The question of how much an American publisher should change the wording of a book written by a British author is not new. It had to be considered when Scholastic Books published J. K. Rowling's wildly popular Harry Potter series. Some readers like those kinds of changes; others don't.

As Discovery House Publishers contemplated what changes to make in this book, written by British writer Russell Fralick, we decided to leave many of the British terms alone and provide a glossary just in case American readers were mildly confused.

For instance, there are some automobile terms, such as *boot* and *bonnet*, that help the author remind us that he is British—so we left them in. We think that context clues explain most of these terms, but in case that's not true, the reader can consult the glossary.

There are also some British products that might not be familiar to American readers. For instance, when you see the words Silk Cut and Shandy, we are pretty sure that unless you have spent some time in the U.K., you'll be clueless. If so, head for the glossary of British terms.

While we retained many British terms, we did, however, make some changes in the spelling of a few British words. For instance, in the United Kingdom, many words such as *anaesthetise* and *realise* and *authorise* use an "ise" where Americans spell those words with an "ize" at the end. Both spellings are acceptable, but we opted for the "ize." Also, we took the liberty to change "whilst" and "amongst" to "while" and "among" to avoid what sounded to American ears to be archaisms that would get in the way of smooth reading. We beg forgiveness of our U.K. friends if that seems awkward to them.

Many other words that have variant spellings, such as *colour* and *flavour*, have been retained with their British spellings—because we think those words help retain the British flavor of the book.

There is one other kind of term that we've tried to help the reader with: words relating to climbing. While we suspect that quite a few readers will know the difference between abseils and *au cheval*, we know that many could get lost in the terminology. Therefore, we have a glossary of climbing terms that we hope help clear up any confusion.

So, with that little lesson in British-American English in mind, we are eager to let you strap on your climbing harness and do us the honour of enjoying the adventures Russell Fralick shares with you in *Over the Top.*

*And David spoke the words of this song to the LORD in the day that
    the LORD delivered him from the hand of all his enemies and
    from the hand of Saul.*
And he said,
"The LORD is my rock and my fortress and my deliverer;
My God, my rock, in whom I take refuge;
My shield and the horn of my salvation, my stronghold and my refuge;
My saviour, Thou dost save me from violence.
I call upon the LORD, who is worthy to be praised;
And I am saved from my enemies.
For the waves of death encompassed me;
The torrents of destruction overwhelmed me;
The cords of Sheol surrounded me;
The snares of death confronted me.
In my distress I called upon the LORD,
Yes, I cried to my God;
And from His temple He heard my voice,
And my cry for help came into His ears."

2 Samuel 22:1–7

PROLOGUE

The steady drizzle quickly drenched my outer fleece and began to penetrate deeper into my inner clothing and down my neck. I could feel it soak further into the depths of my inner resources, stripping them increasingly bare with each fear-laden droplet. Looking down through the darkness, I could barely see beyond my feet, but I knew what was there: over 1,000 feet of absolutely nothing, then cruel, hard rock jutting ruthlessly up at me with the gaping finality of shark's teeth. Teeth that I believed had already claimed the life of my closest friend and had quenched my last flicker of hope.

I could no longer control my arms or legs properly. The shivering was almost constant now, which made handling slings and unclipping karabiners a time-consuming and frustrating task. Still, here I was detaching myself from the rock face. I had to grope in the dark to find a couple of the anchor points, such was the lack of any light in the gully, overshadowed by the looming rock wall above and the rain-filled clouds beyond that.

My fingers worked in slow motion. I had to force them to open out and then grip the gear. My mental state deteriorated with each passing moment. I could feel my heart pounding in my chest and my mind spinning toward chaos. At one point I asked myself where I was going to climb to, and the surge of adrenaline that followed that thought sent me into a state of complete panic. I gasped out loud as I fought to control my body and then force my mind onto the current task.

Just undo the locking ring of the karabiner, I thought.

Grip with your fingers, then twist.

To consider any action beyond that would have killed me, without any doubt. My mind would have completely shut down, and panic would have caused a fall, sending me plummeting down the mountain.

I could no longer distinguish between the shiver of hypothermia and the shaking of raw terror. My heart was clawing at my throat in a furious rage, demanding release, as adrenaline fuelled its anger.

Untethered to any protection, I began to climb across the blank rock face in the darkness. There was nothing on which I could focus: no rock bulges, no tree silhouettes in the distance, not even the smallest of incuts to aim for with my fingers. Everything was by touch. As I progressed, foot-by-foot, my fingers were increasingly anaesthetized by the rain and biting cold. I had no idea of the quality of the rock I was holding, and I could not even tell what size the hold was until I had committed to the move. Certainly, the handholds were no more than one-quarter to half-an-inch deep, and the footholds rarely exceeded an inch. On a warm day up a roadside crag in the Lake District back in England this would have been fine, even luxurious, but not here in the blackness of a Norwegian mountain. Good grief, not here!

The rock suddenly became friendlier. I could place the sole of my boots across a ledge and rest my calf muscles, which had been screaming at me for quite some time. Everything was unnervingly still. The cold and wet had stopped gnawing at my fingers, and at least for a moment I did not even notice the merciless drizzle. Even my heart had stopped its pummelling assault on my senses. I could feel the rock against my cheek as I rested briefly.

I imagined looking at myself, alone on this rock wall. I was miles from anywhere, a tiny speck of colour on a vast, black expanse. I was totally isolated from any living thing; almost unnoticeable, utterly insignificant, yet I was alive. It must have made a peculiar sight.

All at once I became entirely unemotional, though not shut down.

I slowly and deliberately turned around and faced away from the rock. Blackness stared back at me. I could see no lights as I looked down the mountain. I could hear the dripping of water on the walls all around me and the blowing and uncertain gusting of the wind as it swirled in the gully beneath.

This was it. I knew what I had to do. The consequences were irrelevant. I simply had to get on with it.

Strangely, almost ridiculously, I felt slightly nervous, rather like a mild dose of stage fright on the opening night of a school play or like the anticipation of a part-time job interview.

I reached out my hand into the void. I was not reaching for anything, merely stretching out a hand into the night. I was unable to see beyond the reach of my fingers, such was the blackness in the gully, with the trees above and clouds masking any moonlight. I extended my leg. It wasn't glamorous or dramatic; I simply stepped off the ledge. As I lost my balance I felt a rush of adrenaline again, and the stinging stab of sweat burst from my scalp.

Too late . . .

Chapter 1

SMALL BEGINNINGS

▲

The leader doesn't fall."

This was the reply to my question, accompanied by a look of mock horror and a twinkling eye.

It was one of my first outings with a work colleague who was soon to become a close friend. We were standing at the foot of a crag in the north of the Lake District in England. By all accounts Troutdale Pinnacle on Black Crag was a classic route. The weather was idyllic, with rays of early summer slanting their way through deciduous woodland and warming the rough granite that we were about to climb.

Even now, twenty-five years on, if I close my eyes I can still feel the warm breeze against my face and the rock on my fingertips. The roughness of the first touch gave way quickly to a treacherous, almost waxy effect as my palms began to sweat and cover the handholds, which had been polished by the years of time and the thousands of earlier ascendants. These "easy" routes often carried such a sting in the tail; overuse had made the handholds horribly greasy once sweat or rain touched them—treacherous for anyone who did not commit himself to strike upwards with purpose.

My question had been a simple one: I knew that as the second climber I was protected from any fall by the rope above me. "But what would happen," I had asked, "should the lead climber fall?" The answer seemed logical at the time.

The route itself was very straightforward, but for a first-timer whose only climbing gear was a pair of squash shoes and complete self-belief, it was an interesting challenge. I could feel almost every muscle in my upper body stretch and tighten as I pulled myself up the steep sections, unwilling to trust in footwork (as more experienced climbers will), preferring the gorilla approach to that of the ballet dancer.

Later, I would realize that I had never felt as physically satisfied from any other sport as I did as a climber. The burn of the arms and back, the rough abrasions on the fingers, and the sometimes-extreme cardiovascular workout in the walk-ins to a climb (especially in the winter) were always a source of profound joy and deep satisfaction to me.

Feeling my swollen forearms, like some steroidally enhanced pair of lamb chops, reminded me of my rowing days at school. This time, however, I was not reliant on a team (I have never been a team player). It was all so very peaceful as I climbed higher. There was no rowing coxswain barking out commands, no coach on the bank yelling something about straight backs and keeping the rhythm tight, and certainly no armchair experts yelling some inaudible advice from the river bank, apparently aided by their plastic megaphone half-filled with warm, substandard beer. Although I had the rope connecting me to my friend above, an umbilical cord to my advice centre, I felt very much alone, independent, and self-reliant.

It is remarkable and somewhat paradoxical how free it felt being stuck 200 feet up a rock wall with a single 11mm rope as a lifeline and with only the surface area of three or four fingertips plus the inside edge of a pair of squash shoes to keep me in touch with a very poor interpretation of terra firma! Now that I had tasted this new sport, I knew it was for me. I could now marry my sporting ambitions with my inherent love of the countryside.

I was already delighted that Dave had invited me for a climb. We had met only recently. He was working at the same hotel where I had just got a job tending bar. It was simply a money-earner for me during my gap year between secondary school and university. I had become thoroughly sick of studying, and I knew I had to have a break if I were to have any chance of gaining a decent degree at the end of my higher education. The hotel was close to Brookhouse, the small village in which I had been raised, so I could keep living with my parents and thereby pocket more of my wages—an all-important consideration for an 18-year-old.

I had first met Dave in the hotel gym, and a subsequent cross-country run together had established our similar, highly competitive natures. Neither of us would give an inch as we raced to the imaginary finish line; coming second was anathema to both of us, even on a training run. The notion of giving up simply did not exist. It was on this basis, I had learned later, that Dave thought I would make a suitable climbing partner.

The views were spectacular as we climbed. Below me lay the very English valley of Borrowdale, winding its way back toward Keswick with a backdrop of green, rolling hills, the names of which I have long since forgotten. Skiddaw, the Lake District's third highest peak, was visible to my far right—a squat triangle that looked much larger than its 3,000-something foot height. It was pretty feeble in mountaineering terms, yet imposing and impressive on the skyline—until the great, broad footpath, the size of a minor road in places, formed a meandering scar to the summit. In my pride I silently scoffed at the poor minions who had to resort to, or even worse, actually chose to trudge up such a boring, formless lump.

There is a strange-looking hill next to it with new forestry planted between bare areas of grass. It looks like a giant Mohican haircut, and viewed from Black Crag it presented a curious sight. Among the random nature of so much of the Lake District, this sharp-edged forestry project showed the clear, deliberate intrusion of man, no doubt for good purposes, yet it seemed to me at the time a clear case of environmental graffiti. Still, a wonderful feeling of peace enveloped me as I studied each area of my view.

At the stage of the exposed traverse on Troutdale Pinnacle, I had been "gripped," to employ a climbing word. It is used euphemistically to mean focussed, but a closer definition, for my part at least, would be "utterly terrified." As a climber moves horizontally across a rock face, or "traverses," even the second climber can fall a considerable distance if he were to lose his footing. On this route, I had a risk of doing just that, since I had to take a horizontal tack for about twenty yards. A slip would have caused a pendulum effect, resulting in my being slammed into the side of the crag. Happy days!

I have always enjoyed taking risks of any sort. When I was nine, I closed my eyes while sledding down the snowy hill behind my parents' house just for the thrill of it. How I did not break my skull is still a mystery.

Now I was delighted to find out about the risks that were the bread and butter of climbing rock faces. This was a guaranteed way of feeling a buzz, and it was most welcome grist to my adrenaline mill. One thing I could not do, however, was to stand at the top of the crag and look down. A sheer drop of over 300 feet was more than I could manage the first time out. Within months I would stand overlooking thousands of feet without a trace of concern, supremely confident in my invincibility, daring the King of the Mountains to try to find something to scare me! It only took one outing on Troutdale Pinnacle to render me a climbing adrenaline junkie. Being gripped became an essential ingredient to life, and I had found the perfect feeding ground.

As I sat on the top of the crag, I was puzzled—almost disturbed—at what I felt. It was a peculiar mix of sensations, seemingly contradictory, of adrenaline high, physical fatigue, lazy contentment, and total well-being. The walkers didn't come here, and there were no other climbers out that day. The only sounds were the gentle clink of metal climbing hardware and the almost soporific hiss of breeze through the trees. The dull, pleasant ache of tired muscles and the tingle of sore fingertips were therapy in themselves. There was a profound sense of complete physical and emotional satisfaction, which paradoxically made me very uncomfortable. Satisfaction breeds laziness. Without thinking, I knew it was time to go. We finished the climb and returned to the car. Conquest done, spirits soaring, we went off to climb something else, anything else, so long as it was more challenging than the last.

This became my routine: working through the week in order to go climbing on the weekends. I trained almost every day so I could overcome any physical challenges. Training was an obsession in itself. In addition to two-hour stints in the gym, often interspersed with bouts of nausea because I overdid it, there were the punishing cross-country runs and the ceaseless press-ups, dips, and pull-ups, which I would do whenever I was unoccupied (100 press-ups and a load of pull-ups on the doorways during the television commercials was a common occurrence at home, much to the dismay of my mother—God bless her!).

I had found my niche, my role in life. It was to seek fulfilment for its own sake on the rock face. I was going to prove that I could do anything I set my mind to, no matter what the odds. If there were no one else to compete with, I would compete with myself. In fact, I soon became my own favourite adversary.

Soon after my initiation on Troutdale Pinnacle, I was taken on another route, this time near Langdale, again in the Lake District. It was an easy walk-in from the legendary Old Dungeon Ghyll pub, venue of climbing tales for me and myriad others. The route was an unspectacular one on Gimmer Crag called, rather blandly, D-Route. One can always tell the old routes, as they have basic, unpretentious names. In contrast, the newer ones of the time, especially the extreme routes, had names of almost mystical power: "Comes the Dervish," "Cystitis by Proxy," all designed I am sure to instill awe and dread into potential climbers. Still, D-Route provided plenty of entertainment on this day.

I was climbing second again, armed with my squash shoes and wearing some rather attractive running shorts. It was a pleasant, sunny day in the early part of what turned out to be a lovely Lakeland summer that year. The breeze was warm and inviting, not so humid as to be stifling, but welcoming enough to feel safe and relaxing.

There is no more beautiful a place in the world for my money than the Lake District when the weather is right. Balmy summer days with a breeze to keep everything fresh and to bring new smells with it—flowers, sheep, the humid air, or even that strange unmistakeable whiff of climbing chalk on sweaty fingers (a strange notion to the uninitiated, but it really does carry a romance all of its own). The obvious problem is that Lakeland weather is not known for its hospitality. Indeed, it is renowned for its ability to seduce you with a cloudless sky, wait for you to disrobe accordingly, then to close in, whip, beat, and otherwise pound you into oblivion with an inconceivably hostile storm. Finally, the persistent rain will mock and deride you all your sorry, drenched way back to the safety of your car. I had yet to fully appreciate this little nuance of the Lakes. As far as I could ascertain, this would be a pleasant and interesting little route, lasting no more than an hour or so, and then straight back to the pub in time for ale and medals.

The route followed a fairly straight line, meandering logically as the fault line in the crag split its way easily to the top. Gimmer Crag caught the evening sun, and so it was always a favourite destination for a quick route straight after work in the summer months. Its proximity to the Old Dungeon Ghyll did nothing to hamper its popularity either. Dave completed the first pitch and called me up the face. As I started to climb, the reflected heat from the sun felt wonderful. The rock was firm and rough to the touch, and handholds abounded. I could really run up this one and enjoy it. I ignored the first chill on my legs as an easterly wind suddenly started to whip up around me. I hadn't noticed the bank of black clouds appearing over my shoulder, descending on us from out of the shadow of 3,000-foot Great End in the distance.

As I met up with Dave, the rain had started and the wind was insistently grabbing at my naked legs. All my spare clothing was safely locked in the car, a mere half-mile away. We could have done the route in a single long pitch, but Dave had decided against this due to our having only one rope, rather than two. This makes a big difference—especially on routes that are not direct ascents and involve traverses. With two ropes a climber can choose which rope to put his protective gear or "runners" through, which will arrest him in the case of a fall. By choosing which rope to use, the lead climber can make sure the ropes follow as direct a route as possible up the rock, thereby reducing the friction or "rope drag" that results from a rope that zigzags up the mountain. With only one rope, this is not an option. Moreover, the one rope is usually thicker than either of the two (usually 11mm as opposed to two 9mm ropes) and is therefore heavier and more cumbersome to start with. I had not yet bought a rope of my own, so we were stuck with Dave's big, old 11mm monster. It was heavy to start with. Now it was also wet.

As Dave started off up the final pitch, he began to traverse, ascend, then traverse back, following the guidebook instructions and making it all very hard work for himself. I stood beneath him, faithfully holding and paying out rope as was needed, blinking back the stinging rain from my eyes and feeling quite shocked at how cold the wind had become. My fleece was soaked, and the tee shirt beneath now stuck to my skin. In addition, I was wearing nothing of a windproof nature, so these garments simply served to chill me to the bone once they became wet and the wind began to blow through them.

I was miserable. I hate it when a plan falls apart. I had made provision for an easy afternoon out, and this had completely ruined everything. My misery turned to anger toward poor Dave as he struggled up the face above me.

Why didn't he check the weather forecast? I thought. *Then he could have foreseen this wintry squall before I got stuck in it. He's the mountaineer, after all. Where are my tracksuit bottoms and climbing jacket? Who can I blame for neglecting to bring those? Bloody Nora, this is a right pain! Is he not finished yet? It's only graded "Severe," so what's the bloody delay about? Does he not know that I'm standing down here freezing to death? It's all right for him in his fancy rock boots; I have to climb a wet route in sopping squash shoes!*

After what seemed like an interminably long delay, I was invited to join him at the top. It was hardly a relief as I watched the water run down the rock face, so I continued moaning to myself:

Finally! "Climb on!" he says. I only hope my shoes stay on this poxy rock or I'll be sliding and jibbering my way to the top. And it won't be my fault. I cannot recall a time when self-pity was not an advanced qualification of mine.

The rain had become persistent and heavy. My legs were no longer red. They were both a definite shade of blue, stiff as boards, and only slightly less numb than my fingers. I felt as if I was wearing a particularly painful pair of boxing gloves. I was forced to visually check each handhold to see if I was actually holding on to anything. The numbness was an amazing and most unwelcome revelation to me. Before then I had no idea that one could lose feeling so completely and so easily.

It is a strange phenomenon that such numbness to external touch can exist simultaneously with such excruciating pain within. As blood flows into fingers then stops and flows again, the pain of each flow of blood becomes quite breathtaking at times. Within only a year or so, I would accept this as a normal part of life as a mountaineer.

But not today.

On this day I was as mad as a wasp about the whole thing. Mad and scared. My feet rarely stuck onto any hold. I was scrambling at times and cursing wildly at the vile shoes that had become less than useless. Water seeped out of every lace hole as soon as pressure was put on them. The soles had absolutely no frictional qualities against the running rock face, and I could no longer effectively feel an edge of rock on which I could stand and rest.

I looked up toward where I thought Dave would be and yelled something. I have no idea what. Possibly something as inane as, "How far to the top from here?" I just wanted to hear something positive. Instead, all I heard was a garbled voice lost in the swirling gale around us. Then a blood-chilling sight. The rope was snaking away above me, with great bows of slack rope between each runner. Due to the dragging rope, Dave could not effectively feel the rope being tightened as it pulled on my harness. Instead, because he felt a substantial resistance, he had stopped pulling the rope in. Since he could not see or hear me, he was guessing how far I had climbed and had assumed I had climbed at least 20 feet less than I actually had. In short, were I to fall off at this point (a distinct possibility given the conditions) I would have fallen around 15 feet onto a particularly nasty little outcrop of jagged rocks. Injury from such a fall was a certainty. Severe injury, a distinct possibility. This was in no way Dave's fault. I should have been checking the situation as I ascended, but I was far too busy being scared and angry to watch where I was going. Fortunately, I remembered what to yell, and yell I did:

"Slack! Slack rope! Slaaaaack!"

I watched with horror as the bows in the rope became bigger, and the length of my possible fall became a seriously devastating prospect.

"Can you not hear me? Dave! Daaaave! Slack! Bloody Nora! Slack!"

More rope slid down the mountain. I was apoplectic. There was nothing for it. He could not hear me, and if I didn't get moving I was going to fall anyway. Better to fall with as little spare rope ahead of me as possible. I set off at a manic rate, coiling the rope around my shoulder as I caught up with another great loop. In a matter of a minute or so, I saw Dave in the distance and a wave of relief hit me. There was absolutely no anger, just an enormous pressure release as I approached the top of the climb. We both laughed raucously as I handed him a pile of rope.

"Well, you asked for it, so I gave it to you," he said, smiling.

What on earth did he mean? I explained that I was informing him of the swathes of useless slack rope dangling around me as I clung breathless and freezing at the steepest part of the climb. He smiled again. Dave has a warm, full-faced smile that forms glowing wrinkles around the sides of his mouth and eyes. The generosity conveyed in this look made it impossible for me to be in the least irritated with him, even when he was laughing directly at me while calling me a stupid idiot. He then reminded me (he had told me before; I just had not listened) that if you want someone to take in more rope, you shout, "Tight!" And if you want more slack for any reason, you shout, "Slack!" I had been yelling out for more of the stuff that I thought was going to maim me, and Dave had dutifully obliged.

"You've gotta learn, son. You've gotta learn," was the adage trotted out (on this and many other subsequent occasions) as we gulped our pints back at the pub. I had had my first minor epic, and although I would not admit having had such an adventure on such a lowly climb, it was strangely alluring. As Dave had said, I had to learn. Indeed I had learned and would continue to do so, almost invariably the hard way. Unfortunately, I knew of no other way.

This new pattern of life was perfect. My personality was inextricably linked to what I did: *I was a climber*. It wasn't something that I did. It defined me, and that felt good. No, it felt great. I was respected, I was interesting, and I always had stories to tell down at the pub. True, the rugby boys were bigger, the oarsmen taller, but no one could do fifty one-handed press-ups with each hand, followed by the compulsory two-finger pull-ups, and still have room for a few more pints of beer and session number two of "most gripping moments" stories. And let's face it, that's what counts, isn't it? Yes, I had finally made it.

As the weeks went by, I found myself becoming increasingly confident, not to mention capable, as a rock climber. I was also keen to see some improvement in the standard of routes we were climbing. It was all well and good impressing non-climbers in the pub with tales of derring-do on the rock face, but it simply would not do around other mountaineers, so long as I was only doing routes graded "severe" or "hard severe." Anyone who was anyone was at least up to "Hard Very Severe (HVS)" and then, of course, into the hallowed "E" or "Extreme" grades: big lads only, of course (and lasses; very sexy). The fact that I had not led a route yet was a minor detail in my book. I was hooked, and I intended to take this new obsession to the very top.

There was one final experience that confirmed my new way of life. It happened when I saw a mountain that looked impossible to climb, totally impenetrable, and I then promptly went and climbed it. That one event sealed my fate for the following eight years.

Dave and I were driving from Ambleside to Keswick, having set off early that morning from Lancaster. I was looking at the guidebook for

Borrowdale, and we were considering climbing on Shepherd's Crag, a very convenient spot by the roadside (no long walk-ins) where we could notch half-a-dozen routes in the day. I was getting impatient to lead a route, and this seemed the best way of getting into it: do a few warm-up routes, then choose an easy one as my first lead.

Suddenly, off to the right, I noticed a great round lump of a crag, set by itself in an otherwise fairly flat field. It looked like an enormous, disused, overgrown castle, its ramparts long gone. The mound on which it was built still had a commanding presence, reaching probably 400 feet high at the top. On the left-hand edge was a wall that was simply mesmerizing to a climber: vertical in places, with the rest clearly and sometimes spectacularly overhanging all the way to the top of the crag. Some of the angles looked absolutely outrageous, and the notion of seeing a body moving up such a precipice was almost inconceivable. The sweat was already visible on my palms as I pointed over to the rock and said, half-jokingly, half-longingly, "Could you imagine doing something like that?"

"I climbed it with Pete a few years ago, " came Dave's surprising answer.

What? Seriously? No, surely it's not possible! I barely kept the thoughts from blurting out loud.

My mind spun like a whirling dervish. A route like this, so bold, so impossible, so completely out of reach for a mere man. And yet . . . . And yet, perhaps, could I be that figure I had seen in my own mind, struggling up such a wall? I could immediately envisage the walkers who would stop and glass the area a second and third time to make sure their Nikon lenses were not deceiving them. "Could it be that such men as this exist?" they would ask. "I have never seen the like in all my born days!" Simultaneous gasps and applause rang through my mind as my penchant for mental hyperbole ran into overdrive. I had no idea that this was an attainable goal so early in my climbing career.

"That, my friend, is Castle Rock, and the left-hand edge is Overhanging Bastion. It's a VS, but they are thinking of upgrading it to HVS."

I had to have it. More than gaining silver or gold or a Lamborghini Countach, I had to climb that route. Overhanging Bastion became my Holy Grail. I could think of nothing else until we had conquered it.

I have no recollection of where we parked the car or how we accessed Castle Rock. I do not know the day or the month of our climb, but I shall never forget looking up from the foot of the route, examining the guidebook description, and then comparing it to the insane protrusion of rock spiraling wildly up above me, causing me to crane my neck back to its limit. I am sure my eyes were playing tricks on me as I remembered the descriptions of Mescaline-induced hallucinations in the late Hunter Thompson's book *Fear and Loathing in Las Vegas*. This seemed like a granite-induced equivalent: the rock was moving, the angles looked ridiculous, and the final section of overhang would, I am sure, bring guffaws of incredulous derision from me now, if I were asked to climb it.

The first section, or pitch, of the climb was straightforward enough, with plenty of holds in a non-threatening position on the crag. If I looked down, I could still see the lush grass at a comfortably close distance beneath me. The most difficult section, or crux, of the climb came on the next pitch. It involved a step from a huge flake of rock onto the main wall of the crag. It was a move demanding balance, strength, and commitment. Dave pondered the move before stepping smoothly up the wall and onto the final, overhanging section. When it came to my turn, the adrenaline was flowing freely and I considered the move for a long time! This was a different league from what I was used to. This was serious stuff.

No matter what people say about having a rope going above you, it does little for your nerves at the point of stepping out. The thick grass at the foot of the climb was no longer reassuring; it looked like it was miles beneath me. My rucksack was not even visible. It was lost at the foot of the crag, masked by the bulges and overhanging swells of the wall to which I was clinging. I took my time preparing for the step onto the main wall. I checked with Dave that he had the rope good and tight, and was ready should I slip and fall. My heart was beating quickly but steadily; I was not filled with dread.

It was rather like when I went running up and down the hills of the Lake District. However, unlike the wandering thoughts that used to accompany my running, my mind was now completely transfixed by the problem at hand. I was either like a lion about to pounce or a deer caught in the headlights. Either way, nothing else existed but that one great bold step.

And then it was over. Once I had decided to commit to the route, it was done. The move was smooth and delicate, but also firm and strenuous. I loved it. Looking back at the gap I had just negotiated, I laughed out loud. The whole situation was so precarious, so extreme, and so frankly bizarre that it warranted mirth. The ground beneath me was no longer frightening; it was invigorating. I stared and stared down at the foot of the crag. Looking down a crag is a unique sight once the fear factor has gone. All I could see was rock, grass, the odd sheep, and my own rucksack. But it carried the fascination of the world's great vistas to me: examining the rock that I had just ascended, feeling the rush of a problem overcome, and marvelling at the beauty of cold, grey granite from such an angle. It is beautiful.

The crux was over. I looked up at the final section, and filled with confidence, I set off up the great overhang like I was super-charged. Dave had warned me that the holds toward the top of the climb were prone to creak, "but they are really sound, actually," he had assured me. I did not know exactly what creaking rock would sound like and was not sure what he actually meant by "creak." How can rock creak?

The angle of the wall sharpened with every move I made. I could feel the overhang factor kicking in, and the final section of the climb took on an outrageous angle, necessitating long, strenuous arm pulls as my feet strove to combat the natural tendency to be pulled away from the ever-steepening face. Fortunately, the holds were as big as the guidebook promised, but being inexperienced I gripped them with all my strength rather than with just enough to keep hold of the rock. This meant my arms became prematurely tired. I stopped to "shake out" my forearms, hoping to force blood into the stiffening muscles, and as I did, I leaned out and looked down the crag. I imagined how this would look from the road; the stupendous position, the impossible angle of ascent. It was all beyond exhilarating. I was in a different world and could not recall ever being so happy. With arms tiring, I pushed on up the last few feet.

So, what does creaking rock sound like? Very similar to an old door with rusty hinges! Each move created the most horrendous creaks and groans, so much so that I felt for certain one of the rocks would give way, and I would be hurled to my doom in the ensuing rock-fall. I did not know at the time, of course, that just such an event would nearly claim me only a couple of years later. On that occasion there was no warning creak—simply the complete collapse of the tiny world of rock that I was ascending. But that was to come. Had I been leading this route, I would have certainly panicked at such noises. As it was, I reminded myself that this was to be expected, that the route had been around for a long time, and that it would all be over, one way or another, in just a few moments.

Those few moments lasted long enough for me to overcome the creaking fear, and it was a relaxed, smiling, even giddy body that joined his friend at the top of Castle Rock, Overhanging Bastion ticked off in our mental list of "great routes climbed" and later ticked off in the guidebook with a bunch of stars after the date. It was an exhilaration that I spent many years trying to revisit. The pure pleasure of that day, the weather, the company, the lure of the seemingly unattainable, the image of the heroic—these were all nearly impossible to replicate. The Overhanging Bastion had seduced me. I had conquered her, but whereas she has long forgotten the feel of my touch, I will never forget hers. Every wrinkle, every blemish, and every nuance of her granite rendered me smitten back then and pleasantly nostalgic even now. My passion was fully awakened. I had to get more of this wonder drug. Surely I had found what was for me the key to a life fulfilled.

Chapter 2

LEADING OFF

▲

I was eight and a half years old when I lit up my first cigarette.
I remember the age exactly because I wrote it down in a school report for a certain teacher who, for a school assembly, encouraged us to anonymously confess our sins. My various classmates recanted numerous tales of none too heinous misdemeanours, based largely around the themes of sibling persecution or the clandestine evasion of vegetables at Christmas dinner. Even at that age I could not bring myself to be the same as my somewhat ordinary peers. It was all too run-of-the-mill for me. *I* decided to tell something worthy of note, something really shameful, safe in the knowledge that no one except the teacher would ever know the truth.

Until, of course, my father decided one evening to have a quick read of my schoolbooks, just to see how my work was progressing.

Perfect!

It was rather ironic that he was rolling a cigarette as he read it. Indeed, one of my earliest recollections, probably from before the age of five, was watching him make a cigarette. The artistry of rolling up and the pensive skill that it seemed to entail thoroughly captivated me. I was hooked on the image of "rollies" long before I ever tried one. I think largely out of guilt my father did not punish me for my indiscretion. I remember him saying something about ". . . well, at least you have got it out of your system now."

There never was such a wholly misguided case of wishful thinking.

I had seen how appealing and how thoroughly different it was to be a "roll-up artist," so I had to be one as well. It represented to me, in some strange way, individuality. Because my dad stood out from the crowd in this respect, so I too wanted to be different. Besides, this looked impressive even more so because it was forbidden.

To push the limits of what was allowed, of what was acceptable, was another of my favourite pastimes, though, peculiarly, I did not understand this until years later. Sneaking off for a smoke was my idea of claiming my own rights to my life. The very fact that it was not allowed made the whole idea even more irresistible. It served to define my personality. The nature of my addiction was more about pushing limits and proving my uniqueness than any issue of dependence on a chemical. This sad fact only became an unfortunate encumbrance much later.

As I grew older, of course, the odd cigarette no longer gave me the rush I yearned. I had to drink a few tins of beer as well just to confirm my individuality and maintain the secret life of rebellion and thrill seeking. It was therefore disastrous to me when I reached eighteen, the time when both of these pastimes became officially permissible. More importantly, half of my friends were actively engaged in the same activities anyway, so where was my individuality now?

This same mindset affected my other pursuits as well, none more than my new "addiction" to mountaineering. The more I became immersed in the culture of rock-climbing, the more I realized that this, finally, could be the key to standing out from any of my peers. At the same time it could also fulfil my need for an adrenaline rush in a most spectacular fashion. It was also a lot healthier a pastime than drinking and smoking (not that I gave them up), as long as I did not fall, of course! Mountaineers seemed very different, and I was already discovering that most people could not even relate to hanging off a rock wall by their fingertips. This was true individuality, for a time at least.

The only flaw in this master plan was that it became increasingly obvious that, just as in rolling cigarettes, the second climbing route does not quite measure up to that first time out—unless it packs a bigger punch.

Once I had felt the rush of climbing, the feeling of freedom, and the fulfilment of self-expression, I felt at once unfulfilled if I merely repeated the same actions. Indeed, within a month of my adventure on Troutdale Pinnacle, climbing second had become like so much Silk Cut and Shandy. It was time to push the limits further. The real addiction had arrested me, and I was in need of more substantial intoxication. Capstan Full Strength and Johnnie Walker beckoned on the horizon as I looked to becoming a "lead climber."

I had to be the first to go up the rock or ice, the one who takes nearly all the risk. It reminded me of the World War I officer who steps out of the trench to lead his men forward, whistle in mouth, swagger-stick in one hand, and a Webley revolver in the other. Bold, courageous, and some would say completely insane. He would go "over the top" with a life expectancy of, according to some historians, around seven seconds. I saw only the romantic heroism of this, not the horror or the waste. At the very least he was out there in front, not merely following the crowd. I was truly taken with the dangerous and highly individualistic image of lead climbing. For me, image was everything. It was time for me to push on, over the top.

It was the beginning of July, perhaps even an auspicious Independence Day, when I was finally blooded into leading a climb. We had been out for a few days, climbing and camping, marauding around the crags of the Lake District looking for another route to tick off in the guidebooks. I knew I had to step out and lead one. It felt like a natural progression, so I quietly asked Dave if that would be okay. He responded very matter-of-factly in the positive, and so for my first time "at the sharp end" we settled on The Mound on Quayfoot Buttress. It was graded mild VS but also carried a star after the grade, indicating an interesting and fairly classic route.

We were being treated to another superb day in the hills. The elements were kind and the sun shone. The crag itself lay in a sheltered position. The terrain resembled an old quarry, but long years of disuse gave the whole place a most agreeable, natural feel. As we approached the foot of the climb, the only accompaniments to our boots crunching on the gravelly surface of the footpath were the songs of birds and the lilting sighs of the surrounding woodland, blown carelessly by the prevailing southwesterly wind. As a further bonus, there was no one else around, so we were free to pursue our goals in wonderful seclusion.

I had bought a new climbing harness and a pair of specialized rock boots. Loading up my rucksack with my own climbing gear had been a thrilling experience full of excitement and anticipation, and now to pull it out and lay it on the floor before me, hearing the satisfying clink of the buckle on the rock had made me even more elated. As I pulled the harness up around my waist, I could hardly conceal my nervous glee. I tightened the laces on my boots, like some medieval thumbscrew, to ensure maximum sensitivity to the rock. I am still unsure if this actually helped my climbing, but I surmised that anything as painful as that had to be good for me in some way.

Preparing for the job was half the fun of it all. Each piece of climbing hardware was fastened on to the exact part of my harness that I had assigned for it. All the karabiners were clipped onto the belt the same way and were arranged according to the ones with a straight gate, others with a bent gate, and the larger ones with a screw-locking gate. Knowing where to find the perfect-sized wire or wedge for a crack when your arms are about to give up and your fingers are peeling away from the minuscule hold right before your eyes is a vital consideration when preparing for a lead. A delay of more than a couple of seconds in placing the right piece of gear first time could prove most unfortunate as you watch helplessly tired fingers involuntarily losing their grip, peeling you slowly and irreversibly from the rock. Not a pleasant experience.

Once the boots were securely crushing my toes, the rope was then threaded through the harness and tied in exactly the same manner each time, right down to the few inches of spare rope at the end. If there was any difference more than a couple of inches, I would pull the whole thing out and start again. I had a system. It worked for me, and it was my way of ensuring success. It never failed, so neither did I. I always believed that if I put the work into the preparation, success was guaranteed. I was ready to climb.

The route itself was only 100 feet high, so I was going to climb it in a single pitch. That is, the leader does the entire climb in one effort without stopping part way to bring up his partner. In the normal course of a route, especially one that was longer than a climbing rope (typically 50 metres, or 165 feet), the leader would find a safe place to anchor himself (a belay) and then bring up his colleague. He in turn would pass by his companion and carry on up the route, thereby alternating leads with each pitch of the climb. Today, however, I would get to lead the entire route. It was a direct ascent following a fairly straight line up the rock wall with little meandering.

As I began to climb, I was first struck by the amount of moss, lichen, and other debris on the rock. Up until then, all the routes we had chosen had been highly popular, even classic routes, and as such were almost constantly in use, making them clean of any debris—if sometimes a little polished and slippery through overuse. This new phenomenon was peculiar to me and more than a little unnerving, since modern rock boots, although excellent on bare rock, are typically useless on wet, dirty, or otherwise contaminated surfaces; a little like trying to use slick racing tyres on a wet or dirt road. However, this did help me to become accustomed to the terrain that was to come in a few months' time—when smooth, safe rock would be the exception rather than the rule and when deceptive, rotten granite, overgrown with vegetation—would be all I could find. Today's outing, however, posed comparatively little threat. I was only 40 feet up the rock, and since I had placed in some good protection, I pressed on without too much hesitation.

My second revelation of the day was the sudden feeling of exposure one feels as lead climber. Over time this became an appealing, even sought-after feeling, but upon first experience I found it very unnerving. I was almost surprised to find myself in such a predicament—as if I were somewhere I knew I ought not to be and was about to be discovered. It was rather like an errant schoolboy caught with a cigarette dangling from his lips during lunch break. This was coupled with generous doses of physical pain and urgent fear. This peculiar sensation continued and intensified the higher I climbed. I placed some more gear in the rock to protect myself at about 50 feet. Then, after shaking out my tired forearms, I continued to climb.

Third, I began to understand both the risk and reward of leading as a climber. The upper section of the route became considerably steeper, almost completely vertical. More importantly, the holds were smaller, and I could no longer find any cracks in the rock in which to place protective gear. As I edged higher, hoping with each move to find a friendly crack, I only uncovered more of the same blank wall and more increasingly annoying clumps of dry moss, which I had to pull off in order to force the tips of my fingers onto the ripples of concealed rock. These tiny ripples were my only handholds.

My heart was beginning to beat faster. Faster and harder. I had to steady my breathing, which was also becoming increasingly shallow and considerably more urgent.

This was pure fear, not of pain, not of being uncovered, but the ultimate fear of falling off a mountain: a fear of dying.

In an instant I became aware of how precarious my position had become. That I had exposed myself to such risk was foolhardy. I was now some 80 feet above the floor of the crag. A fall now would have serious consequences, even if I did not actually hit the bottom.

Would my protective gear hold me from a fall of that distance?

My hands were sweating terribly. I stopped climbing for a few moments in order to look for a good hold, the last few having been far too small for my failing nerves, and to find a crack in which to place some protection.

My mind was racing erratically. I was certainly not thinking logically.

Would it be better just to wait where I was and avoid increasing my fall distance by trying to climb any higher? What a preposterous concept! Wait for what, exactly?

It was in this moment, I believe, that the course of the next few years of my life was decided. Push on? Overcome the fear barrier. Or wait? Wait for help or for inevitable failure. I made a decision to override the fear, and in a surge of action fuelled by an unexpected aggression, I moved up. I did not even look for a foothold. I simply decided I would stand on whatever was there, and it would hold me.

I stepped upwards, falteringly at first, which is always a mistake. The only way to climb is to be certain of each move, no matter how delicate it is. Even the most agile and refined climbing moves require absolute commitment if they are to succeed. I could feel my feet move uncertainly on the small hold I had found. Suddenly I knew what to do. I began to force myself to exert more downward pressure on the rock, simultaneously reaching for a handhold and committing myself to moving upwards rather than tentatively testing.

Then came the most curious revelation: an unexpectedly attractive feeling enveloped me. The fear did not diminish, but with each upward movement I could feel wave upon wave of inner strength flowing through me. The catalyst for this seemed to be the fear; the more I battled and overcame it, the stronger I felt inside. It was high-octane stuff, and I began to feel literally light-headed from it. I was now determining my own future on this little piece of crag rather than having the crag decide my fate for me. This was a real empowering. I was still exceptionally frightened, but I knew I had to keep pushing upwards.

I had 30 or so feet to go. My last piece of protective gear was at least 40 feet beneath me, and I could not possibly retreat if I found myself running out of either handholds or steam. The chances of my hitting the bottom of the rock face, or "bottoming out," if I fell were now horribly high, and I knew it. I redoubled my efforts, and with arms and calves straining, I began to run out the last few feet of rope to the top.

I finished the last 20 feet at a speed that had Dave struggling to pay out the rope quickly enough. I tied a couple of knots around a tree on the top, sat down—almost lying prone, actually—and signalled for Dave to climb up to me.

The risk had been real. What of the reward? I had been scared, no doubt. But in spite of a highly questionable technique at times and a few missed handholds, I had done it!

It was not just the climbing of 100 feet of rock on a lovely summer's day, nor was it the gymnastic ability to heave my body round awkward bulges using small incuts for hands and feet. It was not even the fact that I had gone where most of the world would refuse to even try to go.

The true reward was that I had gone beyond what I thought I could tolerate physically, mentally, and emotionally. Before that moment I had no idea what I would do when faced with the prospect of falling off a mountain. I had never encountered that degree of imminent danger before, nor had I ever faced such a severe physical challenge that carried such dire consequences if I failed. More importantly, I had never been so in touch with the feeling of raw fear before: a very real and a very revealing emotion. This was an achievement far beyond even my expectations.

The success was all mine as well. I had no need to share my success and feeling of accomplishment with anyone else. Conversely, of course, if I had failed, that failure could be attributed only to me. I liked the black-and-whiteness of that.

But the moment belonged to me. The thrill, the glory, and the accolade were all down to me and my ability. This was nothing short of spectacular.

From this time on I determined that I would develop, push, and stretch my character on the rock faces of the world, overcoming inner obstacles as I climbed physical ones. The thrill and risk of lead climbing became my gateway to fulfilment. I had no idea that this sport could bring so many benefits. Of course, now that I had overcome my fear, I had raised the standard of what *was* fear; and knowing I could overcome it once, I knew

I could overcome it every time. Apart from all that, the surge of adrenaline lasted for hours. I felt positively Herculean!

The Mound had served its purpose, but now it was discarded quicker than a drunken conquest. Once beaten there was no beauty in her. She was simply not challenging enough to be worthy of recollection. It meant that from now on Dave and I would alternate leads with each pitch of a climb. This not only made the climbing quicker, but more importantly, it also gave me the impression that we were two peers out on the crag rather than the teacher and his pupil. A great future lay before me climbing with my good friend, and we went to all the crags we could get to whenever we had a day off work.

All this would have been just perfect. But then the unexpected almost always crops up and ruins everything. Within a few months we hit a problem. Actually, I alone saw it as a problem, possibly a big one. You see, Dave found himself a new girlfriend, and the rot began to set in.

Now, I was all for girlfriends—in their place, that is—sitting next to me in the pub looking pretty and enjoying my climbing stories. They could even come along if they wanted and have a go, just so long as they either kept out of the way when the serious stuff started or became good enough to climb to the same grade. They were especially welcome if they had a car and liked ferrying me back from the pub or even the crag if need be. And, of course, they smelled a whole lot better than the average rock jock if I needed a post-pub canoodle.

Dave's girl, however, was somehow different from the rest. It would have been a lot easier if she was plain weird, but up to that time I had not encountered a more sunny character—which in itself was annoying. Inexplicably, Dave started to cut short his visits to the pub, and then one day it started:

"We were lucky to find a parking spot by the crag today; it was busy," I said with a thumbs-up gesture.

"We weren't lucky, Russ. We were *blessed*," came the reply.

With howls of derisive laughter I dismissed this ludicrous comment the moment I heard it. An hour later, on the rock wall, I commented, "Lucky I bought that quadcam last week; it fits perfectly in there!"

"You weren't lucky, Russ. You were blessed."

That stupid comment again. What book has he been reading?

A few days later at work, it all became clear.

"Hey, Russ, this is my girlfriend."

"You're a lucky dog, Dave; she's quite a looker!"

"He's not lucky; he's just blessed, and so am I."

Realization dawned: *Oh, no! He's been set upon by the Moonies! How do I rescue my clearly smitten buddy from those evil, batting eyelashes and all this nonsense?*

It turned out it was much more serious than the Moonies. At least I could just dismiss them as a bunch of weirdos. No, this new girl was the vicar's daughter, and not just any old vicar. He was known by my old school history teacher as "Swinging Jim," and he headed up the local "chandelier-swinging" church in town. This was serious. This was old-time religion, and it had an attractive new wrapper. I thought it best to tolerate this new turn of events, as to do otherwise would have clearly alienated my climbing buddy. I had to admit, with enormous reluctance, that all this "blessing" nonsense was somehow quaint. I actually despised the word "lucky" anyway. It smacked of being out of control of one's own fortune, and I for one was totally in control of where I was going.

Fortunately, Dave's new interest in life had no interest in climbing, so I could pursue my ambitions with impunity. I could dismiss these little idiosyncrasies as mere enthusiastic infatuation, spiced up with a liberal dose of testosterone. No real harm done. Still, I remained wary of the situation and decided to keep this religion thing at a good, long distance. I hoped Dave would grow out of it, or of her, or of both. Meanwhile, we had some climbing to do. Actually, we had a lot of climbing to do.

My trips to the crags became more akin to great white shark feeding frenzies, and I had to climb another route as soon as one was finished. I talked with other climbers in the pub and on the crags, and we all seemed to share this compulsion to climb more and more. There seemed to be no room for the occasional or weekend climber. It was an all-or-nothing approach, which suited me perfectly.

But there was another trait about such folk that I found uncomfortable and mildly irritating. The more I climbed, the more I came in contact with a host of "spiritually minded" people. It seems the outdoors, and especially outdoor sports, attracts them. I don't think I was ever an atheist as such, and I did occasionally contemplate eternity, whatever that was. But I never lost sleep over it and had no desire to put a lot of effort into finding out more about it. For that reason I found it very difficult to get worked up about "being one with nature" or "feeling the spirituality of the rock" as you climb. I tried to look interested during such conversations in the pub (especially if she was attractive), but I could not keep my eyes from glazing over after a couple of minutes' drone about "oneness," "energy," and "karma." It simply was not me. I put this Christianity business into the same category and tried to sound interested as I removed myself from such discussions as early as possible, seeking the welcome, familiar camaraderie of John Smith and Joshua Tetley, who were invariably more stimulating company.

I certainly had no time for tree-hugging and the like as I led the second classic pitch of Botterill's Slab, high on Scafell Crag. As the rest of the walking world strolled, wandered, or gasped their way along as they headed up England's highest peak, Scafell Pike, off a little way to my left, I was having an altogether more spectacular journey above them. The 120 feet of the second pitch offered very few large holds, so it took great delicacy with both hands and feet to overcome the various intricacies of the climb. It was so hot that I was bare-chested. The bandolier, which hung from my shoulder and held my climbing gear, slipped around constantly as the sweat ran freely down my back and arms. The exposure of the route was quite extraordinary since the ascent toward the crag was snaking a steep path up Brown Tongue, across the clear stream running down from high up the mountainside, and ending almost at the foot of the crag itself.

Once the climbing started, the full effect of the overall altitude of the crag became immediately apparent. Even on the first pitch it seemed as if I would fall for hundreds of feet if I came off, since the path up to the crag was out of sight. This gave the impression that the steep wall descended all the way to the valley floor rather than merely 50 or so feet to the foot of the crag and thence to my waiting climbing partner. It gave a wild and remote aspect to the expedition, even though the solace of the pub was only a couple of hours walk away. Quicker if last orders were approaching.

As for the climbing, it was classic stuff: three stars in the guidebook. The adrenaline was flowing more freely than the monosodium glutamate in a Chinese Takeaway. I felt simply ecstatic to be high up a rock face. The fear was no longer raw; it was carefully nurtured, moulded into a fuel that drove me on to excel. Now was the time of my climbing ascendancy, in every sense of the word! I was not getting close to nature; I was performing exceptionally strenuous and athletic moves high above the most beautiful valley in England, or in my book, the world. The surroundings were magnificent yet intimate, with views of the imposing scree slopes, mingled with rolling hills washed with bracken and dotted randomly with Scottish Blackface and Herdwick sheep. Ravens circled around the rocky outcrops as their deep, gravely "Caw, Caw!" cries swirled, mingled, and then dissipated with the warm wind blowing from the far-off yet visible coastline.

I laughed as I looked down the route of Botterill's Slab with the severe Wasdale Screes to one side, plunging recklessly into Wastwater, maintaining that acute angle deep into the waters of England's deepest lake. Opposite was the fell of Yewbarrow with the enormous mound of Great Gable overshadowing it and the famous Pillar Rock in the distance. And here was I, pinching holds and smearing feet on the wonderfully rippled granite around me. Tiny and unnoticed but quite fantastically happy. There were no cares up here. This was as good as life could get.

My climbing had become thrill-seeking without dread. Fear had given way to excitement of a magnitude I did not believe possible. Each new physical and mental challenge had me rushing toward it. Trepidation, delay, or any thought of negative consequences had simply vanished and had been transformed into food for the journey to mountaineering greatness. For me, however, this journey had no destination, and the hunger was insatiable. This is in itself a paradox, but much more so was the fact that I was content in this realization, for the striving itself was enough, or so it seemed.

Another huge step on this journey started later in the summer when I met up with one of Dave's friends, and the three of us, together with a fourth I had not yet met, decided on an expedition. The usual climbing "mecca" was Chamonix in France. Year after year, hoards of climbers would descend on the Alps and Chamonix in particular, intent on climbing as many rock or ice routes as time and the horrendous over-crowding allowed. With this in mind we decided to avoid the tourist-climbing destinations and opted for a less frequented area: Norway.

There the climbing would be stupendous, with Europe's steepest and longest rock walls, some of them over 4,000 feet of ascent, including the legendary Troll Wall, a real climbing monster that I could not even contemplate so early in my career.

As we discussed the venture, which was to last four weeks and take in a number of 3,000-foot walls, all in full view of the Troll Wall itself, I found myself sitting with sweating palms and a dry mouth, desperate to read more about the routes, the terrain, indeed anything about Norway itself. To be going on an expedition with three experienced mountaineers was a most unexpected crown to my first year as a climber, and I felt privileged that they had asked me along. I was especially grateful to Dave, who had vouched for my ability and character to his friends. It brought a real closeness that enhanced the respect I already had for him.

It was this respect that found me agreeing to accompany him to church the following Sunday, when my normal reaction would be to run hard and run far. I think I was filled with thoughts of the Troll Wall and fame in Scandinavia when he asked me, so I agreed with a smile, even though I was a little embarrassed at first, probably in case someone heard him asking me. The frowning suspicion and contempt that usually accompanied anything "religious" was absent, though. It should have been there but inexplicably was not, so to church I went. At least we could keep each other out of the clutches of any over-exuberant evangelists, I thought.

I entered the old church, head full of Norway, routes beginning at dawn, and the promise of a few pints later in the evening. I expected the usual drone of an octogenarian standing in an angel costume, interspersed with various dirges and recited ramblings from a Bible so large it must have fallen down Jack's beanstalk. The angel costume was ticked off within seconds, though even my cynical eye could not put the vicar much above fifty. My curiosity was awakened by the overhead projector at the front of the church, and I smiled as the words of the first song were placed on it by the guy with a guitar, accompanied by various others on flute, violin, drums, and the butt of hilarious Pentecostal parody: the infamous tambourine! I looked up at the ceiling to inspect the robustness of the chandelier fittings. At the same time I sat down in my pew, more than a little uneasy at what might unfold, making a mental note of the Exit signs.

My early misgivings proved to be unfounded, since the service followed a fairly traditional Church of England format, except that the singing was altogether more lively, and the congregation clearly enjoyed it. I was now rather relieved that this was no more threatening than any other church service, and the modernness was even quite refreshing. My thoughts, however, were interrupted as my eye caught sight of someone from within the crowded pews shuffling and then standing up, edging to the side of the pew. There were no "excuse me's" or smiles as she interrupted her fellow communicants, but those who were disturbed acted as though they were not.

Suddenly, this middle-aged fat woman took off dancing down the centre aisle of the church. In full view of everyone, with this rather odd skipping, lolloping gait, totally oblivious to the spectacle she was making of herself. Even more odd was that nobody batted an eyelid. Local crank, I thought. They must all know her. I should have laughed out loud.

But I did not. It actually looked peculiarly lovely.

Not the dancing, nor the woman herself. It was the sight of someone expressing herself freely without thinking of her own image. This was something new. This was not a professional dancer performing on stage, nor a well-trained amateur showing her friends what she could do. This was someone just being herself and not caring what we all thought. This was freedom: freedom from the shackles of performance and image.

I didn't laugh, but I did smile. She looked happy and content, and somehow it rubbed off on me. I didn't understand any of it, least of all why she was prancing up and down the aisle with gay abandon. Apparently her dance was an "expression of praise to God," whatever that meant. But the image remained long after the service. Of course, I didn't mention it, but I actually enjoyed everything there that night because of that one lingering image of an unspectacular, middle-aged woman dancing. She was free to be herself among both friends and strangers.

That was the crutch she needed, I reasoned, and I was sure she was really an emotional wreck, but I did not scoff at any of it. It was intriguing, and when asked, I agreed to go again, as a casual observer, so long as it didn't upset my climbing plans. My own image was still being crafted as a mountaineer, and no church service was going to mess with that. The dancing woman, however, was not easily forgotten, nor was the peace she seemed to have.

My inner-peace, however, was being pursued at the sharp end of a climbing rope. I was training hard for our Scandinavian adventure, determined to push my limits on some of the great, vast rock walls that Norway had to offer. My journey had evolved into a race, and it was gathering speed, gaining momentum, and thrusting me forward—this time toward Scandinavia. Where I would go next I had no idea, but it would involve climbing, overcoming both physical and mental obstacles, and achieving goals—all set against the backdrop of the world's great mountain ranges. Life could not provide anything so intoxicating or rewarding, of that I was sure.

Chapter 3

BIG STUFF
IN SCANDINAVIA

▲

The sea remained deceptively tranquil as a stiff breeze blew through my fleece jacket. Folding my arms in an effort to stop shivering, I squinted to stem the flow of tears forced out by the unexpectedly cold wind. It was still August, but the falling temperature heralded the imminence of autumn.

We had set out on our 25-hour journey the previous day from Newcastle, England, on our way across the North Sea to the port of Bergen, Norway. Now after 15 hours there was not a sliver of land to be seen on any part of the vast horizon. Our vessel was by no means a majestic ship, even to the most romantically minded. It was a squat, corpulent, top-heavy affair with rust and peeling paint betraying its lowly rank in the maritime ledger of grandeur. This was nothing more than a box for transporting cars and bodies.

In stark contrast I had just been studying a dolphin as it bounced effortlessly across the surface of the gentle waves. The duel between the ferry and this remarkable mammal, between Nature and Engineering, was a grossly unfair match, clearly demonstrated as the streamlined bullet cruised alongside the ship for a while before it banked off to port, dropped a biological gear, and streaked away, just visible under the surface of the sea. I continued to watch until it disappeared over the horizon, still glancing off the skin of the ocean and finally bounding out of sight, like a startled summer roebuck disappearing from the edge of a field into an oak coppice.

Notwithstanding the quality of the transport, my dream had begun. Each gust of wind, every surge of the ship through the water invigorated me further. I was bursting with energy and wandered the ship for hours, doing pull-ups on every doorway, dips on every set of hand rails, and even going for a run round the deck. I could sense the thrill of being in the mountains, the anticipation of being engrossed on some huge, inaccessible wall of granite and intent only on the next delicate move upwards, all the time acutely aware of the hundreds, maybe thousands of feet of free fall as a punishment for failure. Wave after wave of image brought fresh feelings of expectation. I paced back and forth, each imagined route so clear in my mind that it overpowered the reality around me. I must have looked either insane or possessed—probably both.

The ship stopped first at Stavanger, south of Bergen. We knew then that we would be disembarking in a little over an hour. This was most welcome, as the last few hours on board had tested even my enthusiasm. Since we had largely abstained from eating or drinking on the journey due to our meagre budget, we were looking forward to raiding the contents of the boot of our car, kept secure and off-limits below deck until the ship's engines were turned off. When we were finally allowed to go to our vehicles, it came as a great relief to our dry mouths and rumbling stomachs.

I have read about many expeditions, both mountaineering and otherwise, and they all included details of the planning aspect of the trip and of all the provisions that were necessary to embark on such ventures. However, I have rarely been *on* an expedition where all these provisions were forthcoming. For me, it seemed, an empty stomach and general physical discomfort brought on largely by a lack of funds were almost invariably the norm for an expedition environment. It is certainly safe to say that this general rule was epitomized on my inaugural mountaineering adventure.

As we approached our car, the smell of the ship's engines coupled with a gnawing hunger made me feel sick to my stomach. Those factors, combined with the car exhaust fumes belching into the confines of the lower decks, made me feel decidedly unwell. However, the sight of the bow doors opening and the draught of fresh air that accompanied it brought welcome relief as we finally disembarked, and I saw in front of us the port of Bergen and the city roads beyond.

Our vehicle laboured up the ramp unconvincingly, heavily laden with four climbers, all of our climbing hardware, camping gear, and one month's supply of food. Dave's friend Pete had assured us of the power and efficiency of his old Ford Granada Estate, which was our expedition vehicle. I was not convinced, and the effort it seemed to take just to carry us off the ship did nothing to quell my initial misgivings. Nevertheless, we had no other option. The Great Green Beast had been assigned the job rather by default than by desire.

The one advantage this car offered over most others was its enormous load space. Even though the wheel arches were now perilously close to the tyres, The Beast had swallowed all of our climbing hardware, vast amounts of tinned foods, and in addition, the essential ingredients for life on the hill: two cases of suspiciously cheap beer. With the remainder of our needs loaded onto the roof rack, we at least had ample space for the four of us to travel in comfort, so long as the constant smell of unburned petrol did not make us too queasy. The sight, sound, and smell of our workhorse, together with its motley group of occupants, must have made for amusing viewing for the Norwegians unfortunate enough to cross our path.

Within an hour we had left the city far behind, and our adventure into the mountains was beginning. The map we had bought to guide us to our destination, Romsdal Valley, had indicated a major road almost all the way. What I had not expected was a major road barely two cars wide, necessitating slowing down and sometimes stopping for every oncoming vehicle.

Norway's roads appeared to have been cut out of the sides of great swathes of granite outcrops, the scenery rarely changing from nearly vertical, glistening rock on one side of the car to the black, icy waters of yet another spectacular fjord out of the other window. I could feel the heat reflecting from the rock on one side of my face and a cold draught blowing off the glacial mountain waters on my other cheek—an amazing experience as we drove northward.

Much of the terrain reminded me of the north of Scotland but viewed through a magnifying glass since everything seemed to be twice as big. The crags were taller and much more expansive, spreading across my entire field of view. The meadows, when they appeared, were not cut into patchwork shapes by drystone walls, nor did they have barbed wire fences to slice them up. It was more grandiose than Scotland, equally as majestic, but somehow less endearing, though undeniably beautiful. Others may disagree, and I do not deny my prejudice toward the Highlands, but initially I was merely impressed rather than enamoured by what I saw. My viewpoint did, however, change as I discovered more of the sights and sounds of this wonderful country.

In short, the journey was far from boring. We were also accompanied by the tapping of rucksack straps rattling on the roof—an irritant to most people but an intolerable thorn in the flesh for Pete. He would stop whenever the rattles re-emerged, get out, and spend what seemed like an age trying to find the offending strap before tying it securely to the roof rack and diving back into the driver's seat with a half-irritated, half-triumphant look on his face.

Pete was probably around 10 years my senior, similar to Dave, with an open, friendly face and steel-rimmed glasses that gave him a slightly ungainly appearance. He was the epitome of calmness, however, and I was soon to discover that his patience on the rock face had earned him a reputation for coolness under pressure that was most impressive. Only a few weeks later I would watch him climb a previously unclimbed route near Bergen, where he displayed a calmness and fortitude under pressure that would have rivalled a big-game hunter facing down a charging rhino. I think the steel-rimmed glasses served as his disguise for a much tougher constitution.

His prominent jaw line had earned him the nickname of "Chin," which he took in good part. I did not feel, however, that I knew him well enough to address him as such, just in case his patience ever wore as thin with me as it did with rattling rucksack straps. He was, after all, a fairly robust-looking six-footer.

Dave had warned me of this rattling-strap obsession, and he smiled as he nudged me in a "told you so" fashion with a nod of his head in Pete's direction as Pete once more drove off, head cocked slightly, listening for any remaining taps above his head. I smiled back, but I found myself feeling jealous of them both. They had a relationship that had been forged not only at school but also on many previous adventures to crags around England, Scottish mountains in winter, and even to the French and Swiss Alps. They would talk about earlier trips—days to local crags or epic ascents of Alpine peaks in atrocious winter conditions—laughing to each other seemingly about nothing at all. Yet their faces betrayed an understanding that could only be shared through smell, touch, and that inner awareness of an atmosphere long since departed. All these things were the sum of "experience." Experiences shared and silently reminisced about as smiles and gazes were shared over a pint in the pub or over a brew made by our Trangia stoves by the roadside.

I had neither the experiences nor the friendships to share with anyone, and I was envious of their closeness, though I was grateful that they always included me as part of the team. Certainly I was not in the least resentful, but it did magnify my own loneliness. I reassured myself with the thought that by being here I was also becoming experienced, and perhaps one day I too would be able to share wistful looks with the knowing twinkle of the experienced eye—having felt the atmosphere of electrifying tales on high mountains, of real adventure. At least now I had the chance to start my own mental journal of "experiences."

After many hours of driving, skirting alongside magnificent fjords and climbing several hairpin-laced passes, we finally approached our destination: Romsdal Valley and the town of Andalsnes. We pulled onto a campsite and were at once confronted with our first dilemma of the expedition. The site catered to tents, of course, but it also contained many wooden cabins of varying sizes. We had already felt the evening chill of Norway as autumn approached, and we could almost feel the welcome glow of these cozy cabins as we reluctantly unloaded the tents. Comfort, however, came at a price for which we had not budgeted. We discussed the options and were about to conclude in a most masculine fashion that our gear was more than up to the task of keeping us warm in these conditions, when someone pointed out the advantage of having a place to dry out our kit after a day on the hill. We grasped this excellent and practical cop-out clause with relish and promptly shelled out the extra krona for our own little palace. We were all tough mountaineers, of course, but why waste the opportunity to be dry as well as macho?

An hour or two later, having looked around and gained our bearings, we settled around the Trangia stove, watched the water boil, and planned our assault on the various mountains around us. I felt like Wellington's adjutant, invited along to the general's planning meeting prior to a campaign, and I was genuinely grateful and honoured to have been invited along on this, my first real expedition.

The first mountain was to be a "getting fit" climb, up an easy route on Bispen, "the Bishop." I immediately thought this was a silly idea. After all, I had been training for years in general terms, and for weeks and weeks specifically with this trip in mind. Surely all these guys were in peak physical condition. They were, after all, first-class climbers. It seemed utterly pointless to me, and my silent resentment of such a waste of valuable expedition time would not wane until we actually took to the hill the following day.

After an early dinner, I turned in and slept out in the tent rather than in the cabin, enjoying the smell of the mountain air and listening to the wind brushing the sides of the crags as it rushed and swirled down the valley, past the incredible Troll Wall and on past our camp. The thought that the same air that had just glanced off the side of the most famous rock route in Europe, indeed, one of the most famous in the world, was now entering my lungs was thrilling to me. I smiled as I drifted off to sleep, for once, albeit briefly, totally contented with my life.

The unspoken agreement between Dave and me, by now well-established, held firm early the next morning as a mug of hot tea persuaded me to roll over and sit up. Dave lit the stove shortly after dawn and let me doze to the comforting, low hum of the flame and the stinging smell of methylated spirits. As agreed, I took the used dishes to the tap for washing and replaced them in our hut without a word on the subject spoken between us. Our domestic minds were at one with each other!

Loading the kit was a joy, as ever. More so today as we were finally going climbing in a foreign land. The route was far bigger than any I had ever attempted, and the scale of operations was simply breathtaking. I had bought (or more correctly, my generous parents had bought for me) a new rucksack, of which I was immensely proud. The Karrimor Alpiniste 60-80 was the paragon of packs for the serious mountaineer. With the opening of two zips down the sides of the pack, it immediately expanded into a tremendous, huge hauling pack for expedition work. With the zips fastened it maintained a compact and slim profile, ideal for ice climbing over long routes. The slim build enabled arm movement when placing ice axes while still affording room for sufficient kit to be carried on a multi-day adventure. In short, it really looked the part. All I had to do now was to remove the shiny, new look of it as quickly as possible.

Even though most of this day's route was, according to the guidebook, nothing more than a walk and a scramble, there were certain sections that looked as if they would demand actual climbing. We had decided we would not use the ropes except in cases of emergency but packed all our gear just in case. I secretly hoped we would need to get the ropes out and make a "proper climb" of it. We loaded the car and drove off into the bright sunshine of a stunning late summer morning. Having consulted both map and guidebook, we set off for the start of Bispen, south ridge route.

The chill of the nighttime had disappeared long before we had parked the car and started the walk-in to the mountain. I was wearing three layers of upper body clothing, including a fleece jacket, shirt, and thermal vest. I was down to the vest within a couple of minutes and soon felt most uncomfortable even stripped down that far. I soon came to understand the reason people advised against the famous Helly Hansen thermal underwear: the wearer is invariably both toasty warm and quite breathtakingly pungent within minutes of the arrival of the first sweat droplet. It was a smell with which I became intimately acquainted over the following years, and one that convinced me that climbing was for the single man, as no worthwhile woman would ever look at such a creature who announced his arrival with an olfactory assault of which Wellington himself would have been proud.

We scrambled up most of the route with a few sections of pleasant if unrewarding walking, and then we enjoyed a brief flirtation with some steeper sections that had me hoping we would be delving into our rucksacks for the ropes. But I was to be disappointed. It simply did not merit that kind of attention.

Just when I thought we would be arriving in a most mundane fashion at the summit, we rounded a corner and I saw my first knife-edge ridge. Snaking away from me for what seemed to be around 100 yards was a wall of rock that appeared at first to be man-made; only a few inches across the top in places and hardly ever wider than a foot. This ridge leading to the summit was a splendid little adventure by itself, and it elevated our day out to a status far beyond what I had expected. I felt a wave of excitement agitate my senses, and I hurried on to this deceptive bonus to our outing.

The prospect of tackling the knife-edge ridge had the sweat running from my palms almost as freely as the Norwegian sun was making it run down my back. As we approached the ridge, Dave, who was immediately in front, told me he was going to climb the ridge in true alpine style, that is, *au cheval.*

What is he talking about? I thought to myself.

The next moment he straddled the ridge and began shuffling along on his backside in quite the most ludicrous and, frankly, unimpressive a fashion I could have imagined. All I could see in my mind was the true mountaineer, clinging to one side of the ridge, picking his way up the side of the mountain, finger tips gripping the smallest crevices of the ridge, silhouetted against a huge drop beneath the minimal footholds available to him. *Au cheval* was most definitely not that. I was going to show the old goat how it was done.

The handholds were bigger than I had imagined they were going to be. The footholds were more than adequate. The view beneath the footholds, down the unspeakably steep sides of the ridge, was breathtaking.

Breathtaking, exhilarating, and quite outrageously terrifying.

This was my first experience of real exposure. Lakeland crags are wondrous places and can give any climber the feeling of being way out there, like he or she is dangling over an abyss. However, they are not typically so very big. Norway was on a much grander scale, and my problem was that I was holding onto a ridge that dropped off for several hundreds of feet with a backdrop of mountains on one side and fjords several thousands of feet beneath me on the other. This was bad enough, but the foremost thought in my mind was that *I had no rope.* A slip would mean death without any doubt whatsoever.

My solution to this predicament was to hurry across the ridge as quickly as possible. No hanging around making sure of each hold for me; I charged across as fast as I could, demonstrating graphically my inexperience and my fear. Toward the end, however, I had calmed down enough to actually enjoy the views a bit, even laugh at my precarious situation, and finally, enjoy the feeling of the prolonged adrenaline surge that I always desired. I seem to recall posing for a photograph at one point, which I have thankfully since mislaid.

After the compulsory summit photographs and a bite to eat, we yomped down the conquered Bishop by another, easier route. On the way back to camp in the car, we were already looking around for the next mountain.

Unfortunately, as is all too common in Norway, the weather interceded and rain stopped play for a few days. We moped around the campsite and went into Andalsnes a couple of times, all the while inspecting the heavens for a break in the clouds. But all we could see from just over halfway up the entire mountain range was a shroud of grey. A wet, dismal blanket had engulfed the hills where we wanted to play and had dimmed significantly our hopes for the expedition as a whole. The persistent drizzle certainly had a very English feel to it, for which I was not grateful. On top of this, all the while, the temperature was dropping noticeably. It was now September and autumn had arrived. We could only wait for the weather to pick up and hope the rock would dry quickly to enable us to "tick off" a few more routes in our guidebooks before it was time to head south again.

I do not recall how long we waited for a break in the weather, but I do know that we had all abandoned the tents by this time. We were enjoying the dryness and warmth of our cabin to the full. We awoke one morning to find that the clouds had lifted. We were surprised to see a whole range of hills and ridges all covered in a blanket of snow. This was most unexpected and a tremendous bonus. This offered the possibility of some winter climbing, and I was desperate to try what I considered to be *real* mountaineering. We decided at once on an easy peak to test the quality and condition of the snow, and before long we were headed up the pass to climb our next peak: Breitind, interestingly located right above the finishing point of the Troll Wall route.

The climb itself was uneventful, and the route was nothing more than a snow plod, but its effect on me was profound. I was captivated with winter climbing. Using crampons and ice axes held a fascination for me that I could not explain. I felt so completely at ease in these conditions and so enthralled by it all that I surprised even myself. As much as I enjoyed a day climbing rock in the sunshine, it could not compare to being on a big mountain in the winter. The difficulty of the route was immaterial: an easy route was fun and a difficult route did not faze me at all. I simply loved being up a big mountain in the ice and snow. I still do not fully understand why I loved this environment, but it certainly had something to do with the wilderness feel to it, of being remote, inaccessible, and not only untouched but also untouchable. The added adrenaline factor when it came to serious routes only came later and was a most welcome bonus.

From the summit of Breitind we could all feast on the most stunning views of smooth, thick blankets of snow-covered peaks topping off the dark, almost sinister-looking precipitous walls of icy granite as they plunged into the black waters of the fjords several thousands of feet beneath us. On the opposite side, the mountains rolled into the far horizon, crowning emerald fields beneath them. Cutting through them were the white, sparkling scars of myriad waterfalls and streams, all fed by the melting snows and glaciers all around. This was real beauty, and it washed over me and through me like a flood. I was far beyond elation. I sat down in the snow, mouth open like a child, trying to take in more fully what my eyes were showing me. I felt a peace and a joy that had eluded me for almost my entire life up to that point, and for several years afterwards it still escaped my grasp. It was the feeling of complete satisfaction, and I only knew I had experienced it after we had come back down the mountain.

Strange how one can be so affected by a view of a snowy hill! Strange but wonderful nonetheless.

Steve called the rest of us over to see what he had discovered: the exit point of the Troll Wall route. Climbers who make it up the Troll Wall almost invariably come back down the mountain by the way we had just walked up. We peered over the edge and looked down the final section of the climb. Immediately my eyes began to play tricks on me as the snow caused the light to glare off the rock. The steepness of the rock face, coupled with the various layers of granite overlapping each other, all made the route look utterly impossible to climb. Despite all of my ambitions, I had to admit there was absolutely no way I could even contemplate such an adventure. It looked truly terrifying, and I thought what a miserable death it would have been for me had I even started such a route, for my death would have been inevitable. We all stepped back from the edge, talked about wanting to climb this route some day (I was only half-convinced at the time), and then headed back down our gentle walk.

It had been an exceptional day for me. I could not escape the lure of winter climbing and the desire to go steeper and harder on ice and snow. The spectre of the Trolls was more of a necessary challenge to overcome, rather than a true desire, but still, the Troll Wall went down in the mental notebook of "compulsory routes to be climbed." As we returned to base, I was filled with feelings, memories, ideas, and the whole sum of "experience" that I had longed for. Whatever it was, it felt sublime!

We could not decide what to do next, and time was beginning to run out for us. Pete and Steve wanted to look at a couple of other areas of Norway, for they had read some accounts of good rock around those places. So we decided to stay for just a few more days where we were before moving farther south in the hope of having more stable, warmer weather. However, there was still a little time left to do a couple of good rock routes, so we determined one day to split into pairs and do our own thing. Pete and Steve wanted to find a sterner challenge than I was up to as a novice, and I think Dave was glad to opt for the "roadside crag" option anyway. That evening we looked at the guidebook and saw a straightforward route that started just over the road from the campsite. We decided to have an uneventful day out on some sunny, south-facing rock, and we went to bed looking forward to an easy jaunt up a large lump of granite.

However, even an easy route, when the added factor of scale comes along, makes the whole venture much more serious. I had found this out on Bispen and had been able to laugh about it. Unfortunately, I did not learn very much from it. Big routes bring bigger risks, bigger rewards, and bigger problems. I was about to find this out, almost at the cost of my life.

We set off rather late on our little expedition up a Norwegian version of a roadside crag. It should have been an easy romp up a mere 1,000-feet-or-so of Severe to Very Severe graded rock, and we fully expected to be back in time for dinner and a beer long before dark.

Instead, something profound happened later that day and into that night. It happened both gradually, as events unfolded, and suddenly, in one electrifying moment. It was an event, a moment of time, and a change of state that went beyond time. The events and that moment make a grown man cry even today, half a lifetime later. In the space of twelve hours or so my whole life was turned upside down, and I had no idea how, except that I knew in the core of my being that it had happened. I have spoken to other mountaineers since who have shared similar single incidents, but none who have shared the same catalogue of events all rolled into one experience. I do not say this as a boast, since I did not orchestrate any of it, but merely to indicate that it was highly uncommon, even for those individuals who choose to place themselves in dangerous situations. Certainly, it was a different man who came down that mountain late at night from the youth who set off up it at 9 a.m. on that sunny September morning.

But more of all that later.

I have very little recollection of the last few hundred yards' walk back across the fields from the foot of the crag to our cozy little hut that night. I believe it was passed in silence. I do remember that, as we pushed our way quietly inside the door, both Pete and Steve were in bed in their bunks. Pete looked over from the top bunk and smiled broadly at his friend.

"Davey's had an epic has he?"

He stretched the phrase out as long as he could in an almost chiding school ma'am manner. Clearly, he was pleased to see his friend back in one piece. I did not care that I had not merited a mention. It was hard to feel left out even if I had tried to be offended. I simply shuffled sheepishly into the hut, put down my gear, and set out my bed for the night.

Dinner was in order, and I had two cans of lager and a tin of baked beans, eaten cold straight from the tin. It was a deliberate choice of a hard man's feast. Men who have had a great mountain adventure need to eat basic mountain food and drink alcohol. I could easily have had a nice hot brew of tea and some warming stew, but the image in my own mind demanded beans and alcohol. I had nearly died several times over and still I was concerned with the ludicrous issues of image, even while sitting unobserved in a hut in the middle of Norway. I did enjoy it, though—even the cold beans.

We did a few more mountains after that, including the Romsdalhorn north face. Dave and I turned back half way as the snow began to blow around us and dangerous conditions threatened. Dave did not seem to want to get bitterly cold, and I think he thought I was too inexperienced to face such a challenging possibility. What was truly remarkable was that I did not object even for a moment. I was more than happy to come down and wait for the other two to finish the route and return to us, which they did some three or so hours later. I did not even question my acquiescence until years later. Where had my drivenness, my ambition gone? I was almost disinterested in whether or not I climbed the route, which was a paradigm shift in attitude, indeed in my very personality.

As we were sitting in the car, I rolled a cigarette and had a beer and felt warm and content. I enjoyed thinking of Pete and Steve struggling on the north face of the Romsdalhorn in the snow, not because they were having a hard time of it at all; I simply knew they would be enjoying it and I was happy for them. I was also happy not to be with them. Perhaps the events of the last day or so had made me nervous or scared or at least temporarily gun shy of climbing. I did not know, and I did not care. I just sat in the car with Dave, got out and walked around from time to time, looking up at the hill where the other lads were, and thought about what had just recently happened to me. I did not analyze it, but simply let the events wash over me again and again in my mind.

There was no reason on earth why I should still be alive, yet here I was. This was a bizarre thought. I could not make sense of it. Surely my mind had missed something crucial. Over and over I tried to remember some salient point that would make sense of the whole thing, but it never came. Even more strangely, I never once discussed any of it with Dave.

Pete and Steve interrupted my daydreaming as they appeared on the ridgeline, making good progress down toward the valley. By now the snow was insistently driving into our faces and the wind had a real bite to it.

Steve arrived back at the car first, face almost blue with the cold; and his wholly insufficient, summer jacket blew around him in demonstration of its total uselessness in these almost arctic conditions. I shivered for Steve but should have saved my concerns, for he was oblivious to the discomfort I felt on his behalf. For goodness sake, he hadn't even zipped the jacket all the way up!

"Bloody Nora, it's cold," he said. "I need a drink." He immediately threw open the back of the car, sending a flurry of snow across Dave's face, and proceeded to open and greedily gulp down a can of lager from the remaining case of beer. I could not believe he yearned for ice-cold beer on a day like this after having spent the last five hours or more battling the winter conditions of a fairly serious rock route. Moreover, there was not even the slightest sense of affectation to his choosing a beer; he genuinely fancied a pint, and he proved it by downing a second as he welcomed Pete back to the car by offering him one as well.

This is one tough bloke, I thought to myself.

I should not have been surprised. Dave had regaled me of stories about Steve, all of which confirmed him as both a resilient and resourceful chap. I was just a little taken aback that someone could actually not feel conditions that were hard enough to make me want to go back to bed! I could see that his hands were blue, his clothing was totally inadequate for the very hostile conditions he had just been subjected to, and he was shaking uncontrollably in the passenger seat of the car. But in spite of all that, he was not even slightly concerned. He must have been in considerable discomfort, but obviously chose either to ignore it or merely to accept this as part of mountaineering life. Later I would learn that this mindset was essential as a winter climber, but for now, I was very impressed.

I was also suddenly aware that I had limitations. I was not in the same league as these guys. I had my work cut out for me, and I had to strive harder to become a real mountaineer. I had to shake off what had happened to me and push myself harder to achieve my goals. I knew this feeling of not wanting to push myself further on the rock would go away in a while, so as we packed up our gear and headed south, I began to look forward to some sunny routes of hard rock around Ulvik, our next destination. Before this, however, was the small matter of going over the Jotunheim Pass and the possibility of a spot of ice climbing.

As we motored south I was increasingly excited at this prospect. What I had not expected was quite the little adventure that awaited us; nor was it restricted to events out on the hill.

Our Great Green Beast lurched to a halt at a lay-by, which was located nearly at the summit of the Jotunheim Pass. I knew we had arrived because the smell of petrol stopped its ceaseless assault on my nostrils as the vehicle worked less hard and began to come to a halt.

We all got out and looked around as we made preparations to pitch our tents and get some food on the go.

A blanket of clouds all around us made the "viewing" a very brief affair. Pete and Steve had wanted to find a route in the area. Dave had decided that the two of us would get up early the next morning and go and explore the Jotunheim Glacier. Perhaps there was a wall of ice we could climb for practice, or maybe he could simply get me accustomed to using crampons and ice axes as we plodded around on the glacier. I could not wait, and I was grateful to Dave for taking the time to teach me about winter mountaineering; after all, he had been doing this kind of thing for over 10 years.

After dinner, we set out a pan of water on the Trangia stove for a brew in the morning, set the alarm for dawn, and turned in to our tent. The last thing I noticed was that the stars were coming out and the clouds were lifting to reveal a simply spectacular array of the Norwegian night sky. Breathtaking!

What was decidedly not wonderful was the fact that the clear night meant a plunging of temperature to, in layman's terms, horrible-below-freezing. More importantly, my sleeping bag was designed to keep a man warm on the beach in an African summer. It was only a summer bag made for Scout camps and trips in the caravan, but it was all I had at the time, so I took it.

That night, suffice to say, I truly discovered the meaning of the word COLD!

Fortunately, I did have a good sleeping mat, which meant that if I made a quarter turn every fifteen minutes, the part of me in contact with the mat was not aching with cold; I do not mean that it was warm. What a miserable night! I listened to my friend snore as I shivered for a solid eight hours or more, sometimes in considerable pain. Time has never before or since passed so slowly. I was not angry or upset at all; I was far too cold to be either of those. Even my eyeballs ached with the numbing throb of the freezing air. Between clenched teeth I prayed for the sun to rise!

The dawn came with no bird song (we were too high up the pass) but my relief could have produced a dawn chorus all of its own. To see the first rays of sun appear over the mountains and kiss the sides of our tent—watching the frost turn from matt to silk, before slowly shining its molten path down the sides and dripping off the edge of the outer shell—was utter bliss! I rolled my stiff bones out of my bed and put on the stove for a brew (my being first up was a sure sign that things were desperate). The water was frozen solid, and it seemed to take an age to boil. Nevertheless, after a few minutes we were drinking hot tea, and I felt that I might, against all odds it seemed, have survived the night. Most importantly, the sun had now risen on a completely clear day. We were off to play in the snow, and I was giddy with anticipation.

We spent the whole day wearing crampons and wielding ice axes up, down, across, and through that glacier. Nothing was technical; everything was magnificent! Listening to the creaking groans of this mass of almost living ice and rock as it ground its way down or maybe even through the mountainside made me tingle with excitement. I loved to climb small walls of frozen snow, feeling the positive placement of the ice axe and then kicking the front points of the crampons into the sheets of ice. I knew immediately that I loved being in winter mountaineering gear out on the ice and snow. Everyone said it was much more dangerous than rock climbing, but it held no fear for me at all. In fact, I felt completely safe on the ice, as I reasoned that if you could make your own holds, why should you ever have reason to be afraid? It was not like rock where you could be left without a suitable hand or finger hold; you simply stuck your axe or crampon in the frozen surface and carried on. It all seemed very straightforward yet extremely rewarding.

That one day out convinced me that my future lay in mountaineering, and in snow and ice work. Let's face it, "mountaineer" sounds much better than "rock climber," doesn't it? I returned to camp feeling empowered. All thoughts of fear and inadequacy, of doubt and hesitancy, were gone. It was also tremendous fun, and I wanted to do more of it, lots more of it.

It was approaching dark before we had finished packing the car, and snow was starting to fall. In only a matter of minutes, as we drove carefully to the very top of the pass, a blanket of snow had formed on the road, and visibility was poor. Nobody passed a comment, but we all knew there was a long, steep, and heavily hairpinned pass ahead of us. Pete pulled over to assess the situation just as a Norwegian appeared over the now disturbingly close horizon, coming from the opposite direction. He slowed down to check if we were all okay, and he was as helpful and friendly as almost every other Norwegian we had met.

"How's the road down the pass?" asked Pete tentatively.

"Oh, not so bad really, so long as you have the four-wheel drive and snow chains . . ." His voice petered out as he began to scan our vehicular "facilities."

For a minute the two of them wandered around the old Granada, literally kicking tyres. When Pete jumped back in the driver's seat, it did not require any explanation for us all to realize that the guy had shrugged his shoulders and said basically, "Well, I wouldn't risk it, but what else are you going to do? It's your funeral, lads!"

He waved and pipped his horn as he drove off, clearly convinced he would never see any of us alive again. Pete put the car in gear and then drove down that pass in much the same way he handled a difficult ice route: slowly, steadily, utterly unflappable, and without slipping once. I will not say it was not hairy, though. At times we lost the road completely. On several occasions we knew that we had picked up speed and braking was not an option. However, after an epic descent we arrived at the foot of the pass, teeth still gritted, sweat on our brows, and buttocks clenched into a death-lock. Few rock routes have grabbed my attention more! Another experience under the belt, another story to tell, and ahead of us was our next granite wall to conquer, weather permitting, of course. We were on our way to Ulvik, a crag rat's playground, so we had been told.

The weather interceded yet again, unfortunately, and made Ulvik a fairly uneventful place in mountaineering terms, with rain and low clouds continuing to scupper our plans, save for a day spent top-roping a few routes with a group of tremendously friendly and jovial Norwegian climbers we met.

I spent most of the time down there distinctly "out of sorts" without really knowing why. The problem was I did not want to climb, and that really bothered me. After all, I had just been fuelled with high-octane ambition from my jaunt on the Jotunheim Glacier, complete with all the plans that it entailed, and now suddenly I simply did not want to do it. This made me angry. Rather than jumping at every chance of having a go at any top-roping route that was offered me, I chose instead to mope around the foot of the crag doing bits of bouldering here and there. While Pete and Steve did route after smiling route, chatting effortlessly with our new Norwegian pals, I stayed in the corners, morose and skulking, darker than the clouds above us and colder than the increasing gloom of autumn on the granite walls that were our, or at least their, playground. "Disaffected" was not a word in my vocabulary at the time, but it was certainly in my attitude.

Despite my sullen temperament I found the Norwegians we had met to be quite the most friendly and hospitable bunch of guys imaginable. Before too long we had been invited to a slide show of one of their colleague's trips to the north of the country on an ice-climbing expedition, and then on to the pub for a few beers. However, with beer at £4.50 per pint, even back then, we declined, as funds simply prohibited such extravagance. To our amazement, one of them offered us the keys to his apartment, telling us to make ourselves at home, and that they would all be back later for a party. This chap had only known us for a matter of four or five hours, and here he was leaving us alone in his home. Quite remarkable!

We spread our gear across the floors of various rooms, rummaged around for some food, and than a curious event unfolded. I went to answer the call of nature and was at first puzzled as to how to work the strange, chromed Norwegian toilet this guy had. More specifically I could not lift the lid, nor indeed, could I find any means with which it might actually detach from the base unit. Then I noticed that the pipe work from the toilet went up and certainly not down through the floor. I laughed out loud and called to the lads in the living room. This was no toilet; it was a still! The guy was distilling moonshine!

We all were amazed at his ingenuity and speculated on the quality of the brew that such a contraption could make. As we continued to speculate, I looked up at the shelving that went around the entire perimeter of our host's living room. Row upon row of empty bottles; every sort of beer and wine he had ever tasted, no doubt.

All with their tops still on. Strange.

I picked up one of them and was surprised to see it full of water, as was the one next to it. Indeed, all of them were full (my naïveté was quite remarkable). It took the wily Steve to put the puzzle together, and with a shout of glee and a spark in his eye, he removed the top, took a sniff then a stiff swig of the contents.

We were all thoroughly smashed within a half hour or so. It was like releasing a pack of hunting dogs into a pet shop full of rabbits—the drinking equivalent of utter carnage. Our host returned to find four buffoons smiling inanely around a sea of empty bottles. He was quite pleased, it seemed, from what he discovered: "Ah, I see you have found it. Excellent. Now we can all have a party!"

It was only later that we found out that nearly all Norwegians mixed this rocket fuel with coffee to make a rather pleasant tasting brew with it. We had shown no such sophistication, but thankfully the effects were not as brutal as we deserved them to be. The next morning all of us arose none the worse for our escapade. We bid our generous host farewell and headed off toward our last port of call: Bergen.

Despite my melancholy in Ulvik, or perhaps because of it, I felt a need to push hard in the last couple of days of our expedition—to finish on a high note if possible. We camped quite close to the port of Bergen, only a few minutes away by car, and yet still a secluded and very quiet little valley. The weather had picked up considerably, so hopefully we could get a few routes under our belts before heading for home.

During this time Pete set up a new, unclimbed route, which was a real privilege to witness. His poise on the rock was exemplary, never looking pushed or frantic, always careful in placing gear and planning his next move. He graded the route a modest VS, and in all probability he has never listed his ascent anywhere. Pete was never one to shout his achievements from the rooftops, despite his considerable ability.

On the same day, Dave and I set off up a small, straightforward climb that had a difficult and unprotected start. After several attempts, Dave finally overcame the first obstacle, only to be defeated almost immediately by the second. With no gear in place, this defeat meant a fall of around ten feet or so. He landed safely enough but was clearly angry about this whole state of affairs. It had taken quite some time already for him—only to get back to ground level in an awful hurry. As he had struggled up the first section, I had noticed from my standpoint a couple of holds that he had missed. I ventured a question:

"Would it be okay if I had a go?" I knew I could do it, and I was keen to lead off.

"No, it would not," came the very terse reply. I would normally have been angered by this flat refusal to allow me what was actually a perfectly reasonable request, but I wasn't. I did, however, start to realize something: my ambition to succeed was very much intact despite my earlier waverings, and I knew at that point that I would soon be outstripping my early mentor, as I had the drive in me that was now somehow eluding Dave. I saw this as a failing on his part, rather than even considering the possibility that he simply may have been maturing.

Eventually, Pete appeared and asked how we were getting on. Dave let his old friend lead off, and we climbed the route as a three. I did resent that. I could have led that route, and I was going to bloody well show them all that I could do it, and a good deal more besides. Focussed aggression has always been both useful and enjoyable to me, and I could feel that this would be excellent fuel for my ambition.

It is quite possible that this experience, mixed with the heady fuel of ice and snow work that I had tasted on the Jotunheim Glacier, combined to give me the drive to pursue mountaineering for years afterwards. A drivenness took hold of me that was most certainly lying latent already, but here was an outlet where drivenness was essential to success—at least as far as I could figure it.

The ferry trip home was simply a time for me to plan my next expedition and map out the coming year of training and preparation for all the great routes to come. I could see university, which was only a couple of weeks away, as the best way to become an excellent mountaineer. This was where I was going to find my niche, my role in life, and thereby achieve ultimate fulfilment. I might even get a degree at the end of it as an added bonus.

Chapter 4

PUSHING THE LIMITS

▲

By the time I arrived at university in October 1987, I had climbed a good number of routes in the Lake District and beyond; I had been on a serious expedition to Scandinavia; and I was a confident leader of VS standard routes. The vast majority of my packing had been of climbing gear, all of which showed the clear signs of wear. It was official; I was no beginner. I marched with confidence to the stand of the Leeds University Union Mountaineering Club and signed up on day one of Freshers' Week.

One of the first things I did after that was to go out and buy a packet of tobacco. I returned to my hall of residence, got changed, and went for a five-mile run followed by some weight training. Finally, I finished off the day with a good number of beers down at the student bar. In short, mine was a life of contradictions.

In fact, even though I was completely unaware of it, my life was awash with paradoxes. As a student of Chinese, I soon realised that other parts of the world, including China, have no issue with paradoxes. Indeed, the Far East is full of them, all bubbling away happily together in the same pot. It is only in the West that paradoxes seem to be disliked; our Greek-ordered minds always want to see one side of the paradox disproved or discarded so we can keep a semblance of order in our cozy little lives. Later on, when I lived in China, I found such supposed contradictions both freeing and infuriating.

The blindness to my own inherent paradoxes was complete; I simply wanted to live in an extreme manner. My main outlet for this was mountaineering. It was the logical solution to my driven nature. The biggest contradiction, however, was that this driven nature made me increasingly dissatisfied, and the more I fed it with the fuel of "being a mountaineer," the more dissatisfied I became. I was sucking myself into a paradox that was highly self-destructive.

In the meantime I continued to nurture this new identity with relish. I made it clear from the outset what I was. The choice of clothing, the conversation topics, and the style of training in the gym all gave the desired effect: I was a climber, and I was serious about it. This pleased me enormously, but it also made me nervous—not a gut-wrenching nervousness, but a slight disquiet that permeated my consciousness. *I am a mountaineer, but I'm not that good. In fact, I am distinctly average. I should keep my mouth shut, really; at least until I climb my first E grade and lead my first serious ice route. Then I can raise the volume a bit.*

Such were the awkward niggles that crept in to ruin my ideal world and brought me crashing down to earth. I could see the problem: I had to get some serious routes under my belt so I could relax knowing I was a *proven* mountaineer, and then no one could shout me down or prove me a liar and a hypocrite. In the meantime I would work out so that I was as fit, indeed fitter, than anyone I came across, no matter how good a climber that person might be. That would prove I was serious.

In all these pursuits I looked like a determined, able, and focussed individual. Everyone knew within minutes of meeting me what I was about, and they could see I was going to succeed at it or die trying. The latent and profound insecurity beneath all that froth and bubble was soon to become both obvious and crippling. At first, though, all I had to do was pursue the next route, and for that I needed a climbing partner—someone to hold the other end of the rope while I led harder and harder routes, someone to keep pushing me on to higher levels of mountaineering excellence.

Andy Lowe lived two doors away from me in my hall of residence—in distance about ten feet, door to door. Like me, he was relatively new to climbing, but he also shared my zeal, and we hit it off famously from the outset. Within hours of our first meeting, we were planning trips to local crags and comparing climbing gear so we could spend what remained of our student grant on the essentials of life: kit. The local climbing shop owners must have rubbed their hands with glee every time their jangling doorbells announced our arrival. It was simply impossible for either of us to step inside one of these Aladdin's caves without parting with yet more of the government's handout. Soon we were amply stocked with metal gear and gaudy clothing, and once we had borrowed Andy's mum's car we could begin our ascent to glory (or so it seemed) on one of the myriad local crags.

Yorkshire contains hundreds of rocky outcrops, havens for climbers to explore on most weekends and bank holidays. "Yorkshire Grit" is the name given to the Gritstone crags that dominate the Yorkshire climbing scene, renowned for wide, parallel cracks, rough surfaces, and above all, a lack of sharp, incut holds that climbers crave—the holds that make you feel warm and cozy inside; that you can swing on and look impressive from. There is none of that on a typical Yorkshire crag. Most of the holds for both hand and foot rely on friction and precious little else, except for a generous helping of boldness. In short, Gritstone can be a seriously scary place.

Nevertheless, it was riveting stuff, and we raced up route after route, following our guidebook descriptions, hurrying on until we were either exhausted (rarely) or lost the light. Running back down hills in the twilight, loaded down with a full climbing rucksack swinging awkwardly from side to side became the norm for us. People assumed we ran to avoid getting caught out and lost in the dark. The real reason was simply that we wanted to get back to our preferred pub in time for a pint before our usual "double-pint" at the bell of last orders. We were living the student dream, at least according to some publications.

Halcyon days were spent that first summer, with day after glorious day (it was a heat wave that year), week after week during vacation times, on such crags as Ilkley and Armscliff, or further afield, on Peak District limestone, Lakeland granite, and Welsh slate. Guidebooks became well worn, ropes became increasingly supple with extended use, and most importantly, we began to push our technical limits, both on the indoor climbing walls, and more crucially, on the mountains. I deliberately repeated routes that I had done the previous year with Dave, only this time I led them all. Following that I would lead an adjacent, harder route just to prove I had outstripped my former mentor. I did not tell anyone else what I was doing—this was a competition with myself.

But it was more than a competition; it was a war. It was a war that I could not win, since every new route was a fresh battle to face, and every route climbed no longer qualified as a victory as it was relegated to ignominy the moment it was finished. I had to improve all the time. I had to overcome every obstacle. If I was to be defined as a mountaineer, then I had to be a brilliant one.

It was a war that could not be won, but it could be lost.

The first time I lost my footing or a handhold failed, and my gear did not arrest the fall, then I would have lost, and there would be no second chances. This almost happened on one of those delightful sunny days in the Lake District. It was in Borrowdale, on Shepherd's Crag. Andy and I had been climbing all morning, having done both "Eve" (a re-climb by me to show I could lead it) followed by "Adam," the harder route of the same grade just next to it. We were excited and confident and wanted to push our grade up, so I looked at a steep, impressive crack line to our left, graded HVS. This was only one step beneath our goal of leading E-grades, and I was brimming with confidence.

"You up for this one, then?" There was even a swagger in my voice, let alone my stride, as I had already begun uncoiling the ropes at the foot of the climb.

"No worries," came the reply, with a boyish wink. "Do you want the sharp end, Ted?"

"Don't mind if I do, Ted," I replied. We called each other Ted all the time. It is a long and tedious story not worthy of explanation, except to say it became funnier by the pint.

The first moves required boldness and strength, and I relished every moment, placing a good piece of gear at about ten feet above the ground. As I moved powerfully and smoothly upwards, a couple of older climbers approached and began chatting to Andy. He replied politely to their comments, but he was always bad at hiding his annoyance with people, and for Andy, climbing was about supreme concentration—always a very serious affair requiring total focus. These old codgers were in the way, and they soon knew it, no matter how "polite" Andy's answers were! Still they stuck around and watched, and that suited me fine.

Forty feet up, I placed my third piece of gear. It was becoming difficult to stop and fit the runners in place due to the lack of comfortable resting places and the unrelenting steepness of the route. Every second spent trying to wedge the protection into a crack or loop a sling around a flake of rock proved to be increasingly tiring, and I could feel my strength being sapped by these delays. My forearms were swollen, and my heart was beating hard with exertion as much as with adrenaline. Holds were positive but almost always small, and I now realized how the route justified its harder grade. The angle of the climb was almost invariably vertical, with a few overhanging bulges, and there were precious few easier sections where one could take a break.

Nevertheless, I shook out my arms, looked down at Andy, and grinned, just as I heard one of the spectators say, "It gets tiring about now. Just above where he's at is where I saw a bloke get tired out and lob off there. His gear failed and he bottomed out. He smashed his ankle."

All said very matter-of-factly and all very unnecessary. *Get stuffed, you pain in the backside!* I thought as I scowled to myself and looked up for the next hold. I could, however, feel a nervousness start to pervade my thoughts and feelings. In truth, I was scared. Perhaps these old guys actually helped a little, as their comments turned my fear into both anger and determination. I could focus this fear and use it to my advantage. I told my body to do what it was bloody well told and keep climbing, and I swore that no piece of rock was going to beat me. It was time to dig deep and get on with the job at hand.

In a matter of only a moment or two, I raced through a whole range of reasons and arguments just to overcome my physical pain and mental angst. People were climbing harder routes than this all around me, even today, so I was determined that I would not fail now. I even felt angry that I was struggling at all on this climb, as it should be easy. It wasn't even an E-grade, for goodness sake! It did not even occur to me that I had only been climbing a little over a year, that some people never climb this grade of route after thirty years on the hill, and that grades do not matter anyway. As a good friend has said since, "There are only two grades of route: those you can climb, and those you can't!" But as usual, the only criterion to qualify as a success was "just a little better than you are now."

Even perched on that steep wall of granite, fingers and toes barely keeping me alive through gritted teeth and sweating brow, I was applying the lash to my own back, never satisfied with my efforts. I looked up the wall, the sun-kissed rock twinkling and glistening back at me, inviting me up with an outstretched hand. This was not a friendly hand, however. It was a hand offered by a tormentor, and it was filled with mocking derision. This untrustworthy hand still glistened with the blood of past torments. And I chose to grasp it, just to prove I would not be defeated. I could almost feel the whip come down again across my shoulders, and I swear I heard a cackle in the distance, spitting out the words, "Work harder, fool, then you'll be happy!"

I surged upwards, the pain in my arms increasing, and the sweat on my brow and back not entirely due to the summer sun reflecting off the sparkling rough granite that was my world—a world to which I was only attached by finger tips and boot edges.

A few feet higher I was forced to pause while I looked for the correct route up the rock face. One way looked relatively smooth and fairly steep, but I could not see where to go after that. The other way was a steep overhanging bulge that looked extremely exposed and that carried on out of sight above the bulge. The most alarming aspect of this side was that there was clearly nowhere to place any protective gear. The first option did have a couple of cracks in the rock, which would take a runner or two. My problem was that if I took the wrong route, there was no way of retracing my steps; it was simply too steep a climb, and this particular part was exceptionally precarious. My mind was beginning to race, as I knew I had to make a decision very quickly before my arms finally gave out and I peeled off. I was now over 60 feet up the route with nearly 40 feet to go. My last piece of gear was almost 20 feet beneath me, but I knew it was good; I had placed it carefully. But a fall of what would be 40 feet was not appealing . . . not at all!

If I took the wrong way at this point, I might get off route and find myself trying to climb an E-graded route, which in my present tired state could prove disastrous. I had to decide which way to go, I had to decide immediately, and I had to get it right!

People spend years running companies, trying to tell people how difficult it is to make the "tough decisions" and how they need to take time to assess all the options before finally making the move that may or may not decide the future prosperity of their organization. Many know little of real pressure: there are thousands of crag rats in England alone that make such decisions and judgments daily and are prepared to stake their lives on those decisions!

Now it was my turn. The bulge was the way to go. It was risky, exposed, and required total commitment to the move. I did not delay; it was time to launch myself "over the top" and face the unknown on the other side.

Then came "The Surge." Actually, it was surge after thrusting surge and wave upon wave of pure adrenaline that accompanied that move. The physical pain actually intensified the adrenaline, and coupled with the burning ache of lactic acid in what seemed like every muscle in my upper body, the effect was completely euphoric, almost overwhelming.

Suddenly, all the pain momentarily ceased, and I was moving past the crux move as if on a conveyer belt, arms flexing and moving, legs delicately shifting my body weight from one side then on to the other foot—all the while accompanied by the dull ringing of climbing hardware on the grey granite of that bulge, that beautiful, bold, buxom bulge!

Oh my, oh my! It was simply extraordinary. I was light-headed with the thrill of it all. The cocktail of adrenaline, success, fear, pain, and exposure, coupled with the physical exertion that the climb had required, was an altogether new feeling for me, and it was far beyond ecstasy. It was simply spectacular, and it was coursing through my veins like a flood through a parched land. It seemed as if it was everything I could possibly need; all life's fullness flowing in one colossal wave, and it was absolutely impossible to get too much of it.

And then in an instant, in the quietness of my mind at first, but quickly becoming more urgent, I was suddenly aware of something being wrong, terribly wrong. The alarm bells were ringing, but I did not know at first from which direction they were coming. It was a little like hearing the police sirens close by but being unable to locate the direction they are coming from—giving rise to an uncomfortable nervousness, a fretfulness that will not go away. There was almost a twinge of guilt thrown in for no good reason, except to suggest that whatever had gone wrong might have something to do with me. In this case, it did.

What was it? Why were my hands not working as they had been?

I must be wrong, somehow seeing things. Perhaps the heat shimmer is deceiving my eyes. My fingers were opening up.

"Stop it; just stop it and grip the hold. What the heck is happening?"

The fingers on my left hand were letting go of the tiny hold that they were gripping. I had raced up a further 20 feet of the route, powered by the elation I had felt at overcoming the crux of the bulge. I had not placed any further gear, and I was still 20 feet from the top of the climb. A fall now would result in my hitting the ground before any of my gear could be put to use. Basically, a fall from this height might well prove fatal.

I had used up all the strength in my arms. I was almost completely physically spent, so much so that I simply could not grip the rock. The mixture of the heat of the day and the fact that we had already climbed at least two quite long routes immediately before this one had effectively sapped my energy reserves. I was watching my fingers let go, and there was absolutely nothing I could do about it. Unless I had a reserve tank of energy somewhere, then I was about twenty seconds from death. Twenty seconds maximum, that is.

As I tried to shake an ounce more energy into my arms, I prayed, which of course is the typical refuge for a scoundrel: wait until all hope is lost and then rub the rabbit's foot and hope God himself behaves like a genie and does whatever is asked of Him, even if I lived the rest of my life like a sorry little ingrate!

But I was immediately aware that I was not asking someone for help whom I had never met. There was a familiarity to it that made it feel like I was asking a friend rather than rubbing a lamp. I was having a conversation and not reciting a desperate mantra. Strangest of all, I *knew* there would be an answer, either way, and I was content with that. Either way.

All of these thoughts took a matter of moments. I am sure my pleas were heard, but I also discovered after those brief seconds the truism that we are never really spent when we think we are. Our bodies seem to have an override switch that kicks in when we really need it (and as a climber, I *often* needed it). It is what is known as "the head game," and you either learn it or you fall off! All climbers know about it; I am sure most adventure sports participants know about it as well. It means a lot of things, but in such instances as this it basically means you refuse to accept this is your limit, and you decide to override your physical problem and your mental anguish. It may sound odd, but it's true and it works (most of the time).

Having learned this in practice before I ever heard of the theory, I was able to push on up the last section of the route, moving smoothly and strongly up a strenuous crack-line. I stepped over the top of the route, sat down, and smiled broadly to myself before tying off the rope and calling down to Andy:

"Okay, Ted, I'm safe. You can take me off now!" I was grinning by now, standing over the top of the climb and looking down the route as Andy made himself ready to follow me.

"Those two silly old gippers can be impressed now, and go and tell their stupid mate that they saw a guy who did *not* fall off, *or* break his ankle." I boasted to myself and examined my bleeding fingers and swollen arms with enormous pride. On reflection, it does sound all rather silly, not to mention arrogant and self-centred. Still, that was how it was, and I was very pleased with myself.

Andy climbed the first half comfortably and made some pleasant comments on how bold a lead it was. We both used this ploy while climbing second to the other. It served two functions. First, it was a genuine compliment to a friend, and second, it illustrated to all around us, anyone who might be watching, that we were finding it a pleasant route that was not too difficult or strenuous. A person having an epic never engages in conversation, especially when about to fall off! This bantering made it clear that it was a route well within our own capabilities, and we could have led it ourselves, given the chance. Put another way, it was macho posturing, but we evidently enjoyed it!

By about the 60-feet mark, Andy had stopped chatting, and at 70 feet he was complaining at the length of time it had taken to remove some of the gear I had placed. He had a chiding air to his tone that made me laugh.

He did not like that and swore at me. I stifled another chuckle, as I realized his arms were now as tired as mine had been, and I tried to urge him on with words of encouragement. He responded somewhat melodramatically in my view:

"Keep that bloody rope tight. I'm coming off!"

"No you're not. Just shake out that left hand and reach up. There's a decent jug hold just a few feet away. You're doing fine!"

The rope suddenly went tight, and I felt a lurch around my waist.

He wasn't doing fine.

He had just fallen off and was so tired that he was content to swing in the air for a few seconds to shake out both arms at once. He was clearly in pain and had given it everything.

Good thing he hadn't been leading, I thought.

Andy soon finished off the route and complained about the gear that had been jammed lower down. I conceded how tiring a job it is to have to mess around and remove someone else's gear, and I apologized for my excessive yanking on the runners in order to make them safe. As my tongue had been firmly in my cheek, he noted my mocking tone for daring to do all I could to prevent my own death, and we both laughed out loud on the top of the crag. We grew closer together that day and would frequently remind each other in following years of those glorious summer days and of pushing each other's limits on those routes on Shepherd's Crag.

I was grateful for the divine help I had received in the last 20 feet of that route, but I did not mention this to anyone else, of course. I did ponder the event in my own mind, however, and often wondered why I deserved such paternal attention when I gave scant external recognition of it in between crises. I suppose my problem was twofold: I did not understand fully who or what I was talking to, and I still enjoyed the prize of accomplishment and acclamation that went along with my success. I was in no way ready to share this glory, especially in a fraternity that would have derided such notions without mercy. I had to fit in, and I wanted to continue to build my climbing curriculum vitae and my mountaineering "experiences."

So I kept my mouth shut. But the wrestling match was already underway, and I knew it. I knew it enough to know I had to stifle the thoughts that were beginning to affect my everyday life. I could best keep these notions at bay by continuing to do as I was doing: climb harder, get more accolades on the rock, and be a mountaineer. "After all," I argued, "how could a Creator God not be happy with a guy who enjoyed His creation and simply wanted to be closer to it?" I fooled myself with this line for ages.

During these days of prolific climbing, many evenings were spent in pubs and around camp fires in several different countries, let alone towns and villages in England, where we would re-live myriad climbing moments while others shared their own experiences and many more just sat and listened. Frequently, non-climbers expressed their envy at what we had done (the experience rather than the climb itself usually), and I enjoyed the fact that now it was me with the stories, the knowing looks, and the distant smiles, rather than Pete and Dave sharing that which I had no part in while we had been in Norway. I was beginning to have my own experiences, and it seemed to give me my identity.

One evening Andy and I were discussing what we should do for the summer break. It was usual for every serious mountaineer to head off to the Alps and do some of the classic Alpine peaks. Chamonix was the usual destination, and already several members of the Leeds University Mountaineering Club were making preparations. We could have tagged along quite easily and possibly "ticked off" such peaks as Mont Blanc, The Grandes Jorasses, or perhaps even my personal favourite, the Matterhorn, if we ventured into Switzerland.

But I felt deeply uncomfortable about going along with everyone else. I said that the Alps were always very crowded, the weather unpredictable, and the chances of our getting a lot done and thereby improving our abilities was minimal. With this in mind, I argued, we should head to Norway as I had done the year before. In truth, I simply did not feel comfortable around a load of other climbers. I found the constant talk of route grades and incessant posturing incredibly tiring and tedious. Frankly, I was at least as guilty as everyone else in doing this. I was in a state of constant competition, and while loathing it I found myself driven to play these games almost all the time. Whereas I looked the part with the clothes, attitude, and focus, I certainly did not feel it. I felt awkward and out of place in the climbing community. There was a horrible niggling feeling that it simply wasn't me. This concerned me, as I desperately wanted to belong, to be defined as a mountaineer.

Still, Andy agreed on Scandinavia with relish. We would visit the same place I had been the previous year, Romsdal Valley, and do some more serious routes. In addition we could visit some friends of his in Sweden. The fact that it was an extra 24-hour drive for us did not even slightly deter us. Sweden was next to Norway; therefore, by definition it was close enough to pop over the border and visit them. We talked about our trip until late, then Andy went off to bed, turning as he went:

"Are you coming to church tomorrow, Ted?" he asked.

"Yeah, great. What time are we leaving?" My reply was alarmingly natural. We made arrangements for "Ted" to wake me up as usual, since he could get himself out of bed while I always seemed to be glued to the mattress. All I had to do now was train him to bring me some tea, and he could be the perfect replacement for Dave. I fell asleep in my room dreaming of the Troll Wall yet again.

About a dozen of us walked the mile or so to church the following morning. Most of them were very clearly Christians. I had no idea what I was, but I did know that I was slightly embarrassed to be among them. Not because of them, but because of me. I did not really act like a Christian; that is, I frequently went with Andy to church armed with a slight hangover, a packet of mints to hide the alcohol breath, and an overall guilty conscience from yet another misspent Saturday night. I never used to feel guilty. It only started after I came to university just a couple of weeks after I had returned from my first trip to Norway. I hated the guilt, and I hated being unable to stop doing the things that made me feel guilty. So I kept taking it to church on a regular basis. Strangely enough, no one ever made me feel guilty. I simply knew I was. No point trying to deny that. "Guilty as charged, m'Lord!"

Sometimes I felt simply too filthy to show my sorry face, and I usually spent the rest of Sunday trying to "clean myself" with a healthy lifestyle and a five-mile run. It helped for the duration of the run but could not leave the dark corners of my mind once the lights went out and I tried to sleep, often without much success. A day on the hill was the best cure for that, I argued. Get out on the crags and get tired, doing what is truly fulfilling. Then I'll feel great again.

Sometimes that worked.

But if I actually got to church and sat down, the fact was that I felt truly at home. I felt like I fitted in, not only with those around me but also with the entire situation. This made no sense at all. How could I possibly be a part of all that was good and pure and, dare I say it, holy, when I knew what I had been up to the night before? More importantly, He knew what I had been up to the night before. Yet I *knew* I was welcome. The people, the place, and the Person all made me know I was welcome. I was both welcome and I *belonged*.

I truly fit in, and there was no earthly reason why I should have felt that way. What a contrast! I had all the right gear, clothes, language, and desire to fit into the climbing fraternity, but I felt invariably uncomfortable and out of place in it. And then here I was with all the wrong behaviour, thoughts, and emotions, fitting in just perfectly with not only a bunch of "holy rollers" but also with the One who made them such! It was all wrong. This was a paradox that I could not even begin to fathom.

Was He making me one of them as well? Impossible! Time to go climbing again. The more I climbed, the more I would fit in. I was off to Norway in a few weeks, and it was going to be impressive. I imagined our triumphant return when we met the Club members the following September. They would have climbed a couple of routes in the Alps; we would have countless, massive rock walls in Norway to report back on. Maybe we would do a pitch or two of the Troll Wall itself, just to make them jealous.

The start of our Norway 2 venture had an uncomfortable feeling of déjà vu to it: the same old bus for a ship, the same stinking fumes, and the same dubious-looking mode of expedition transportation. This time, however, it was a smaller version.

Our expedition vehicle, a 1967 Triumph Vitesse, had been hand-built from nuts and bolts by Andy and his elder brother in their garage at home. It had an old Triumph Spitfire engine under the bonnet and had been hand painted in light blue Hammerite paint, the stuff you use to cover up rusting metal. How appropriate! They had finished working on it in the small hours of the day we actually set off, so there had been no time to test their little invention. However, tootling along the English country lanes around my home and even opening her out a bit on the roads up to the ferry terminal at Newcastle proved to be unproblematic. A little later, though, when asked to do some work up the steep passes in Norway, the Little Blue Beast—laden with food and climbing gear—started to complain. We dealt with these knocks and rattles the best way we knew how: by turning the music on the tape player louder. In the end, however, the car's noise did attract our attention enough to contact the RAC, but that was almost four weeks later—after we had returned to England. What we found out then was interesting, but that is another story.

Disembarking from our North Sea ferry, I rolled my eyes as the gaudy, shiny, Blue Beast laboured out of the lower deck of the hull, wheels almost scraping the wheel arches, before we blue-smoked our way toward the hills. My cheap tape player droned in the back seat, trying its best to overcome the engine noise. I think the two settled for a draw eventually, about two weeks into the trip. More likely, that is how long it took for my ears to focus on the music rather than on the engine!

Andy and I were in our element. We spent most of every day grinning at everything. I was a happy chap as we sped on to Romsdal. The familiar sights of the fjords, the smell of the water and the mountain air, and the whole feel of the country were deeply invigorating. I loved the country by now and gabbled to Andy endlessly about the crags, the meadows, and the hills around us. He could, of course, see all that I was seeing; yet he never betrayed any feeling of impatience at my incessant rambling. Either he enjoyed it all as much as I did, or he was being especially gracious to me. I suspect both are true.

We arrived at the same campsite I had stayed in the previous year. There was no point in even pretending to pitch a tent; we immediately grabbed ourselves a "hut with a view" and spread out our gear in warmth and comfort! This was great. The weather was warm (we had come in late July this time to avoid the lousy weather I had encountered the previous year), and it was a balmy evening as we sat on our little veranda soaking in the view of the Romsdalhorn in the distance, drinking a couple of cans of Tetley's (a fine choice of expedition ale), and planning our trip.

Two very attractive Norwegian girls seemed to be in charge of running the kiosk where we signed in and paid our camping fees. We were soon flirting shamelessly with them—poor girls. We were awkward around females at the best of times, but dressed in the extremely unattractive garb of the mountaineer we must have looked quite a sight to anyone we came across, let alone the young women who were the target of our affections. How much greater must their dismay have become as we continued our efforts to woo them two weeks into the trip, having seemingly lost the ability to bathe or shave during that time. They continued to smile politely, despite us. Young men and testosterone, though intrinsically linked, often make for excruciating viewing!

We decided on a number of routes as "definites," including Kongen (the King) and a re-run of the Romsdalhorn, north face. This was the route I had turned back on with Dave due to bad weather the year before. I was determined to climb this mountain above all the others. Having made our plans, we drank a couple more cans of beer and retired to our bunks. The breeze from the mountains was still warm as we gazed out of the open door of our hut, watching the wisps of cloud turn from white to yellow to deep orange before the final departure of the sun left them as grey as the granite of the crags beneath them. The Romsdalhorn, bright and pointed against the pale blue sky, turned purple and then blue as the clouds blended their colour tones with it. Then, as if by design, the sky deepened its hue until orange and purple stood out from a cobalt blue backdrop to finish off this perfect artist's palate. I closed my eyes and breathed in deeply; sleep was not elusive that night.

I awoke to the sound of Andy cursing up a storm. He had just burnt his fingers while trying to put out the flame of the Trangia stove. I thanked him for my brew and told him to stop whining. Once I had put on my shirt, we packed our gear prepared the night before, threw in some food, and dived into the car. Even though we were setting off well before seven o'clock, it was already warm. Since we were so far north, it had been dark for only three or four hours, so the sun had already had time to warm the air and dry off any morning dew that had formed. We were down to our t-shirts before we even started the walk-in to the foot of the climb. Today we would conquer Kongen, and tomorrow, the Romsdalhorn.

The "today" route passed uneventfully, except that it was a long, very pleasant, and thoroughly enjoyable affair. It was certainly more difficult than any of the rock I had climbed in Norway the previous year, but very little of it of it was overly technical, with none of the pitches rating much above Hard Severe by English grading. Still, it was the scale that was impressive, and even doing an "easy" route when we were 2,000 to 3,000 feet above the fjords and fields was fairly gripping stuff. Warm sunshine and blue skies all the way made the whole adventure feel friendly and safe, though. We returned triumphant and ticked off a good route in our guidebook.

It was the "tomorrow" climb, the Romsdalhorn, that was to prove a learning experience. Everything began much the same as the day before, and when we set off on the walk up to the ridge we were to follow to the beginning of the face proper, we were accompanied by more of the wonderful weather of the day before. We observed the fabulous views as we strode out along that ridge: mountains rolling away into the distance, some dusted with snow, others spiking the skyline with grey granite teeth, and icy fjords leading to the North Sea, stretching out to a curved blue horizon to our right. In an environment like this I soon forgot the initial strain of the steep slope that we had climbed to attain the ridge, and we both pressed on at quite a pace.

Soon we were approaching the break in the rock, the step onto the north face of Romsdalhorn itself. This was where I had turned back the year before. We stopped, looked up the vast wall ahead of us, and began to uncoil the ropes. As I set off "at the sharp end," I spat on the rock. There would be no turning back today. I would not let any mountain beat me, and the very notion of giving up seemed to be inherently spineless. About two hours later, however, the Romsdalhorn spat back, and for a minute or two up on that face I thought I was a dead man. It is curious how things can change so quickly out on the hill.

The first few sections of the climb were enormous fun but uneventful. The problem we were discovering was the vagueness of the route description in the guidebook. On first reading, as we had planned our ascent, the book had seemed to be sufficiently accurate to make route finding fairly straightforward. This was, in reality, not the case. In truth the writers of this part of the guidebook gave a new definition to the term "vague." I was to discover this fact even more so later in life as a winter mountaineer. Many descriptions are little more than "start here and climb till you get to the top. It's very dangerous at about halfway, then again near the summit." Great! Thanks for the tip.

When one reads such comments in a guidebook away from the climb itself, it does not seem to be all that bad. But when faced with a huge wall of featureless granite or ice, it becomes more than a little disconcerting. Here at the Romsdalhorn we were constantly faced with choices that we did not want to have to make. Here is a typical example of this:

Guidebook description: Follow the crack line from a large flake, up two rope lengths to a belay.

Reality: Twenty different cracks, ten of which start next to a flake and the rest start from *almost* next to a flake. Two rope lengths later, there is a blank wall of rock and certainly no belay. Guess what? You just picked the wrong flake and the wrong crack line! However, you were still almost on the route, so you basically meander upwards, more or less according to the guidebook, but often not quite on the exact route, according to the description.

This may sound like fun to some people, and in theory, the thought of climbing on previously untouched rock is quite exciting. In reality, however, a great deal of this lovely, untouched rock was not simply granite. It was rotten, decomposing granite, and it would fall and crash all around you if you had the temerity to place all your weight on it. To make life even more exciting, it did not give way when pulled on just a little. It liked to wait until you were committed to a move before collapsing on you, causing great consternation to the hapless climber who had dared to disturb the mountain's slumber, not to mention terror to his second waiting beneath him, on whom the rock was about to land at almost terminal velocity. We soon learned to test every hold carefully and to knock on the rock to listen for the telltale hollow thud that would betray its looseness.

All of this not only slowed our progress but it also meant that we frequently found ourselves on some pitches where the climbing was technically harder than if we had stuck exactly to the guidebook description. It became a strange blend of playful fun and abject terror. This was Norwegian mountaineering. This was big rock wall climbing, and here was our first real baptism into it. At least it was for Andy. It had already happened to me once before, and I was uncomfortable with this reminder for a host of reasons. We carried on upwards, taking it in turns to have the lead, and eventually we found ourselves on an obvious face that was in the guidebook. It was good to be back on route.

I set off on the next section with a new confidence, knowing we were exactly where we were meant to be. The sun was warming both my back and the rock. Holds were big and abundant with just a few delicate moves to make the pitch interesting. It was a sufficiently easy section to avoid putting in very much gear, and I figured that we ought to crack on since earlier we had lost more than an hour by getting off route. There was still quite a long way to go and then a long descent that was not straightforward involving, according to the guidebook, multiple abseils and difficult route finding. I hated complex descents, so I was eager to make up for this delay.

I realized that I was making fast progress, so I relaxed and took in more of the surroundings and our spectacular position. From our campsite the Romsdalhorn looked impressive, but from up here it looked awesome! We were completely alone on a vast rock wall, with the pass we had driven up some 2,000 feet beneath us. I had looked out of aircraft from heights less than this, and here I was now clinging to a mountain with nothing but fresh air between my feet and the valley so far below that I could barely make out the livestock that I knew were there, grazing contentedly in their fields.

I looked down the mountain at Andy, some 100 or more feet beneath me, and I leaned out from the rock face with one hand holding on just beneath a huge flake of granite. I enjoyed the warm glow of the sun reflecting off the rock, and I imagined my impressive position on the mountain as I looked down at my friend, who in turn, smiled back at me, completely aware that I was posing for the imaginary camera.

I slipped some gear, a huge cowbell of protection, under the flake of rock and tugged on it several times in order to be sure it was secure and was properly wedged in place. Turning to Andy I shouted, "That's bombproof!" As I did I gave it one more triumphant tug on the rope.

It was just at this moment that the mountain spat back at me.

My first realization was the deep rumble I heard the instant I gave that final pull. Then came excruciating pain as the wall of rock around me fell away, and the point of the huge triangular flake of rock, under which I had threaded the cowbell, came loose and fell onto my hand, splitting my thumb open on both sides of the digit and hammering my hand against the anvil of the mountainside.

The pain was quite exquisite. I have rarely come across such an excellent example of agony; nor did it pass in a moment. Proof positive of damage having been done was the steady trickle and then stream of blood flowing from behind the flake of rock where my hand was still held captive by the boulder, to my visible wrist, and then down the arm. Before long there was a steady drip, drip of crimson fear splashing from my elbow onto the rock several feet beneath me.

The wound was not serious: my thumb was not severed and I could move my fingers. The problem was that ever since I was a young boy I have reacted very badly to the sight of my own blood, especially coming from my hands or fingers. Strangely, other wounds do not bother me nearly as much, and certainly someone else's blood does not bother me at all. But watching my own bleeding fingers was, and still is, serious business for me.

Specifically, it makes me pass out. At this moment I was clinging onto a mountain with no gear in place for over 100 feet, with several dislodged boulders now resting against my chest and systematically trying to push me off the crag. And my own blood was dripping off my elbow.

I began to feel woozy.

I knew that the moment I lost consciousness I was a dead man, and the resultant fall, complete with boulders, would probably kill Andy as well. He would either be struck by rocks or my bodyweight falling at speed would pull him off his belay stance and probably dislodge his belay gear as well. I suddenly knew that I was almost certainly done for. I had never been able to stop myself from passing out once I had reached the stage of the spinning head, the prickly, sweating scalp and palms, and the overwhelming feeling of watery-mouthed nausea—all of which I could now feel in my countdown to disaster. Death was a matter of seconds away.

Meanwhile, Andy waited below me. I think I warned him to take cover, that I was coming off. He never wavered. He knew my weakness, that I would almost certainly pass out, and he never let go of the rope, nor did he stop looking up at me when he could have been taking cover.

Later, he told me he was waiting for me to come off, at which point he was going to try to take in as much rope as possible as I was freefalling toward him, (I would probably have bounced a couple of times on the way) in the hope of reducing my fall and thereby hoping to save my life. Top man.

I should have passed out. I always had done so before that day, and I have almost invariably done so every time since. I thought what a miserable end it would have been. Not so much dying on a mountain in Norway, and probably dragging my friend to his death in the same instant, but the fact that I had died because I could not stand the sight of my own blood. Pathetic! At least no one else would have known. It would have been reported that I was killed in a rock fall, high on a mountain in Scandinavia. That sounded more like it! During the event, however, none of it sounded very comforting at all.

Moreover, my hand hurt. It hurt *a lot!* I was being forced to hold on with the damaged hand as my right hand was holding the loose rocks against my chest to stop them from falling onto Andy directly below me. After several minutes of complete silence between the two of us while I fought to stay awake, I began to realize that the spinning head and the feeling of nausea were beginning to subside. I forced myself to breathe deeply, in through the nose and out through the mouth, and eventually I could look up again, after having concentrated on one tiny piece of rock down by my feet for the last few minutes trying to make my head cease its spinning. Finally, after what seemed like hours to me, I shouted down rather shakily:

"I'm okay. My hand's busted and it's bleeding. You need to get out of the way so I can throw these rocks past you. Are you safe?"

Andy checked that his belay was secure and moved under the shelter of a small overhang to his left. I began to push the rocks off my chest and down the mountainside.

The noise was dreadful: a second of silence, perhaps the slight swish of displaced air before the deep crash, more of a harsh grumble, a hollow thud, as the rock glanced off the side of the mountain, just beneath where Andy had been standing. The acceleration of each rock, the smallest as big as my head, the larger ones the size of a five-gallon drum, was quite shocking, and I grimaced at the thought of any one of them hitting my friend had I let go of any of them without warning. What a mess that would have been!

Moreover, I thought about what it would have looked like had the boulders been my own body rather than just rock. Each glancing blow against the mountainside would have rendered me more and more unrecognizable, and then, after the crunching thuds had finished, the final silence as the horrific free fall began, all the way to the fields, 2,000 feet beneath me. I hoped there were no animals in the fields when those rocks finally landed. What a nightmare it would have been for a poor hill walker, had it been me, rather than a rock he or she discovered in that field, possibly weeks later! It was a disgusting thought, and I felt, at least momentarily, ashamed. Selfish and ashamed. What on earth was it exactly that I was so desperately trying to prove?

With the rocks out of the way I was free to anchor myself to the face and then call Andy to climb up to join me. It was painful forcing my left hand to grip the rope and take it in as Andy climbed higher. Blood was still seeping from the wound, even though by now I could see that it was not a serious injury. Andy and I chatted on the belay stance and discussed whether or not we should retreat. We agreed that down climbing the route would be more hazardous than continuing to the top, especially since we had already climbed the hardest sections of the route. The rest was very easy by mountaineering standards, so Andy put a dressing around my hand and we carried on.

By some miracle we stayed exactly on route, and a little while later we were posing for summit photographs, me proudly showing off my still bleeding hand! We sat in a little hut on the summit, and as I warmed up further (a brisk wind had developed as we had neared the top) my thumb began to throb slightly. We grabbed our guidebook and began to look for the route down and soon became aware that this too was not such an easy task as a typical crag in the Lake District. It involved finding some specific abseil points and then carefully down-climbing a labyrinth of rock gullies on a very steep slope. If we got off route, we may well have found ourselves looking over something of an abyss without any anchor point to abseil from. On top of that, the breeze we had started to feel had now become a serious wind, and the wind was bringing some weather with it. I looked out of the hut and saw black clouds billowing in from the mountains. Was that forked lightning in the distance? Surely not.

Our disquiet was interrupted by a knock on the door even though it was already ajar. Three Norwegians appeared, smiling warmly, as I think all Norwegians do. It must be trained into them from childhood: "If ever you see an Englishman, smile, shake his hand, and be genuinely pleased to see him." I can think of no other explanation for the genuine warmth I received from these people.

"You are English, yes?" He seemed to be the leader of this triumvirate, and he was a few years older than his colleagues.

"We heard your voices on the north face route. We followed you up. We also heard the rock fall." I looked up in alarm. *Did one of my bloody boulders nearly kill them,* I wondered.

"Who is the injured one? We have followed your blood trail up the mountain!" he continued with a smile and a very singsong, Norwegian laugh. I was delighted. This was suddenly heroic stuff. All sense of guilt and shame was replaced by rampant egomania! I almost wanted to have something more severe to show them than merely a bandaged hand.

"That blood-stained rock over there; do you see it? That's *my* blood!" I mapped out the story in my own mind. This had real mileage down at the pub, without a doubt!

"And here I am still alive to tell the tale," I continued the formation of the legend in my head. "Rock hard; that's me!" (I left out the part about my almost passing out at the sight of the above-mentioned blood. That would not be so heroic and may have tainted the overall flavour of the tale).

After inspecting my hand, our new friends, satisfied I would survive, sat down and we ate some food together.

Andy and I soon learned that the leader had climbed this route many times before, and neither of us needed to communicate our relief to the other: we had found our much-needed guide down the hill. Here was a saviour indeed, and I barely tried to hide my relief. By now, the rain was coming down, lightning was striking the top of the peak, and visibility was down to about 100 feet. Before the arrival of these three, I could feel another most unwelcome epic coming on.

I recalled the last epic with dread: just over a year ago in the same valley. The rain, the darkness, the impending doom were all too familiar. I was glad that I was not going to have to repeat it. Andy and I followed our new leader gratefully to the first abseil point. We would certainly have missed it had we been by ourselves, and the lightning strikes on the summit were already most unnerving. We wanted to leave that place in a hurry!

As the rain came down steadily, all five of us trudged carefully and deliberately down the side of the hill, placing gear to protect each other and roping up when things were a bit hairy. We did not get off route once. This guy knew his mountain incredibly well. Andy and I exchanged a few glances that we only verbalized back at camp that night, along the lines of, "If these fellas had not shown up we would have been knackered! There is no way we would have got down here in one piece in these conditions!" I think Andy recorded in his diary something like, "It would have stretched us to our limit." I remain unconvinced that our limits would have stretched quite that far!

As we neared our car some two hours later, we said our goodbyes to our Norwegian friends. The two of us ran to the Triumph, relieved and giddy with excitement, both at having climbed the route despite experiencing a bit of an epic and at managing to get down safely in what had turned out to be absolutely atrocious weather.

More déjà vu. Almost a year before, I had been guided down a mountain in filthy weather by an unexpected Saviour. This time I was not alone, and the help was in physical form, guiding me down in an obvious manner and choosing the correct path for me when I could not see the route clearly for myself. Last year was very different; it was colder, darker, and altogether more sinister as a situation, but the help had been just as real, though intangible. I thought on these things for a long time, both on the way back to camp and much more in the quietness of my own thoughts while lying on my bunk later that night. What had really happened last year on that route?

I did not answer that question. It was too uncomfortable to answer in a way that gave me a get-out clause. But it was beginning to get under my skin, and whereas I was not happy about it, I somehow knew it was not going to go away. What I did know was that the next day we were going to do some bouldering routes right next to the start of that climb; The Climb from last year. I wanted to look at it. I did *not* want to climb it again. The very thought made me shudder. Moreover, I determined that I was not going to tell Andy about it. It was all still far too raw in my mind.

I drank a lot that night. And I did not sleep well. Can't imagine why.

We went bouldering the next day. The sun still gave out a summery warmth, and its brightness, twinkling off the mica in the granite, made my eyes smart, though it was far too pleasant for me to raise any objections. And what a bonus: we met Chris Bonington, one of Britain's greatest mountaineers, on the bouldering site! I did not recognize him at first, but Andy clocked him immediately. I helped him top rope a couple of bouldering problems, and I won a great accolade when I climbed a technical problem that he could not get up!

Andy and I both laughed later on that day as we concluded, tongues firmly lodged in our cheeks, that my success on the bouldering problem must have been due to my greater abilities as a mountaineer over our legendary colleague. I doubt very much that he remembers me, but I certainly remember him! We spent a very pleasant morning together. He was with a Norwegian colleague, with whom he had recently climbed Everest. Perhaps, after all, he still had the edge over me as a mountaineer!

I looked at the foot of The Climb. The start, just next to an old tree, with the first pitch going so close to it that you could use some of the branches as holds if you wished; the steep chimney going upwards toward the right then out of sight. I turned away with a knot in my stomach. I did not want to re-climb this one. No way. I could not pretend that I had conquered this route. I had been rescued from certain death, not probable death, far more than merely a risky situation, and it was not Dave who had saved me. Repeating this route would be utter folly, nor did I want Andy to climb it with me. It was somehow too personal. It also represented complete loneliness and loss of hope to me—that point of absolute solitude and absolute surrender. Moreover, if events repeated themselves, if the same disaster struck, would I receive the same deliverance or would I get what I really deserved a second time around? I turned and walked away after making excuses why we should not climb any routes today. "Better to have a rest day before we head off to Sweden, eh?" Andy agreed and we said our goodbyes to Romsdal that evening.

Perhaps it wasn't that climbing was no good or inherently wrong in itself, but that I should not insist on being defined by it. My problem was that I could not do things by half, and climbing had become an all-consuming desire, which would inevitably cost me all my spare time, and ultimately, possibly my life. I had been more than content with that thought, but now I began to consider that perhaps that thought was wrong; not just wrong as in "incorrect," but much more seriously, wrong as in "a mistake," or dare I say it, "a sin!"

As we returned on the ferry to England after our side trip to Sweden and back, my mind was grinding through such issues almost constantly. The whole realization began to sweep over me: I simply did not share this all-embracing zeal for the next rock route that I saw in other committed mountaineers, even though I constantly forced myself to *look as if I did.* I saw for the first time why I did not fit in with the whole climbing scene that I had tried so hard to become a part of. This was an awful thought—a thought I tried to stifle for many years. I loved the outdoors, the mountains, the hills, but I began to realize that I did not live to find the next E-grade or wall of ice.

I started to see that I had set my course in the wrong direction, but I refused to accept this fact and turn around. I was going to climb all my life, and no one was going to change that. This was my one chance at looking good and being seen as a success, and I was not going to be robbed of it. All I had to do was to keep practicing and go and find something harder to climb. In fact, I argued with myself, what I really enjoyed was big mountains and snow. If rock was not the answer, then surely ice and snow would be. I convinced myself of this during the ferry ride home, so much so that as we headed across England, Andy and I were engrossed in planning our first Himalayan adventure. If rock had ceased to satisfy, surely the ice and snow of the big mountains would.

After we started for home aboard the Triumph, we were interrupted after only a couple of hours by the noise I referred to earlier of our shiny blue chariot becoming intolerable. It had begun not long after we had arrived in Norway, but since the car had not broken down, we had carried on regardless, assuming it was something unimportant, like binding brakes. Finally, we admitted defeat and phoned the RAC. The mechanic came out and informed us within a minute or so that both back wheels were about to fall off, and we should drive the car onto his truck ramps *"if it will make it up them!"*

Good grief! In Norway we had driven up ferry ramps and over several very steep passes laced with hairpin bends, and now this guy is telling us our wheels are almost off!

It turned out that Andy and his brother had installed the wrong size differential onto our little rocket, and it could have collapsed on us at any moment. Our blue chariot was, in fact, a death trap, a disaster waiting to happen. Had a wheel come off, a distinct possibility according to our RAC man, there was a very good chance we would have died. There would have been no ropes to arrest a fall over the edge of one of the hairpin bends on the many mountain passes we had driven over! You could argue quite effectively that we were indeed being protected throughout our expedition.

We ended our adventure laughing at yet another little mishap, just as we had spent most of the trip grinning at whatever Norway had thrown at us. My misgivings about my future were put at ease for a while as I considered the big mountains and ice climbing as a way to gain true satisfaction in my life. I knew that I was, deep down, a profoundly dissatisfied person, and my drivenness to excel on the mountains was ultimately a destructive influence. Still, onwards I went toward the next goal: a Himalayan adventure.

Chapter 5

RUDE AWAKENINGS IN THE KARAKORAM

▲

DIARY ENTRY:

24ᵗʰ December 1988

LOCATION:

8,000 ft up Emei Shan, Sichuan Province, Southwest China

WEATHER:

Snowing.

What a waste of time. This hill is nothing more than a walk up a path. For goodness sake, there are guys being carried up in cots! What a waste of time. No point even bringing my ice tools. Am heading down in the morning. Maybe if I run all the way I'll get a bit of a workout. Maybe I can even get rid of these two women clinging onto us. Waste, waste, waste.

There was no point going further up Emei Shan, because there was no challenge to it. It was not technical, and the hill itself was a mere

10,000 feet high, with a path all the way to the top. I would not be pushing any mountaineering limits here, and I resented the whole exercise. I felt like a fool, having taken my climbing hardware all the way from Beijing down to the Southwest of China just to plod up a formless lump that any unfit person could do just as easily.

It was all a far cry from my expectations three months earlier when I had run to catch a flight from Heathrow to Beijing, China, where I was going to spend a year as part of my university degree course. I arrived at the check-in, moments to spare, and proudly threw down my rucksack containing all I needed for a year in the Far East: one change of clothes, toiletries, underwear, and every scrap of my climbing gear, including ice axe, crampons, rope, and harness. I did not even have a climbing partner. What on earth did I need a rope for? In a word: image. I was a mountaineer, and somehow I was going to do some climbing in China, just to say I had done it.

Back in Sichuan province, Emei Shan was killing this ambition. I had hoped to see an ice wall on one side of the peak, so I could climb this and meet my friend on the summit. In reality all I could see was a blanket of clouds and a line of people plodding up a path, some literally being carried in litters. I was both despondent and angry. My whole experience in China up to this point had been a catalogue of disappointments and difficulties that had left me disaffected with the country and dissatisfied with my life. Whereas some of my colleagues had built some excellent friendships with students and locals, I had found myself feeling alone and isolated, contentment only being found in trying to work out every day and trying to get drunk every night. A day without either or both of these was the exception proving the rule. I was having a bad year—that much was true.

It was perhaps unfair to blame China for my malaise. Indeed, many of my colleagues loved the whole country and their experience there. However, bearing in mind that in the 1980s China still had many remaining vestiges of a Stalinist society, with grey drabness and hostile indifference as seeming prerequisites for fulfilling the Socialist ideal, it was very easy to feel downcast in such conditions. My overriding feeling was almost invariably anger, aimed like a scattergun at anything and everything

The one thing that kept me focussed and helped me to keep on training during this turbulent episode of my life was the brilliant, shining light at the end of this dark, unfriendly tunnel: Andy and I had decided on a Himalayan expedition at the end of my year away in China. He would do the bulk of the planning from England, and I would join the other three members of the team directly from China, either by crossing into Nepal or taking trains and buses through Xinjiang province and over the Karakoram Highway into Pakistan. This exciting prospect had filled my imagination all year!

Shortly after my disappointing trip to Emei Shan, I received a letter from Andy confirming that he had decided we would go to Pakistan (climbing was cheaper there than in Nepal, apparently, with more unclimbed peaks to explore). So I began planning my overland adventure to the northwest of China and then into Pakistan, aiming to rendezvous with the rest of the team at Skardu, gateway to the hills and stopping-off point for most of the climbing expeditions going into the Karakoram Range.

China then managed to ruin the whole thing by orchestrating what became known as the Tiananmen Square Massacre of June 4, 1989. The gunfire could be heard from just a short distance away on the campus where I lived. As a result, most of the foreign students were evacuated in a hurry on June 6, having been instructed to bring with them hand luggage only. I packed some underwear, like a good son, and my climbing rope, like a good climber, and walked out of my bedroom expecting to be back in a couple of days.

Our specially chartered Boeing 747 took us to Hong Kong the following night, the fires from the violence of the days before still visible and burning as the plane circled around and headed south to Britain's then-favourite colony. I arrived back in Heathrow on June 8, thoroughly disillusioned with a country that had decided to kill its own just as I was beginning to warm to them. Of more immediate concern to me, not to mention more selfishly, I now had to contemplate a Himalayan trip without any of my gear.

China was incurring my considerable venom. During my time there I had formulated a plan that would entail me making a living, a career even, out of being a climber. Becoming a climbing writer, even a mountaineering filmmaker, seemed a great way of pursuing my goals while making money at the same time. This past year had obstructed all this, and the final disaster of what had happened on June 4 had really messed up my immediate goals. I had mountains to climb, and if I did not climb them, my whole career—my whole life—would fall in tatters. China had gotten in the way of that, both in wasting a year of my mountaineering life and by stealing my kit, and I could not afford any more delays.

On top of all that, Andy had climbed his first E2 while I was locked in Fortress Beijing, and that stung. I had some catching up to do. I could feel myself knotting up whenever I talked of grades and big peaks. The drivenness was increasing, not decreasing, with every achievement, and the next route was the only way to assuage this gnawing hunger. Within a week of arriving back in England, I was packing gear for our trip to Pakistan, and working three jobs to pay for it all.

It was great to see my friend again, and we caught up on our year apart in about one minute flat. Andy had sent me various letters while I was away, usually updating me on our planned trip and often accompanied by "scratch and sniff" sections, where various ales had been spilled on the paper to remind me of home. We went to his student house, and I found his room chock full of climbing gear and food bins, all being carefully loaded with sponsored goods: dried fruit from local health food shops, chocolate from some other retailer, even Gore-Tex bags (a real bonus) sponsored by some outdoor shop. These bags were seconds, but even so, they formed the jewel in the crown of our scrounged kit. I was very pleasantly surprised that companies would actually sponsor us, even in fairly modest ways, since in reality there was absolutely nothing in it for them.

Looking at all this kit made me giddy with excitement. This was a real expedition! This looked serious and was impressive even before we had arrived in the mountains. I mean, we were even freighting out food and kit in advance! I was so grateful to Andy for all the work he had done in preparing this. He had even checked out some peaks for us to attempt and had decided on a mountain of just under 19,000 feet—with the possibility of a second one if time allowed. This seemed a little small to me for a first peak, but I trusted Andy's judgment, and, after all, he had worked hard preparing it all. It was his call.

Then came the bombshell.

As we made final plans for packing our gear, Andy dropped into the conversation that the outfit that was freighting out our food supplies to Skardu for us, a well-known trekking company, often led people up the same mountain we were attempting, as it was a straightforward trekking peak.

I nearly blew a gasket, yet with enormous difficulty I kept silent. Inside I felt I was about to implode.

A trekking peak. A bloody trekking peak! I was furious.

Has he done all this supposed work to get us to slog up some stupid snow plod, up a bloody trekking peak?

What possible use is it to plan all this, to train every day, to work three jobs at once to get the money together for a stupid, lousy, nondescript bump that old men and school children can get led up every day of the week by a trekking company!

I kept these thoughts to myself, and we continued making preparations for departure, but this one piece of information had severely dented my enthusiasm in the whole venture. I wanted to climb a much more serious mountain, and preferably two, if time and weather allowed. My only consolation was that, in my mind, we could class this peak as a training climb, and if we were quick, we would have sufficient opportunity to do a *real* mountain afterwards. The fact that it was almost 19,000 feet of nondescript bump now meant less than nothing to me. I stayed silent and prepared myself for the trip.

Packing my gear was not nearly as much fun as in previous years. Everything I had, except for my rope, was borrowed. All of my wonderful gear—my ice axes, crampons, plastic boots, climbing hardware, everything—was stuck in my dormitory in Beijing. And now I was loading old, borrowed, and frankly substandard gear into an equally old, borrowed, and fairly uncomfortable rucksack. I was grateful for those who had loaned me items, but I resented having to take such kit with me. It really took the edge off the preparations, something I usually enjoyed enormously.

Soon the date came around for my departure to Pakistan. I was flying separately from the rest of the team because Andy had been forced to buy me whatever ticket was available at the last minute following my unplanned exit from China. I would land in Pakistan a couple of days earlier than the others. Travelling alone suited me fine. I wanted to spend some time not talking to anyone, to prepare myself for the climbing ahead, and to try to make sense of the conflicting thoughts and emotions that were robbing me of peace as well as sleep. I was beginning the whole expedition feeling disaffected rather than elated at the prospect of climbing in one of the great mountain ranges of the world because I believed we had set our goals too low. I would have to get over all this, or I was going to be a nightmare to live with.

Fortunately, arriving in Rawalpindi was just the tonic I needed. The sights, sounds, and most importantly, the smells of a bustling city in the developing world were deeply invigorating to me. I loved the jostling at the airport, where lines of young men tried to carry my bags, often grabbing the straps of my army holdall in an effort to wrestle it from my grasp and then charge me a few rupees to take it the hundred yards to the bus terminal. They were fairly skinny chaps on the whole, whereas I had forearms like lamb chops and the grip of a vice in those days, so their best efforts to unlade me went unrewarded.

What I appreciated the most was that, in defeat, they would smile broadly at me and walk off happily, calling out, "Body builder. Very strong. Body builder" and then go and harangue a more frail-looking westerner. In China this would have been a loss-of-face situation, and the defeated miscreant would have skulked off, sullen and dejected, with no expression of humour at all. I enjoyed this honest skullduggery much more, where a smile and a wave would carry the meaning of "You didn't get me this time, you little crook" on my part, and an understood, "I'll get you next time," on his! I felt at ease almost immediately.

I booked into a clean-looking little hotel close to the main street and went out immediately to explore. Tiny black and yellow taxis filled both sides of the road. Often open-backed affairs, these vehicles provided the bulk of the motor vehicle transport for the local people. At a cost of one rupee I could go almost anywhere in Rawalpindi, if I could stand the heat, the smell, and the insanely dangerous antics of the drivers long enough to reach my desired destination. In addition, having twenty or more people in a vehicle designed for four was the norm, so taxi rides were cramped, to say the least—especially when the sun was beating down an easy ninety-five degrees on my pasty European scalp! I spent the bulk of my first afternoon back in my room, regretting that I had made an environmental stand by refusing to book into a hotel with air conditioning. I also did not want to look like a soft westerner when all the locals did without air conditioning. Either way, I was soon regretting my brave decision as I sweated on my bed.

By the following morning I was growing impatient with city life. I wanted to be off into the hills. I kept looking at the plane ticket I had in my pocket, booked for three days hence, which would take us from this stinking city and out into the hills, on to Skardu. I effectively wasted another opportunity to see another culture because all I could focus on was the next hill to climb. Even then, it seemed, it did not matter where that hill was so long as it helped in my insatiable quest to be defined as a mountaineer.

It was great to meet the lads at the airport the next day. We had spent our last day in England practicing crevasse rescue techniques, hanging from one of Andy's parents' trees, and doing a load of pull-ups from branches before taking some team photographs prior to my departure. We had all gelled well together, and I could see us all getting along splendidly throughout the expedition. Having been in Rawalpindi for a full two days before they had arrived, I felt quite the old pro and led them from the airport exit to a taxi, like a responsible tour guide, before enjoying their comments of approval as they all checked into the hotel I had chosen for us.

Andy had brought along his brother, Dave, who, at six feet four inches tall in his socks and weighing sixteen stones (224 pounds) in his underwear, was quite a head-turner for the locals. He had helped build the Triumph Vitesse for my previous year's trip to Norway with Andy. In order to maintain good team relations, I refrained from talking about the car's differential.

J-P was as small and wiry as Dave was tall and expansive. A medical student with a keen wit and a rapier tongue, J-P knew his own mind and did not suffer fools gladly. He was also supremely laid back and took everything very coolly, almost lazily. His cutting irony had me at once laughing helplessly and being fearful of saying anything that may become fuel for his piercing, sarcastic observations. He was also an accomplished climber whom I respected from the outset of the trip, even though I had not been in his company for more than a few hours until we met up in Pakistan.

Along with Andy, this made up the foursome of our adventure. We sat down together for dinner that first night, and I fancied a crisp, green salad, perhaps with a nice, juicy tomato sliced on the side.

What a fool!

Never, never, never eat a salad in a third-world restaurant, no matter how appealing it may seem after slogging around dusty, smelly, sweltering streets all day! No matter how clean the establishment *looks*, lay off the salad! I had lived in China for a year and had never become ill from the food. Why? Because I was always careful. I never ate anything that I could not *see* had been thoroughly cooked. It is a basic rule of life for a Western traveller in such countries.

I had ignored this rule.

Within four hours I was throwing up in a way I did not believe possible; images of power-hosed pig swill come starkly to mind. I was sitting on the toilet at the same time, since that end was equally active. I wanted to die. I lay on the floor, unable to move, even as a cockroach the size of a mouse came running across the room at me and crawled over my head. I was past caring.

The next day the lads left me semi-conscious on the bathroom floor and went to confirm our reservations for our flights to Skardu the day following.

They returned two hours later with the news that the airline had informed them that the weather was unsuitable for flying, and so they would have to return the next day to see if the plane could be confirmed for the day following that. I was used to such bureaucratic bumblings: China was masterful at this, and patience had been born in me because of it. Perhaps that's why they invented Buddhism!

Dave was already fed up with waiting. He seemed to blame the bad weather on the Pakistani airline. I was still puzzling over how he had made this colossal mental leap when J-P slammed him down with a pithy dose of sarcasm, which made me chuckle. Dave was not amused, and Andy stepped in quickly to act as mediator while J-P looked on benignly—as if he had nothing to do with it. This became the pattern for the entire trip. Not an entirely healthy group dynamic, but nonetheless dynamic!

Three days later we were still no closer to confirming our flights. I had already been in Pakistan for a week, and even if we flew the next day, it would be approaching another week until we actually got into the mountains. Patience was wearing thin on all of us, and tempers were starting to become a little frayed. We could see our expedition grinding to a halt before it had even started.

I was feeling better physically, although I had lost around seven pounds in three days. This concerned me, as I would need to be in peak form if I was going to be able to do serious ice and snow at altitude. Andy and I both knew we would need to take some decisive action, and after discussing the issue we all decided to cut our losses and go for a bus, which would take us to Skardu the next morning. We had already paid for our flights and would not see any of this money refunded to us if we chose not to wait for the weather to change, but we had been advised that the weather was not likely to change for weeks, so the bus was the best option. Tickets were cheap, and by dawn the next day we were boarding our brightly painted charabanc, together with all our climbing hardware and some hastily bought food supplies. Finally, we were leaving the city behind us and heading off into the hills, knowing that we should be in Skardu in around twenty-four hours.

Twenty-four hours on a bus. Twenty-four hours on a *crowded* bus. I was fine simply sitting staring out of the window. Of course, it was uncomfortable and it was smelly and it was occasionally boring, but I could accept all of that. Andy did not like it and was a little tetchy at times. Dave hated it and was asking the adult equivalent of "Are we there yet?" from the first hour up until our arrival. In truth, he was altogether too large to be sharing his seat with several others, all the while his knees were putting dents in the seat in front of him. J-P was as phlegmatic as ever. I do not think he uttered a single word of complaint for the whole journey!

Soon, however, Karakoram vistas started to open out around us as the bus wound its way often precariously around mountain dirt roads, invariably with a sheer rock wall on the left side of us and a vertical drop-off to our right. At the bottom of this gorge the mighty Indus River would be crashing and tearing its way down the valley; churning the thick, sand-coloured water with its terrific power. I was fascinated at this spectacle of one of nature's powerhouses and imagined the appealing suicide mission of trying to paddle down it in a kayak.

Our occasional tea stops were great, made at the whim of our driver. The whole busload of occupants would disembark and follow the driver to what was little more than a mud hut, outside of which were wooden bed bases with a lattice of ropes for springs. We would all huddle onto a few of these and then be served "chai." This was a delicious blend of water taken from the river, boiled up with a huge amount of loose-leaf tea, an equally robust serving of sugar, and a mound of dried milk. This was all placed over an open fire, and the mixture was left at a rolling boil for a good while before serving. This meant it was perfectly safe to drink, even for our delicate western constitutions! The result was a brew of extraordinary strength, sweet and creamy, with sediment at the bottom of each mug of tea leaves, sand, and silt. I always had second servings!

By early evening we arrived at Gilgit, a wonderful mountain town. We were all told to get off the bus and take our gear with us, as this bus was going no further. When we asked about the bus to Skardu, we received our next installment of bad news: the road to Skardu had been destroyed in a flood due to the unexpectedly heavy monsoon rains, and there was no way to get there by road.

Disaster! Did we have to return to Rawalpindi and wait for the plane, if indeed it would ever actually take off? We were never even going to set foot on a mountain at this rate. Amazingly, we came across what would very loosely be called a travel agency run by a larger-than-life gentleman named Mohammed Iqbal, who, as J-P wryly put it, "had an ego the size of K2!" He was a charming gentleman who assured us that we could get all the way to Skardu by jeep. If we would only cross his palm with silver, he would furnish us with said jeep and a driver—and we could set off in the morning.

What an adventure! A jeep journey over a pass into Skardu sounded like great fun. We questioned Mr. Iqbal further, just to make sure the jeep could indeed get us all the way there. His assurances gave us no need for any more doubt. Our hope was restored! We would be four-wheel-driving our way into the mountains, past the Hindu Kush mountain range, which includes Nanga Parbat (one of the world's fourteen 8,000-metre peaks), and onto Skardu, where all our food and supplies awaited us! Even though we had few supplies left, we departed the next day brimming with enthusiasm and laughing all the way out of Gilgit and onto the mountain roads.

Viewing the scenery from our rag-topped jeep was an extraordinary experience. Bright sunshine and blue skies filled with billowing white clouds meant that we travelled in T-shirts, with the famous Pakistani towels wrapped around our heads to keep off the withering heat. We stopped to take photographs of Nanga Parbat, a huge mound of snow, rock, and ice dominating the horizon, and though still far off, its massiveness was hugely impressive. I thought of Reinhold Messner, one of the great mountaineers, who had climbed it solo on his way to climbing all of the world's 8,000-metre peaks. I wanted to go above 8,000 metres as well. I knew I could not just yet, but it was no longer a dream; it was an intention.

After many hours of fun-filled four-wheeling, we approached an area of greenery, an oasis amongst the brown, arid landscape of the foothills. This emerald patch stood out in stark contrast to the boulder fields we had just been circumnavigating, and it glowed even more invitingly when positioned against the backdrop of the huge mountains capped with snow above their own dark grey faces and ridges. Random huts, rather than houses, dotted the edges of the green miniature fields, manufactured out of mud bricks and a type of straw thatch roofs. Whoever lived here had a meagre existence, that was for sure.

We came to understand that this village was called "Chilam Chowki." I cannot vouch for the spelling and have never seen mention of it in any guidebooks before or since. The driver of our jeep stopped and urged us all to get out. At once I was looking forward to a "chai stop." But then I noticed that there was no road out of there. Even the track we had been on just seemed to peter out, and it became a footpath, with no evidence of any vehicular activity having ever been over it.

Why did I sense those little alarm bells ringing? We were in the middle of nowhere, and as the inhabitants of the huts emerged it occurred to me by the looks on their faces that they were unaccustomed to receiving visitors, let alone western mountaineers. The four of us looked around nervously for a bus stop, an airfield, or at least a sign saying, "Skardu, half a mile this way."

"Jeep go no further. I get man to come with horse for you," said our driver.

Hmmm.

Unless that man happened to be the Lone Ranger himself, along with good old Silver, we were up to our eyeballs in trouble. We had a day's food supply, maybe two if we went hungry, a great pile of climbing hardware, and our own personal rucksacks with us. We were in the middle of nowhere, and there were no phones, radios, or smoke signals to send for help.

At this moment I half expected the driver, at the behest of his boss in Gilgit, to offer us a return journey back there at the tidy sum of oh, let's say, all the money we had left. He did not, however. Moreover, he made sure we were all comfortable and introduced us to the village leader before sharing some chai with us and starting his engine. As he drove away, I experienced a brief jolt of fear, almost panic. We were very much alone, and entirely dependent on the arrival of our horse and guide. If he did not show up, we would sit here and die. We had no map of the area and could not communicate with anyone except in sign language. It was a brand-new experience, and despite my fears, it was very stimulating. Another amazing twist to our already outstanding adventure!

We pitched our tents, and after a dinner of *chapattis* (a Pakistani flatbread) and particularly inedible pasta, we turned in, chatting about our horse and guide and speculating on when they would come.

Our guide turned up through the mists of a cloudy, drizzly morning. We had been informed some two hours earlier that "weather cloudy, man not come." Our despair, therefore, had turned to almost excessive joy as we saw a palomino pony arrive alongside a frail-looking and clearly quite elderly guide. The Masked Rider and his trusty steed they were not, but we were delighted to see them nonetheless. He had almost no luggage of his own, no sleeping bag, no extra kit, hardly even a bag big enough for food. This meant, we assumed, that the way to Skardu must only be a short hike away, and we would be there by nightfall. Our jeep driver had told us that it was a one- or two-stage trek across a plain, and we therefore surmised that, in our excellent condition, we could make it in a day. We all smiled at each other and began to load up the beast. Soon we were striding out along the path into new territory, and visions of a hot shower and an excellent curry dinner at the K2 Motel in Skardu that evening beckoned us on.

More than eight non-stop hours later, the pony stood still yet again to catch its breath. I was pleased that its owner coaxed it forward with gentle words and a delicate touch. I had seen some horrendous brutality toward creatures in China, and I was not willing for a beast to suffer because of me. I leaned into its rump, and with J-P at the other side, we both tried to help the hardy creature along. Whether I was helping or merely leaning on something for a rest, I cannot say. What was true was that my lungs were screaming at me in a way I never thought possible. Both of my quadriceps were on fire, and my shoulders, weighed down by my rucksack, were aching so badly that I could feel the pain from my neck down to my groin.

And still the path grew ever steeper, steeper and rougher, as it snaked around boulders and up into the mountains and finally around the corner and out of sight. The majestic scenery around us was now a curse. I hated looking at it. Rage was spurring me on, and I would swear out loud as I stumbled again on a rock, since I could not lift my heavy-booted foot high enough to get over it. We were all wearing our ice-climbing boots in order to save on luggage space and weight, but on a path, these were cumbersome, not to mention painful for the feet. I could already feel several blisters forming on both feet, and I knew they would have burst by the time we ended our day's walk.

As evening approached we were all despondent. We could not ask our guide, "Are we there yet?" for he did not speak a word of English. He simply kept trudging forward, seemingly oblivious to all of us. Finally, we rounded a bend and the path flattened out. Surely this was just prior to the descent into Skardu!

But what was that shimmering just a few hundred yards away? The late sun was glistening off the path just ahead of us, causing the light to dance around and dazzle our eyes.

It cannot be. There is no way to avoid it. Good grief, it's big, too!

A glacial river stood in our path. It was not huge but it was fast-flowing, around 30 yards wide, and deep enough to wash us away if we lost our footing. We waited for our guide to point out the bridge, which was clearly the only way over this hideous obstacle.

But in fact it was not hideous. The glacial waters were a glowing turquoise and crystal clear. The sound of the river, chattering and friendly in the shallows, then grumbling and sinister toward the middle sections, was both exciting and friendly, with just enough threat to be deeply alluring. The speed of the flow was very deceptive, and if you cared to observe for more than a few seconds, which I did, you could see quite a torrent spinning, twisting, and rushing down the side of the hills, disappearing miles away over the edge of our false horizon.

I was beginning to enjoy the view for a moment and briefly forgot the task at hand when I noticed our guide stop and remove his shoes. I laughed. The poor old guy is jiggered and wants to cool his aching feet, I thought.

That poor old guy then walked into that freezing, and I mean *freezing,* glacial river without even breaking stride and led his poor old pony with him, stopping several times to help the beast keep its feet as the torrent around it seemed to wall up behind the substantial barrier of its girth. In bare feet he just stood there and talked to his horse, all the while fighting to keep his footing as the waters fought to send him crashing down the hillside, under its gin-clear surface, and on to his undoubted death.

You must be bloody joking! I thought, possibly out loud. This was now a preposterous turn of events in our little adventure, and none too welcome at that! I had precious little energy left, and now I had to fight a river as well. We decided to team up and help each other over in pairs. I teamed up with Dave. We stripped off our boots. It was the first time I was able to examine my feet: several of the blisters were already bleeding, and I did not even bother to count how many I had in total. It might have depressed me.

I strode into the icy waters and gasped at the immediate rush of the glacial assault on my previously toasty toes. Within seconds the intense pain of freezing feet was almost surreal. I literally gritted my teeth to avoid any further expletives and to focus on the job at hand. Again, anger became my ally as I determined that no stupid little river was going to stop me. After all, that old man over there, seemingly detached from the whole situation, was unconcernedly putting his shoes back on. This river was now my enemy, and I was going to give it a good thrashing!

A split-second later I felt a huge weight on my shoulders that almost caused me to fall and sent a shock wave through my system. I thought at first that I had been hit by an object flowing down the river. I struggled to keep my feet and with all my remaining power fought against the crushing load on my upper body that was threatening to send me under the water.

Then I heard crying—not the tears of a child but great sobs of someone utterly terrified. Dave had stumbled, almost losing his footing, and was hanging off me, all sixteen stones of him. If I was not literally carrying him, I was certainly holding him upright, and all the while he just hung there and sobbed, unable to pull himself together and carry on.

I felt disgusted. Disgusted and repulsed. To admit defeat was bad enough, but to cause someone else discomfort in that defeat was quite simply bereft of backbone. When we arrived at the other side, I removed Dave's arms from my shoulders and silently put my boots back on.

Dave wanted to talk about his experience.

I wanted never to speak to him again.

The poor guy had been scared. I deliberately walked briskly to put a few yards between us so I could avoid starting any conversation with him. He seemed happy to hang back and talk to his brother about his "near-death experience." Little did I realize that the situation would be entirely reversed in a matter of weeks, and I would face the most difficult challenge of my life: Could I live with myself, knowing I was an abject failure as a mountaineer?

Now we had to rest, as darkness was approaching, and we needed to eat something. Actually, we were about to eat the last of our food. Dave said he needed food enough to fuel a sixteen-stone body, so he argued that his ration was not enough. I gave him mine. Perhaps I felt guilty about how I had thought of him a few minutes earlier. I like to think that it was the old me that had been cruel, and one of the first signs of the new me that showed compassion on someone. Whatever it was, Dave ate his fill and I went hungry. And I was genuinely fine with that.

We *had* to be near Skardu now. Not that we just *wanted* to be near, but we *had* to be near. We had no more food. We were approaching exhaustion, and we had been going uphill (so much for a flat walk across a plain) all day. Andy drew a line in the sand, pointed at one end, and getting our guide's attention, said, "Chilam Chowki" (the name of the village from where we had set out that morning). Then he pointed at the other end and said, "Skardu." Finally, pointing at the ground around us, then at the line he had drawn, he said, "Here?" and gave him the stick to indicate.

We repeated this three times because the answer we received the first two times had made our hearts sink. The third time confirmed that we had covered around one third of the distance to Skardu. Put another way, we had more climbing to do, actually double what we had already done, and we had to do it *without food*.

We were in a serious predicament. The only thing to do was buckle down and get on with it. Little was said that night. I bivouacked in my Gore-Tex bivvy bag rather than sleeping in a tent, but I enjoyed the sound of that river and the mountains around us. Of course, life was serious at the moment, but I certainly knew I was alive!

The chill of the river was as nothing compared with the icy chill I had felt two years before in Norway. Memories of a desperate struggle and a waterfall came back to me as I looked at the dense blanket of stars in the vast and spectacularly clear night sky in the Karakoram. Two years ago there was not the faintest twinkle of light. All lights had been snuffed out, as had all my hope. For now, life was merely a little challenging, not like in Norway that horrifying night of The Climb. The fear I had felt while crossing the river earlier was almost laughable compared to the stark terror of two years before in Romsdal. That night, life had seemed completely without hope and yet here I was, still alive. I smiled and slept well, though the blisters did try to keep me awake for a while.

Like soldiers on a mission, we route-marched the whole of the second day, and despite some difficult and steep sections, the hardest part had been putting on my boots at the very outset. The blisters had objected quite strongly to being covered up again by rigid, plastic boots, and whatever protective membrane that had formed overnight was stripped off the instant my heel reached the back of the boot. With a grimace I had set out, gingerly at first, and then, by force of will had increased my pace, until we all looked as if we were in boot camp being harried by a particularly sadistic lance corporal! We must have been quite a sight.

We crossed four more rivers on the second day, but by river number three, it had become routine: boots off, grit your teeth, get over quickly, and do not slip! More importantly, around mid-afternoon we had begun our descent, and we could see ahead of us fields and a wider horizon, rather than more and more mountains concealing from us our destination. As we camped by a gentle stream, the non-glacial variety, we were in high spirits, and we ate our "meal" of two boiled hard-candy sweets each with laughter rather than the sombre silence of the night before. We also made a boiled-sweet tea, which consisted of, unimaginatively, sweets brewed up with boiling water. If that was not bland enough, not to mention insubstantial, it was also quite a weak brew at that!

Shortly after noon on day three we entered Skardu, having bid goodbye to our guide on the outskirts of the town. He did not wait for a moment and set off exactly the way he had come, pausing only to argue with us over the amount of *baksheesh*, or tip, he should receive for his efforts. I thought he deserved a medal, but still, in the spirit of good negotiation, Andy haggled with him until honour was satisfied on both sides. I expected him to stay with friends for a day or two and stock up on supplies, but off he headed back into the hills. I still have no idea what he ate during our time with him, but he certainly taught me a thing or two about the hardiness of these people and of the relative fragility of supposedly tough, athletic mountaineers from the West!

It was four bedraggled and hobbling men who pitched tents on the grounds of the famous K2 Motel that night, walking around the campsite barefoot so as to promote the healing of our blisters. All of us ate a marvellous curry in the motel and relaxed by our tents until the sun went down. We were now almost two weeks behind schedule for our expedition, but on that day we were merely happy to have full stomachs and a lie down.

We found out later that we had completed a known trek over the Deosai Pass. Far from it being a one-day walk along a plain, it is apparently a five-stage trek, usually completed in four or five days, which goes from 8,000 to 17,000 feet. Small wonder we had been out of breath! We had marched this trek in a little over two days, carrying full rucksacks and with almost no food. On reflection, this was quite a feat. At the time, it was just a pain in the neck. All this before we had even started our expedition!

Over the next three days we recovered as best we could, and I was very thankful that, against all expectations, by the time we set off into the mountains, my feet had completely healed—despite having had more than a dozen bleeding blisters when we arrived. We assembled all our gear, collected the supplies that had been freighted out to Skardu, and having hired a climbing *sirdar* (a leader of our porters) and a cook, we headed out in our hired jeep.

Our *sirdar* was the jewel in our expedition crown. Abdul Karim was no more than five feet tall and cannot have weighed more than seven stones (98 pounds). He had climbed Nanga Parbat carrying a paraglider that the famous mountaineer Jean-Marc Bouvin had used to fly all the way down the mountain! Karim had also been on K2, the world's second-highest peak, six times. On two of these occasions he reached the highest camp, missing out on a summit attempt only because the weather closed in on the expedition. This was quite a climbing pedigree. He showed us sleeping bags he had been given from various expeditions that had hired him, one bearing the name "Messner" across it. Karim talked of Reinhold Messner as a friend. He was not a boastful man, and I am still convinced the two of them were certainly well acquainted. And now Karim was on our team!

We almost lost him as our *sirdar* the day before departure, as we were informed that he had fallen off a jeep and had broken his collarbone. Our hearts sank: not another setback! An hour later the little man appeared and assured us he was fine to continue. He showed us the arm in a sling, and just when I thought there had been an exaggeration of his injury, he revealed his collarbone to us. I saw it clearly moving under the skin in the middle as he moved his arm. I grimaced and asked, stupidly, if it hurt.

"Little pain, sah, little pain. No problem!" He agreed to take some Ibuprofen we offered him for the pain, and that was all he received in terms of medical treatment. This was one tough little man! Only a week or so later I would see him wade through chest-deep snow, working his arms and shoulders with two snow poles, fighting through the wet, clinging drifts that were in our way. Not only did he not complain, but also none of us could keep up with him! A western mountaineer would have been wild with pain in the same circumstances. Every ounce of his seven stones was an inspiration to me.

Finally, at dawn the following morning, we were really starting our expedition up Gondoro Peak. The previous two weeks could all have been avoided had our flight left Rawalpindi on time and brought us here to Skardu. It took several years for me to realize that all that "wasted" time was what made the whole trip memorable. All I could focus on now was getting on with the task ahead of us: climb the easy peak, and then look for an impressive notch for my climbing belt. Down came that whip across my back again! We jumped into the back of our jeep, and with all of us standing, we set off.

Within only an hour all substantial habitation had been left behind, and we were now officially on our way to the big mountains. These came thick and fast, with spectacular views mesmerising us at every turn. The villages we passed through became more and more remote as we stood in the back of the jeep, on top of our kit, and marvelled at the almost prehistoric way of life for some of the people out there. Donkeys threshed the grain that had been harvested, and it was clear that no electricity was used, even from a generator, nor was there any gas power. We helped ourselves to clusters of apricots, hanging ripe and succulent from the trees just above our heads as we motored through the tiny dirt streets. We quickly realized, however, that these were probably the local people's only cash crop, and we felt immediately guilty, resisting any further temptation. They were quite extraordinarily delicious, though, which probably had as much to do with the way we harvested them as it did with the fabulously fresh taste of the fruit itself!

By evening we were arriving at Karim's hometown (I use the word in the loosest possible way) in the Hushe Valley. From here we would pick up our porters and begin our trek into the mountains and on to our base camp, at around 17,000 feet. I stood and gazed at our collection of men who had been hired to hump all our kit up into the hills. They were both young and old. Some looked well over sixty, though it would be impossible to make an accurate guess; their difficult lives in a hostile environment must surely have worn a body quicker than our cushy, padded existence in Britain.

Most of them used an old, blue polypropylene drum, the kind used to carry non-toxic chemicals and suchlike, as their "rucksacks." These were tied on to their backs by rough hemp rope. As we went about adjusting the straps of the ergonomically comfortable back systems on our rucksacks, these men merely threw their barrels on their backs and set off, tying a knot in the rope as they went! I could never understand how they were not crippled with back pain from it. I found out that they were farmers in the climbing "off season" and spent all the climbing and trekking season being used for myriad expeditions as porters. The very best of them, like Karim, became high altitude porters and could earn, by their standards, huge sums of money in this occupation. Becoming a high-altitude porter carried an enormous amount of kudos for them presumably because of the money they earned rather than anything to do with the mountaineering prowess it represented.

Once we began our climb, I kept up with them as best I could (which was not very successfully most of the time!) and was always the first on our team to reach our rest area. Then I would try to run back and take a few photographs of the team as they approached. Watching the porters ahead of me and the lads behind was thrilling. It all looked so professional; a real expedition, and the scenery around us was unlike anything I had ever seen. We had passed the huge peak of Rakaposhi early in our trek, and now we could see K6, K7, and the enormous bastions of the Trango Towers. These massive rock routes are quite extraordinary in sheer size, and to climb them requires the most superlative fitness level imaginable.

I could feel the effects of my recent salad-induced illness when I walked. I had lost a certain spring in my step, as if I had less in reserve when I started to feel tired. Doubtless some of this was due to the altitude, but I could certainly feel there was more to it than just that. I did suffer from quite severe headaches, which was to be expected as a normal aspect of high-altitude walking, and these things started to weigh on my mind. I felt that the best treatment was to ignore them and force myself to walk faster—to try harder to keep up with the porters. I made it an imperative to be the first member of our team to reach the campsite each evening.

We stopped for a night at the last village before starting onto glacial walking, at the point above which there would be no significant vegetation. It seemed the whole village came out to meet us, and soon we were swamped by children asking us for either a rupee or a pen. We had been warned of this and were armed with a bunch of cheap biros (ballpoint pens) brought from England. These were received most warmly, but apparently, having "earned" one so easily, the little rascals rejoined the queue to claim a second, doubtless to sell or exchange to a less fortunate colleague. It seemed that we should have made it more difficult for them to obtain their gifts, as an easy victory was received as being a sign of weakness on our part, which deserved their exploitation! I was at first annoyed by the lack of gratitude on the part of these children. Why, after all, could they not be content with the one gift they had received? I laughed when I heard my own pomposity. I would do the same thing if offered something for nothing. I knew I too would try to exploit generosity and in far greater ways than merely taking a second pen!

I lay awake that night pondering this further as I gazed up at the broad white band of the Milky Way, clearly visible, stretching over the whole night sky. The moon, at this altitude and so far from any artificial lights (the village was pitch black, with no sign of even a fire burning), was bright enough to hurt my eyes if I tried to stare at it, yet it was so stunning in its glow that I wanted to fix my gaze on it all the time. The trees hummed and moaned gently all around our camping area, and the gentle cool breeze flitted sporadically through the leaves, prompting them to hiss and clap lyrically into my tired ears. I found myself, in such a place of peacefulness and solitude, talking to God. It was a most natural thing to do—not forced or out of a sense of duty.

Along with those pen-wielding children, I too had received something for nothing. Two years ago I had been given something that I could not even begin to pay for. I had been kept alive when I should have been dead. But there was more to it than just that. Since that event I had been living as if I could now exploit that act of kindness and see what else I could get from Him whenever I needed a favour. I believed I could live just as I wanted while taking for granted what had been done for me and what He would continue to do for me. This did not seem altogether right, but I was just beginning to understand what I was doing wrong. It was like I had been bought but was living like I was still self-employed. I was still trying to call the shots in my own life when deep down I knew that I had relinquished that right back on The Climb.

This realization was at once very uncomfortable and a source of great relief to me. I was starting to make sense of all the conflict I had been feeling for the past two years. There were things that I could not even start to explain, yet they were a basic part of my everyday life. Why did I not fit in as a climber, even though I looked the part; and why did I fit in at church, even though I looked anything but the part? Was it true that in the core of me was not a climber, but a Christian? Perhaps even, according to God's will, I was not even a Christian who climbs. Maybe I was not meant to pursue climbing as a lifestyle or even as a pastime.

That last thought was not acceptable, though I did take hold of the fact that I needed to be a Christian on the outside as well as one on the inside, the bit that only God saw! I was keeping a diary of this trip, and most of it was taken up with crying out to God over all of the angst that I was desperately trying to process. Lying awake in the open in that village that night was a pleasant awakening for me. I decided to be more real about what I now believed. After all, He deserved it. I would even ask Him if it was right before I made life choices, so long as I could keep climbing. Surely He would not object to that.

My ponderings were pierced abruptly by one of the most desperately eerie sounds I have ever heard. From out of the pitch-blackness, a couple of hundred yards away, I heard a woman's voice. Beginning in a low moan, it transformed quickly into a rapid crescendo and then into a full volume wail of hideous intensity. Just as I thought someone had found a murdered child, the voice was joined, first by one more female then by several men, their masculine sounds adding an almost primeval roar to the monstrous choir, which by now sounded as if it was surrounding me. I could clearly see a fire at the farthest point of the village, though I could not make out what was happening. The wailing continued and intensified until it had masked completely the beautiful sounds of the wind in the trees that had been lulling me to sleep. I lay rigid and literally wide-eyed in my sleeping bag. What on earth was going on?

It must have been a full two hours later that I finally managed to fall asleep. The noises had not stopped, but I had managed to convince myself that nobody was coming to ritualistically dismember me. I discovered the next morning that the village was "celebrating" a festival to commemorate the long-ago deaths of Mohammed's sons, whom we were told were named Ali and Hussein. Apparently, they had both been torn apart by wild horses—lovely! Furthermore, as the wailing intensified, there was also talk of self-harming going on with knives, perhaps to get into the whole "torn apart" theme.

I have no idea if this festival is true or if indeed Mohammed had two sons named Ali and Hussein. What I do know is that whatever they were doing that night was extremely disturbing to a young mountaineer bivouacking within earshot of it all. It was an unforgettable experience! Despite that event, however, I felt a sense of calm concerning what I had been thinking about the night before. I began to see a new purpose in my life, so I set off into the rocky moraine of the glacier fields with enthusiasm and a renewed spring in my step.

The next few days of walking were filled with stirring vistas, breathtaking peaks, invigorating hiking, and spectacular sunsets as we approached our base camp on the Gondokoro Glacier. There were so many peaks around us that were over 6,000 metres that our chosen peak at 5,650 metres was decidedly ordinary in comparison. I fought the feelings of despondency and anger that accompanied this realization. Most days were spent in a familiar routine: up at dawn or shortly thereafter: A breakfast of chai with some fresh *parathas* (Indian flatbread), usually smeared with some sponsored marmalade, followed by hours of trekking through spectacular scenery, accompanied by the chatter of the porters and the sounds of creaking glaciers or the crunch of feet over snow, ice, or boulder-strewn moraine. Despite my daily headaches, it was magnificent!

On one occasion we met a few goat herders, and our wily cook, Haqim, persuaded us to buy one of the goats for around one hundred rupees, I think. He cooked up a goat curry for us all that evening, which I was really looking forward to, until that is, I was served the knee joint, complete with gristle, cartilage, and a liberal sprinkling of hair. I crunched and gnawed through it as best I could but could not help feeling that it was not worth all the effort for the paltry amount of meat I actually had to eat at the end of the ordeal.

We lost a couple of days from our expedition when our porters all left us to return to their village to finish the last day of the Ali and Hussein festival that I described earlier. As they departed for their little celebration, I wondered if they would all survive the night! Fortunately, I did see the same faces return the following evening, none the worse, at least on the outside. A couple of days later we arrived at base camp on the edge of a glacial lake, and we could finally unload all our gear and make preparations for our summit bid. I was hoping to get over Gondoro Peak in the next day or two, so we might have time to do something worthy of report.

Sitting outside of our tent one morning, the deep blue sky contrasting starkly with the amphitheatre of massive snow spires on three sides of us, I was trying to take my mind away from the griping stomach pains and the imminent arrival of yet another mad dash to the "latrine" (a boulder to sit behind, to be exact), when I heard a hollow crack in the distance followed by a deep grumble, slowly intensifying in depth and volume. I looked up toward the top of the ridge that faced us several miles away on the other side of the lake, and I saw simultaneously an almost hypnotically captivating and yet terrible sight. A huge section of snow had just broken free from one of the mountains, and an avalanche was plunging down the side of the face, billowing like a cloud formation and accelerating with an intense roar that was filling the entire valley. What looked like cloud was in fact thousands of tonnes of snow and ice hammering down the mountainside and stripping it of more snow as it went.

Then in an instant, all was silent again. A dark grey scar marked the area where snow had been displaced. It did not look that big from where I sat, but I knew it was actually an enormous amount that had fallen away. Half an hour later, tiny specks of snow were still landing on our tents, dusting them like icing sugar before the breeze caught them and sent a swirling cloud away up the valley. It was a sobering experience considering there had been no warning of the avalanche, and yet it had a devastating effect on the look of the mountain. This was indeed a serious place, no matter how easy a peak we were attempting.

We decided on a summit attempt the following morning, leaving at half past midnight so as to reach the top at dawn, thereby reducing the risk of the sun melting the snow, which would make it harder going and increase any risk of avalanche (even though this was a small risk for our peak). I tried to get some rest, but my guts were in a terrible mess; the food poisoning was still active in my system, and I knew I was still losing weight because of that delightful salad back in Rawalpindi.

To add to my expeditioning pleasure, sleep had not been coming easily to me over the past few days. I was using one of Karim's expedition sleeping bags; that is, one that he had been given on one of his many famous expeditions. I was forced to use it because we had lost one of ours during our jeep ride into the mountains. We liked to think that it had fallen off during the journey, rather than it being pushed off by a light-fingered local. Either way, one of us would have become rather cold had not Karim saved the day.

The cold was not what robbed me of sleep, though. What impeded my slumber was that the bag was made for a person five feet tall, and I could keep warm only if I adopted a fetal position all night. More importantly, I was not sleeping alone. I was sharing my bed with an unknown number of tiny, crawling friends. I was being bitten to pieces every night, waking up to find more welts on my tired, aching body. Two or three hours of fitful dozing was the norm while I listened to Dave's abundant, satisfied snores as he lay next to me. I was not in a good way. In fact, I was drained. I prayed for strength, for the ability to keep going, and for this foul illness to go away.

We all got up and loaded our kit in time for the agreed 12:30 departure. The weather was simply awful. Snow had come down all night, and now it was accompanied by a strong and bitter wind, pulling and biting at our clothes and stinging any exposed skin. I pulled on my last layer of borrowed clothing. It was a pitifully inadequate polyester hooded jacket, and I was at once envious of the others, all of whom had well-fitted, well-insulated Gore-Tex jackets. My hat did not fit properly and soon became wet; the wind then chilled my head in a matter of minutes. As I walked into the knee-deep and then thigh-deep drifts of snow, I could feel the sweat start to form. Since my waterproofs were not breathable, all the sweat simply sat on my skin, and if we stopped it would become icy cold and chill me to the core. It was just profoundly uncomfortable and unpleasant from the outset. I was determined, however, to keep up with Karim as much as possible, and I strode into the snow, kicking fresh holes and ignoring the pain in my stomach and the desire to vomit. Within minutes of setting off, though, I was aware that all was not well.

About two hours had passed. I could see Karim in the distance, just ahead of Andy and Dave, with J-P alongside them. The snow was up to my waist in places, and I fought to keep my balance on occasions, cursing at the wind as it threw yet more icy snow into my face, stinging my eyes and blurring my vision. They turned and stopped, looking at me. I remembered Karim's broken collarbone and how he was simply ignoring the pain he must have been in. The pain in my lungs was substantial, but I had felt this before; the ache and lactic burn in my legs and back was severe, but this had become an old friend to me. All of this was acceptable. What I could not understand was the inability to raise my leg out of the snow; I simply could not take another step forward. As I cleared my eyes of the ice that had blown into them, I noticed that my vision was still blurred. I could not make out my friends, who were only fifty or one hundred yards away. What was going on? I rubbed them again, but still they were not functioning properly.

The realization hit me in a devastating wave.

I was utterly spent. There was nothing left in me. I could not go on.

In disbelief I sat down in the snow. How could I be like this, and the others still be standing? I was without doubt the fittest on the team; I had trained harder than any of them, and I could dig much deeper mentally than anyone I knew. This was not possible.

More than that, it was just not right. It was not fair. I did not fail. I never failed. "If you put the work in, you get the result out," is what I had always said, and I was sure I had put the work in and then some!

Hot tears of rage and despair stung my eyes and fell down my cheeks. I punched the ground, for I did not have the strength to raise my foot to kick anything! The lads came to me, and Karim asked if I was all right. I could not even look at him, I was so humiliated. He had always called me "the leader" even though it was Andy who was officially the team leader. He would come and sit and chat with me by the campfire, telling me stories of his expeditions on K2 in a beautiful, broken English that I loved to listen to. I had been delighted that he had chosen to guide us, and our rapport was both friendly and mutually respectful. Now I had let him down. How could a man like him even look at a failure like me?

My words to myself of a few months previously came flooding back, chiding and shaming me further: "It's only a *trekking* peak!" In an instant I was back in that river, hating Dave for not being stronger. Now, when it really mattered, I was the weak link! It was the worst disaster—the greatest nightmare I could ever have possibly imagined.

"I will come down with you," said J-P almost cheerfully.

"No, no way!" I bellowed back. I would not cause anyone else to fail because I was a failure. Andy insisted. If I had had the strength I would have hit him—my best friend. He was insisting that I should be further humiliated. He was right, of course. I could not see straight and I could hardly stand. I would have to be accompanied down, just to make sure I actually got back to base camp. Pitiful, pathetic creature!

The others turned and headed into the foul weather, soon disappearing out of sight on their way to the summit. I sat in silence, too weak to make conversation and still disbelieving what had transpired, almost as if I was watching events from the outside. It could not possibly be real.

Yet it was. J-P talked about his being knackered anyway, and that he was on the verge of turning back himself. I appreciated his lies, but I could see he was absolutely fine. I considered turning back around and going for the top, but the instant I tried to walk back uphill, I could feel all my strength draining away to nothing again. Downhill was the only option.

We arrived back at camp as the grey of the dawn silhouetted the tents from beside the lake. Haqim smiled and offered us breakfast, presuming we had reached the top and come back first. How I longed, how I ached for that to be true. Why hadn't I slowed down in the walk-in? Why did I not pace myself better? Why wasn't life a lot more fair than this? I slunk off to my tent, dreading the return of the rest of the team.

I slept for several hours and awoke to see Dave's head poking inside the tent. He was very gracious.

"I'm absolutely knackered, Russ. Andy and I made it up, but only just. The conditions were terrible! You okay?" I nodded and expressed my congratulations. I was surprised and pleased that I was genuinely happy for them, and for the first time, I felt that *the team* had done well. Two of us had succeeded, and the third had helped me to get back down safely. That was good teamwork, and I felt satisfied with it. All I had to do was adjust my mindset to accept the fact that I was no longer the leader, the pacesetter, or the pioneer; I was the back marker, the apprentice, the hanger-on. I wrote fluidly on this experience in my diary. I started to face up to some difficult realities, mainly around the theme of, "How will I base my life on a career that I am no good at? I am not going to be defined as a mountaineer, because I am a lousy failure as a mountaineer."

The bottom had fallen out of my world, and I needed time to reflect on this. Out of the recesses of my mind, another thought cropped up: "Why didn't God help me out of this and strengthen me to go on?" It was almost as if He had abandoned me and doomed me to fail. Yet that was out of character to the God who had shown up two years before on The Climb. It was a different kind of solitude that I was feeling. Back then, it was black as pitch, and I was utterly alone. This time, however, I felt as if He was watching me, not in a sick "I told you so" sort of way, but more in a waiting-for-me-to-get-it sort of way.

After a few hours wrestling through all of these ideas, I decided to get away from camp and spend some time alone. I would get up the next morning and go for a wander, if I had recovered sufficiently. I tried to get some sleep and was obviously so exhausted that I slept like a log!

I awoke to the sound of a flask falling over in our tent. As I rolled over, I felt like I was in a waterbed; sitting up, I found out that I *was!* The weather had improved dramatically overnight, with clear skies and a wave of warmth sweeping down the valley. This had caused all the recent snow to melt, and the consequent run-off from the glacier had flooded the lake, which, in turn, had risen and enveloped the entire camp! Fortunately, all our kit was suitably protected, and we laughed as we moved the tents to higher ground while a dazzling sun baked our faces and caused steam to rise from our gear, the rocks, and everything in the campsite, drying out the ground around us within just a few hours. I found myself smiling and affable—the sinister, melancholic bear of the day before hibernating for a while.

I also felt physically fine, to my enormous surprise, and ate a hearty breakfast for the first time in days. Later in the afternoon I packed my bivvy bag and went above the snow line, following the route of the summit trek.

I lay out my bivvy gear and had some food, then sat down in the snow, using my bag as a couch to relax on. It was so warm that I was bare-chested as I wandered up and down the slope taking photographs and testing to see if I was capable of walking uphill, or if my strength was going to fail me again. I was surprised to find that I could actually run up the slopes and carry on running around at a decent pace for quite a while before the lack of oxygen at over 17,000 feet took its toll. I could not understand why this was possible so soon after the disastrous summit attempt, but I was thankful.

As I looked around, I saw Layla, a mountain that had been beckoning to all of us since we first set eyes in it. It was just opposite our camp and was the most obvious landmark in the area, as the summit was so distinctive. At a little over 6,000 metres and with a pinpoint summit so sharp it was impossible to stand at the very top, this mountain had quickly become our goal for a second peak. I think deep down we knew it was not a possibility on this trip, as we had neither the experience nor the equipment to make a reasonable attempt on it. Nevertheless, it was the stuff of dreams, and I must have snapped at least a dozen photographs of the piercing tip, like a titanium lance thrusting up into a cobalt sky, so thick and dense in colour as to be almost drinkable! The contrast of brilliant white against a background of deepest glossy blue made the whole panorama almost look artificial, like an altered picture postcard, with only the wind, blowing shards of spindrift across my face, to remind me that this painting was a reality that most of the world could only ever dream about.

I stayed out all night, watching the sun disappear, and the cobalt of the sky turn to grey, then suddenly pitch black, as all light from the sun was extinguished. I could still see clearly, though, as the stars and moon shone so brightly as to dazzle. I saw shooting stars literally every two minutes, streaking across the entire night sky, sometimes visible for several seconds. It was truly amazing, and I felt so privileged to be up there witnessing a beauty that so few people get to see. The temperature dropped well below freezing, so I pulled the drawstring on both my sleeping bag and my bivvy bag as tight as they would go; all that was exposed of me was my eyes.

As I snuggled into the duck-down of the bag, I felt safe and at peace. Up here I was alone, and that was fine. Up here I was not going to screw anything up, get things wrong, or live a life that was not pure and simple. I do not know why I was thinking like that, but I decided I wanted to live a clean life. I wanted to do things differently. I wanted to be a better person. It was not that I was a hell-raiser or a devious criminal or even a plain nasty piece of work. But I knew that my lifestyle was not how God wanted it to be. I had been writing in my diary about how I did not feel right about my lifestyle, and how I felt constantly worried or guilty about all kinds of things. This had started after my Norwegian experience on The Climb, and I was only now starting to make sense of it.

Was He trying to get my attention in a very gentle way? Was He saying that I had to live my life differently? That I could not do things the way I used to? It then occurred to me that my failure the previous day was perhaps the start on the long, long journey toward humility.

It was a profound and deeply enriching night, and I came down the next day feeling positive and excited. This was helped further by the news that the lads had decided to climb the same peak again, mainly because they had not seen any views the first time, with the weather being so bad, and they wanted some pictures. Also, time had effectively run out for us to try anything new, so we were just going to stay in the same spot for a couple of days before heading back home. J-P and Andy decided to go again the next morning. I decided to wait another day just to make sure I was fit and then go up with Dave. After my cruel attitude to him earlier, it would be good to be able to share a pleasant experience together.

My pleasant thoughts were dashed by an unexpected source later that day. As we were packing gear for our respective summit attempts, I overheard a comment by J-P to Andy. It was one of his throwaway sarcastic lines. Andy laughed out loud then tried to stifle it. I was shocked to realize that J-P was quoting one of my diary entries, and he referred to my talking to God. He made a few other comments, and they both chuckled and carried on with what they were doing.

This was an awful jolt. They had been reading my diary! All the weeks of entries, as I had described my wrestling with so many issues; of discussions with God and crying out to Him; all the deeply personal thoughts and emotions that I had expressed in the privacy of my journal were now open for public dissemination and ridicule.

My closest friend was laughing at my walk with God and at my insecurities in my embryonic faith. That one minute in my life effectively destroyed one of my greatest friendships and ignited an anger and resentment that took me several years to get over, by which time our relationship had deteriorated past the point of redemption.

I have never felt so betrayed before or since. My best friend, who had helped introduce me to God, was now laughing at my relationship with Him. The peace I had enjoyed the day before was washed away in a torrent of blame and resentment.

It was a simple throwaway line, a silly bit of fun, but I was far too fragile in my faith to be able to take it. My pride and inability to forgive swamped me. I decided that I would not let my guard down again and that I would tell no one about my so-called faith. I would prove to everyone that I was better than they were, and they could all get stuffed! Needless to say, in true British style, I never mentioned it to Andy. "Least said, soonest mended," as my father used to say. No idea where he found that one, but I was brought up on that adage, and it left me a relational cripple for decades! It certainly meant that resolving this issue through discussion was never going to happen.

I marched up Gondoro Peak the next day and I enjoyed the walk. I went to the summit and back in record time, just to prove I could! I took pictures of Dave and genuinely enjoyed his company. I slid most of the way down on my backside, picking up enough speed on my seated glissade to melt a hole in my salopettes!

On the following day I marched back down the mountains, trying to be civil and even friendly and sometimes succeeding, but I knew in my heart that this trip had been about failure and about not fitting in. Moreover, it signified that I was alone, and I had to go about proving myself all over again. If my best friend would betray me, then the best thing was not to have a best friend; and if having faith was a thing to ridicule, then the best thing was to keep my mouth shut about having any faith. To do otherwise would invite ridicule from outside the church for being a supposed Christian and from within the church for not knowing enough about God to live a godly life.

By the time we returned to England from our Karakoram expedition, I had found reasons to be angry at all of my teammates. From a climbing perspective I was a broken man and viewed myself as a charlatan. Instead of enjoying the trip and the experience, I merely felt ridiculous, and my ambitions were in tatters. I felt guilty about my feelings of hostility, and peace continued to elude me. I had gone back on my decision to consult with God before I made life choices. I was still unwilling to sacrifice mountaineering and the desire to be defined as a mountaineer, despite believing that I was an utter failure at it. I forced from my mind the notion that I had felt peace before, especially back in Norway, when I had had it, even in my darkest, most hopeless hour when failure had been proven to me many times over. This image only served to make me feel more guilty and uncomfortable, so I pushed it away as best I could.

Yet I knew I craved peace! Despite my continuing to pursue my climbing goals for the next two years, this expedition had broken the camel's back. I had to accept what had happened in Norway and acknowledge it. The feeling of guilt at my disobedience gradually intensified. God was turning the screw of conviction, and I could not enjoy anything the way I was trying to, especially if I insisted on pursuing happiness at the end of a climbing rope.

It just was not working; Pakistan demonstrated that. It was not meant to, and He would not allow it to. My rebellion began to wane gradually, but there was still one more spark left. I had to push one last door to make sure I was on the wrong path. Perhaps God wanted me to succeed and be fulfilled this way after all.

I had to try to be excellent on the ice. Maybe that would make me happy.

Chapter 6

THE LURE OF THE ICE

▲

The old 2-litre Cavalier engine roared as we accelerated up Kirkstone Pass. It was 3:30 a.m. The reverberating beat of Yello's "The Race" resonated loud and hard in our ears; a great explosion of sound and emotion, raucous and urgent. We were already wound tight, buzzing with excitement, even though we would not be climbing for another five hours. The cacophonic chorus of saxophones belted out the same riff again and again as we replayed the song at least a dozen times. Luke sat in the front, head bobbing frantically to the rhythm, hands a blur of "air-drumming" prowess. In the blackness of the car, his face lit up only by the reflection of the headlamps on the dull road, he took on a demented choirboy look, with his boyish face made wild by dishevelled hair and unkempt beard. It all added to the unbridled, not to mention largely unplanned, nature of our trip. We were men on a mission!

After leaving university, delighted with my academic studies yet despondent with my mountaineering achievements, I had decided to return to the Lake District, a climber's mecca, for a year to concentrate on my climbing before "getting a proper job," as I was frequently reminded I ought to be doing! I wanted to explore the possibilities of some kind of career in climbing, and notwithstanding my own feelings of inadequacy due to my disastrous Karakoram exploits and my complete dissatisfaction with my climbing progress to date, I wanted to make it work somehow. The Lake District was the place for this to happen, as I could make some useful contacts and really progress with my abilities. I had to prove that I was up to the challenge and could climb with the best of them. Success had to be at the end of a climbing rope, or all my plans and all my efforts for the past few years would have been in vain.

Six months later, and I had spent most of my days alone—no climbing partner, precious few routes done, and an outlook that was day by day more gloomy and pessimistic. I trained hard, I drank hard, and my disposition darkened with each passing, uneventful week. I was beginning to feel awkward around people when they asked what I was doing and what my plans for the future were. I had no real answer—certainly none that rang true in my own heart. There were some bright moments, some great days out on a number of crags, and a few friendships were formed, but these were the exception to the fairly depressing rule.

One of the few highlights was my friendship with a couple of lads who frequented the pub I worked in. They were excellent climbers, yet they seemed to be able to enjoy life and other people without constantly going on about grades and crux moves. This was an unexpected and refreshing change, since it meant I did not have to try to compete in this manner either. Not that I could anyway. They were far beyond my level, but they never made me feel that way. Over time I began to relax around them, and we spent many an evening talking about all sorts of things, including but not exclusively, climbing.

It was on one of these nights when we had been bored in the pub, me working there and the others drinking as much Hartley's beer as our meagre funds allowed (which meant we usually went home sober), that Luke suddenly effervesced his way into the room as only Luke could. His ability to be upbeat and enthusiastic always surprised me. I have never shared his positive outlook, playing my Eeyore to his Tigger on most occasions. Tonight, however, whether I shared his outlook or not was immaterial, as it was clear he had a plan and the mental sparks were fizzing and popping all around him.

His objective, he explained with a broad grin, windmilling arms, and saucer eyes, was to drive up to Scotland and back in one day. This in itself was not a particularly spectacular feat, of course, considering we were well under an hour from the Scottish border. However, there was the small issue of his suggestion that we drive up to Ben Nevis, Scotland's highest peak, and then climb the legendary Zero Gully: 1,000 feet of steep, often vertical ice and snow, renowned for the lack of available protection in its upper sections. At grade V this winter route means nothing to some of the ice dancers of today, but to me back then, it was serious stuff: gripping, terrifying, and absolutely essential for the climbing CV. I could envisage endless pints in store, regaling my adventures on the ice, holding court to wearied travellers, too young or too timid to dare to tackle one of the ogres of British winter mountaineering. It was the King Solomon's Mines of ice routes, and here was my chance to become Allan Quatermain himself! *Pompous* is not the word. It was downright *egomania*, and I loved it. I took no further convincing, and with Andy also on the team (not my original climbing partner Andy; this one was a National Trust employee, lean, tough, and staving off a bout of the flu), we were all set.

The very prospect of ticking off a route of this stature would mean I would have progressed into the realms of technical ice climbing. Plodding up a snow slope was all well and good, but no matter how high the mountain you were on, it was still, at the end of the day, only a walk. True accomplishment and real satisfaction could only be had on extreme ice. In my drivenness, I could see this offer of redemption for my wasted months in the Lakes in one adrenaline-filled episode. It was infinitely more ferocious, more dangerous, and more of an adventure than merely clambering up crags by the side of some Lakeland or Pennine road. Once I had Zero Gully on my list of climbing achievements, I would finally be starting up the ladder of mountaineering respectability. It made all of my fading aspirations at once credible and attainable again; it was my springboard to greater things.

However, there was ice climbing and then there was Scottish winter mountaineering: an altogether different animal than any other kind of rock climbing. Notwithstanding the smaller scale of the hills compared to their rivals in the Alps, they are at least as treacherous, and often much more so, than their European counterparts. The main reason for this is the typically awful weather north of the border. One minute driving gales try to sweep you off your feet and plunge you over the nearest precipice, the next a swirling miniature tornado whips up ice like a million tiny shards of glass, able to sting eyes and cut any exposed skin, which would be already smarting from the drenching, biting cold. These little Scottish nuances, however, did not appear on any part of our "risk assessment." All we needed was commitment and ability, neither of which was in any doubt. We had decided on our miniature expedition. We were all geared up to set off the very next morning.

We had only one sticking point to the scheme: none of us owned a car. Even if we could have borrowed one, the prospect of driving for hours, walking and climbing all day, then taking a long, tired, night drive back seemed a bit extreme even for us. We were still discussing our vehicular dilemma when a new voice suddenly piped up just to the side of us. Enter David, standing at the bar, ale in hand, completing approximately the forty-eighth hour of his forty-second birthday celebrations. He had overheard our plan and evidently liked the sound of it.

"I'll drive you to Scotland, lads," he drooled. "I like Scotland; gives me a chance to clear me 'ead a bit."

David hailed from nearby Hebden Bridge. He was a writer by profession and after a few warm-up pints, a skilful raconteur and most entertaining orator. His stock beginning to most sentences of any import was, "I'll tell you how it is . . ." This commanded enormous respect, since in *Hebdenese* this phrase signified that whatever followed was not merely fact but absolute truth.

We murmured something about his being totally smashed and unable to find his car, let alone drive it. "I'll tell you how it is, lads . . ." he began.

We ignored the rest. The edict had been passed, and more importantly, we had a ride to Scotland.

Later on, I learned that four hours rest, a trio of triple espressos, and a liberal dose of Guarana is the perfect remedy for rampant alcohol abuse over a sustained period, apparently. We agreed to meet at 3:30 a.m. for our Zero Gully expedition. I went home to check over my gear and was in bed by midnight, since I knew I would need a good night's rest!

Shortly after horrible o'clock, having slept only sporadically, we were all bundled inside the car, climbing gear stuffed into the boot with the excess wrapped around us in splendidly disorganized fashion. Inside the vehicle the heater had made the atmosphere close and even humid. There was the faint tinge of petrol in the air, mixed with a far too generous dose of exhaled alcohol breath. Coupled with the familiar nose of climbing hardware and well-worn rucksacks, it made for a truly exciting and heady perfume. There was a real buzz in the air. The crowning touch of the thud of Yello's music had us all wound like coiled springs. The banter raged effortlessly for the whole journey.

We were treated to some extraordinary sights as we headed north, which gave me more evidence that this was going to be a remarkable day, a day to mark in red in whatever journal I would keep. We saw a group of five badgers bumbling up the side of the road on Kirkstone Pass. All of them formed a line as they muscled their inimitable jog along the edge of the verge. I had never seen a badger before. Their muscular stockiness took me by surprise, and I leaned forward excitedly, crying out and pointing eagerly toward the first shape as it was lit up in the headlights.

It was enormously comforting and made for a warm feeling of comradeship to see and hear the same excited, boyish reaction from all of the other occupants. I was at least five years younger than any of the others and did not want to be seen as the weakest one, so to see the delight on all of their faces was reassuring. Unlike many of my earlier experiences, I did not have to live, eat, and breathe climbing in order to fit in. Certainly at university, the urgency to be "a rock jock" was terribly stifling and filled with latent pressures, which had instinctively repulsed me. It was wonderful to be able to enjoy the badgers together!

We talked about our five masked friends for quite a while, exchanging tales of first sightings and expanding the conversation to cover other countryside issues and interests. Andy talked about building paths for the National Trust high on the Lakeland fells; Luke discussed his landscaping and tree-felling exploits around the area. I enjoyed the lack of pressure. I was allowed, or perhaps I had allowed myself, to just listen with no pressing need to interject my experiences. They were not competing, and for the first time, neither was I. There was no sign of the knot in my stomach that had begun to accompany all of my climbing outings for the previous three or more years. I was actually enjoying myself without achieving any tangible goal and without beating someone else or overcoming my own limitations. This was most welcome and most unexpected, especially considering the calibre of climbers I was sharing the car with.

The time passed very quickly in such a warm environment. By dawn we were approaching the historic site of Glencoe, Scotland. As we rounded the bend that first reveals the glen stretching away into the far distance, we gasped and let out a collection of unrehearsed, simultaneous cries of "Whoa!" "Wow!" "Look at that!" as a herd of red deer stags charged down the side of the glen at the gallop, sweeping over the ground effortlessly, resembling a dark russet shadow of some great cloud formation, brushing the heather, and deceiving the eye into thinking that the hillside itself was rippling its way down to the valley floor. They were huge beasts with their great antlers silhouetted against the pale grey of the dawn.

The deer swept down the mountain and through my very soul it seemed, holding me mentally and emotionally breathless until they surged as one body round the bulge of the hill and out of sight. The speed and course of the car as it cruised along the road seemed pitiful in comparison. We had no chance of catching up to steal a second view, and suddenly fifty or more deer disappeared forever. I felt so privileged to have been allowed to experience such a sight. This really was going to be a day to remember.

The scene stayed with me, together with all the excitement it had caused, for the rest of the journey. I could never have imagined how alive I could feel just by looking out of a car window. How peculiar the satisfaction that was wrought from sitting down, looking, and drinking in a moment of time! It negated the need to pursue the adrenaline surge and had an infinitely lower risk factor.

The car pulled up outside the youth hostel at the foot of Ben Nevis at around 7:30. We hurriedly put on our gear, checked our packs, and set off at a simply blistering pace. It was a case of heads down and march. We were oblivious to the crystal-clear day that was starting to unfold around us. David waved us off and went to look for a place to spend the day. He actually saw a lot more than we did, as he would describe to us later.

Apparently, it was such a exceptional day that he had walked up the mountain a short distance and had sat down at a vantage point from where he had seen the Cuillin Mountains over on the Isle of Skye to the West, and almost down to the borders of England and the snow-capped tops of the Border Hills to the south. These views are only available on Ben Nevis a few days each year, as the clouds usually veil any decent panoramas. According to David it was absolutely incredible. We, conversely, had seen nothing but the next few feet of ice and snow in front of us for the whole day (and into the night, as it transpired). Yet another stunning vista wasted on this purpose-driven mountaineer!

By 9 a.m. we had arrived at the backside of Ben Nevis, close to the Clark Inglis Hut, a popular stopping-off point for climbers. Luke had walked up the slope to ask a couple of climbers who were already there what routes, if any, were in suitable condition to climb. He returned to us beaming:

"The world is our oyster. Everything is in condition. Shall we do Zero Gully then?"

Even though I had prepared to do this legendary climb, when he said those words I could hardly believe it: we were actually going to do it! All three of us scrambled briskly up the snow-covered scree and then consulted the guidebook to find the foot of the climb itself.

The starting point was straightforward enough, but as I looked up there seemed to be any number of ways to progress to the top of the mountain. I looked again at the guide:

"Climb the gully to a stance below a left-facing chimney to the left of the main gully."

My untrained eye could hardly make out any of this. It was just a mess of ice and snow; *very steep* ice and snow.

"Ascend the chimney then traverse right to an amphitheatre in the gully," the guide continued. "Take the narrow gully above to easy ground by a long pitch."

That was it. That was all the help we were going to get. Basically, "Start here, go to the top. Oh yeah, try not to fall off!"

I loved it. This was the stuff of dreams!

I rushed to put on my harness and began to uncoil the ropes. Part of me wanted to lead off, but when Luke began to thread the ropes through his harness and went to stand at the starting off point, I was actually quite relieved that he would get us going. At least this way, I figured, we would stay on route. His experience and skill were a huge comfort.

Moments later we had started to climb the famous Zero Gully. As I paid out the rope for Luke, I was chuckling, almost giggling to myself, imagining what we looked like: three lads grinning as we stuck ice axes and crampons into ice and snow high above Fort William. No one could see us (the other climbers we had seen earlier had gone, presumably ensconced on their own little adventure) but that did not matter. We were following in the crampon prints of some great mountaineers, including those who had first climbed this classic: Hamish MacInnes, A. G. Nicol, and Tom Patey. Andy and I chatted excitedly as we watched Luke move smoothly up the first chimney and then boldly and steeply climb off to the right and out of sight.

Before I knew it, it was my turn. Each swing of my ice axes felt tremendous. I prided myself in making each placement secure with a single swing of the axe to conserve energy, minimize damage to the route for those after me, but mainly, to look impressive and professional! The sharp, clean crunch of the blades entering the packed snow a couple of feet or more above my head, and the duller thump of my boots as they drove home the front points of my crampons, sounded deep and resonant against the silence of the face all around me. The grey light of the Scottish winter's day never brightened. The glorious sunshine that David could see on the other side of the mountain did not rise high enough in the sky to offer us any substantial illumination or warmth. Whereas the brightness would have been nice, the warmth could have proven problematic, as melting snow mixed with gullies is a recipe for avalanche disaster.

The steepness of the gully proved deceptive. Looking from beneath I could see that it was a steep and sustained route. But when I actually started up the first pitch, it became immediately evident that most of it was nearly vertical, and sometimes the snow bulges made certain sections slightly overhanging. Moreover, when I swung my ice axe into the compacted and hardened snow, it often only entered an inch or so, giving my body the feeling of being in an overhanging position as I pulled myself up on the tips of the blades.

Even when going second, it is important never to take your own safety for granted when climbing ice. In this brittle arena, any sudden jolt can easily pull someone off his belay stance; gear can break out of the ice, and ice screws can sometimes melt the ice around their own anchor points, making them strip out after only a few minutes. With all this in mind, I made sure that I advanced both purposefully yet carefully. I did not presume on my being safe just because I had a rope above me.

This newfound sense of exposure and fear was accompanied by an equally unexpected and entirely new definition of pain. The strain of exertion, of burning shoulders, forearms, and especially calves was stronger than I had anticipated, but I had long found such feelings welcome. The burn of a workout was as comforting to me as a warm blanket! The sharp pain in my throat and lungs of cold air rapidly moving through my panting mouth was proof of my situation high in the mountains. I enjoyed it.

Even the sting of the icy wind on my wet cheeks and forehead was bearable, despite the headache that was creeping into my consciousness as a result of this. No, the real pain, the overriding and unexpected agony, was in my hands. This was my first real adventure with "hot aches," as Luke called them after I had grimaced on the first belay stance with him and explained my suffering.

"You get used to it and gradually accept it as a normal part of winter climbing," he explained casually as he smiled and squeezed the water out of his own fleece mitts simply by making a fist with each hand. I was in pain wearing Gore-Tex mitts with fleece liners, and here he was, without any windproof outer layer for his hands. The bitter wind was thereby allowed free rein to chill his sodden fingers, and all Luke did was make a fist and grin! I was impressed, but still my fingers throbbed. As it turned out, on three or four occasions during that ascent, I had to stop mid-climb, put the ice axe straps above my elbows, bend my arms, and make fists with my hands just to help get the blood back into my fingers. All the while, the hot aches were so awful that on two occasions I actually blacked out momentarily with the pain. I pulled my straps above my elbows simply to make sure I did not let go and fall off if my blackout caused me to lose balance!

Once Andy had joined us at the belay, we set off again and soon came to the crux pitch of the route. Luke led it. There was hardly any place to put protective gear, and the position was so exposed that it felt extremely fragile and precarious as we clung to our small perch and paid out rope as Luke moved effortlessly higher. We could only view the whole expedition in superlatives as we talked over what we had done so far.

It was good to be sharing the stance with Andy. Winter climbing is not nearly as friendly as summer rock. I had been on mountains in the winter many times, of course, but a whole new dimension kicked in when I was high up a very steep wall with a long way to go. Feelings of isolation mingled with the awareness that my position was far from safe. Clearly, the weather and fading daylight were both fighting to prevent my success. Also, the pressure of being in a constantly dangerous situation never abated. I could not claim to be safe until I was back in the car. This had a tiring and draining effect all its own. I suddenly felt rather isolated, so it was good to have a warm body next to me for reassurance.

Andy, however, was not doing well. The flu he was fighting off was winning the battle, and his shivering was not entirely related to the biting wind and hostile environment we had chosen to place ourselves in. I was a little concerned for him. I wanted us to push on quickly and finish off the route so we could be back before dark.

Soon all three of us were together again, sharing a belay stance and having completed the hardest part of the climb. It was a superb lead by Luke, and both Andy and I thanked him for taking us up this amazing experience. He was as humble as ever and almost rebuked us for the thanks, saying we were a team and all in it together. What a smashing bloke! Congratulations and backslapping could wait, though, for we now realized that because there were three of us, we had taken twice as long to climb to our present point, compared with climbing as a pair. We still had 400 feet to climb.

"So who wants to lead now?" Andy and I looked at each other. I knew it would not be him; the poor guy was knackered!

"Come on, it's someone else's turn!" Again Luke smiled as he spurred us on to greater heights.

I relished the chance to lead, but the crux section had challenged me somewhat, and I was aware that I had little experience in finding gear placements in winter conditions. The words of the guidebook came ringing back in my ears: "the lack of belays meriting the V grade."

Oh, how I hope I can find some belays and some gear placements, I thought as I took my turn at the sharp end and began to lead off on Zero Gully.

The first 50 feet or so made me feel more than comfortable; I felt fantastic. I was suddenly into my stride and enjoyed the steep but straightforward climbing in hard, sound snow. I found a couple of rocks bulging out of the snow and had managed to place some protective gear in them, which gave me enormous comfort, as I was now convinced that I could find placements and keep myself relatively safe, even at "the sticky end."

I spent a few more minutes of highly enjoyable climbing, humming to myself and generally having an awful lot of fun. Then, after a while, I paused and looked up the gully and immediately realized two things: I could not see any definite route to take (it was all a vast expanse of snow and ice), and my eyes were starting to play tricks on me—the kind of thing your eyes do when the light is fading and dusk is approaching.

My heart sank, and I became dry-mouthed with fear. It was getting dark, and I did not know where I was going. In an instant everything had changed. This was no longer a great day out; it was about to become an epic. The adrenaline was pumping fast and the thumping of my pulse in my ears signalled that horribly familiar arrival of fear and dread. I stopped climbing and shouted down to Luke, telling him the totally obvious, that it was getting dark!

He shouted back to me and down to Andy that we should all put on our head torches. I flashed back to Norway just a few years previously when the light was fading fast and the fear was much more heightened. The utter dread of being in pitch black in a place of unspeakable danger had rushed over me in an almost engulfing wave. Back in the present, having anchored myself, I took off my rucksack and almost in a rage I thrust my hand into it, scrabbling around inside, feeling without looking, as the memories almost caused a panic to set in. The relief I felt as I discovered the cylindrical light and the rectangular battery pack was extraordinary.

I set off again and picked up the pace as best I could. Within minutes it was pitch black, and I was not even trying to find a route. I was simply going "up" in as straight a line as possible.

The problem with climbing in the dark was that I could not see any belay points. As the words of the guidebook echoed yet again in my ears, I heard a voice call up to me, saying:

"You've got twenty feet of rope left. You'd better find a belay!"

Fat chance, I thought. *I couldn't find an elephant up here. It's black as coal.*

I wandered to the right and to the left for a few minutes, but I knew I would not find anything. It was just steep, hard snow, wherever I looked. The head torch only lit up the ground immediately in front of me. Anything farther away was nothing much more than a blur.

I called down this news to Luke, finding it hard to cloak the fear in my voice.

"We need to move together as a three then, and keep a full rope length apart," came the reply. I knew this meant that we were not going to be well protected at all. If I came off, I would fall more than 300 feet before the rope pulled tight around Luke. The chance of his making himself secure in time to withstand that kind of fall without being pulled off by my plummeting carcass (approaching terminal velocity no doubt, if I had not been bouncing a few times beforehand) was almost nil, and therefore Andy, a rope length beneath Luke would also be doomed.

I was not a happy man. I started to climb with my old friend Dave's words ringing in my ears: "The leader doesn't fall!" I would have no second chances if I failed to heed his advice tonight, that was for sure.

The farther I climbed, the more hopeless I felt. I could not see any evidence of the top of the route. Each time I looked up, all I could make out was more snow, more of the steep face above me. I strained to see beyond, past the feeble beam of my head torch, but all I found was my own deepening despair.

We were climbing well into the night. I had been leading for what felt like over an hour, and I sensed the solitude enveloping me as coldly as the chill wind swirling down the gully. I was clinging on to the hope that I would see the summit ridge at any second. Looking up dashed my hopes yet again. I increased my pace and surged onwards, spurred on not only by my old friend, Aggression, but also by the raw fear that was threatening to get the better of me.

Rather than moving one point of contact at a time, either an ice axe or a cramponed boot, I was moving one hand and the opposite leg together as a way to climb quickly up toward the summit. It is not as safe a technique, and especially in the dark it can force errors. Any error in my position would be fatal, but I was becoming desperate and simply hated the dark and hated even more that our fantastic day out was turning into a nightmare. I thought again and again of the drop beneath me and the incredibly precarious position I was in. I had never before led out such a long pitch without any secure anchor, especially not on ice, and not just ice but near vertical ice in the dark!

I kept thrusting the axe blade into the snow, not knowing if the placement was sound or poor, unable to judge if my crampons were going to hold my weight as I stood on them. I just wanted to finish the climb, and do so quickly, before my nerve failed me.

Luke called up: "You have to slow down! Andy can't keep up."

Poor Andy. He must be hurting by now, I thought. I knew I had to slow down as well, but it took the last vestiges of my self-control to go along with his request. I was desperate to finish the route before the fear overcame me. For a few minutes I slowed down, took some deep breaths, and tried to control my emotions.

After stopping for a moment and regaining my composure, I looked up as I was about to set off again. I blinked and looked again. There was a slightly different hue to the snow slope about 100 feet above me, just visible in the light of my head torch. A clear, sharp line defined the slope I was on and another, different brighter slope behind and above it.

It was not a slope; it was the night sky! I was looking up at the summit ridge.

Hallelujah! What a relief! I groaned out loud with the release of the strain I had been under, and suddenly I found myself powering for that sharp line—the line that signified the end of the route and the end of my terror ordeal.

As I neared the ridge, around ten feet beneath it, I could hear the wind, blowing hard, directly toward my face. I had not felt it all day, except for a swirling, gusting chill that had accompanied us for most of the climb. Ben

Nevis had been protecting us from the full extent of the bone-chilling gale that had started in the middle of the afternoon, but I was introduced to it the instant I dared to poke my head over the summit ridge.

Whoosh! I was nearly blown back down the gully to my death as a storm force gale smacked into me like a brick in the face! It took me completely by surprise, and my environment changed instantly from the deathly quiet of the steep, dark, ice wall, to a roaring bear of a wind trying desperately to repel my assault on the top section of the mountain.

Falling to my knees automatically, I pressed my head to the snow and began to crawl up the shallow slope to find a safe belay point. Despite this sting in the tail, I found myself laughing out loud as I found an anchor point, placed some gear in it, stuck my ice axe in the snow, and tied the rope off around that as well.

I laughed and laughed. All fear, all dread vanished, and a euphoria kicked in that I did not believe possible.

What a climb! What a route! What a day out!

"Zero Gully! I've just climbed Zero Gully!" Over and over again I repeated the phrase.

I loved it up there. I loved the night sky and the wind, and the 1,000 feet of free fall that I had just conquered. Terror no longer existed. It had been replaced by giddy, schoolboy giggles, by euphoria previously untapped, and by a pure joy that had eluded me for years!

I brought up Luke on my rope, and he in turn took in the rope for Andy, who seemed to forget his discomfort as soon as he had joined up with us, for we all laughed and shouted to each other over the roaring gale, as we coiled the ropes and set off down the walking route of Ben Nevis, going past the observatory, and carefully avoiding the treacherous Five Finger Gully.

We ran down to the car park, rucksacks banging our backs and rubbing our shoulders. It did not matter.

I have no idea how we found David. It must have been by homing beacon, because he was in a pub and we went straight to him. In fact, we all had time to join him for last orders!

By 4:30 the following morning I was unpacking my gear back at my little cottage down a quiet lane in Ambleside. No one heard me drop the latch on the front door. No one knew where I had been. But I knew what I had just done, and it was difficult to get a sensible conversation out of me for a full three days!

But why was I so happy? Was it the conquest? Was it the danger? Was it the reputation established? Could I now start to pursue my climbing career in earnest? As I sat in my room back at the cottage, I knew instantly that it was none of the above.

Climbing Zero Gully had proved nothing. I had been terrified. Luke confirmed to me on the way back that most of winter mountaineering is about "jibbering" as he put it. I felt most comforted to know that even he felt scared.

"Oh yeah, that's just the way it is on the ice!" So matter of fact, so straightforward, and completely without affectation.

It was an extraordinary adventure, and I was happy for it to be finished at that. It was a remarkable little expedition among the very best of company and in the very best of British landscapes! That was all that mattered.

I climbed a few other ice routes during this time in Ambleside, and I thoroughly enjoyed all of them. I always felt confident on the ice, more so than on rock, despite its inherently more dangerous nature. I wanted to do a more serious route similar to Zero Gully, and this time to do more leading. There was still a part of me that yearned to know that I was technically competent. Zero Gully had served a purpose, but there were still points to be proven; proven to myself, that is. The ebb and flow of my need to push harder was still dictating much of my life, and certainly most of my mountaineering life, despite my realization of the reasons I had been so overjoyed with Zero Gully.

The chance to prove myself again centred on Ben Nevis. This time a group of us went, and once more I paired up with Luke.

We chose a route based on the "looks all right, dunnit?" principle. That is to say, we could not find a route description in the guidebook, but the first section looked clear, steep, and rather exciting, euphemistically speaking. We had already been warned by some locals that some of the routes "were a bit thin." This means that in some sections of the climbs, due to recent marginal weather, there was insufficient snow or ice, and so the climbing would be a lot more serious than the guidebooks said, since there was less ice to secure our axes, crampons, and protective gear, such as ice screws and the like. Put another way, we could find ourselves climbing up a section and suddenly find that the ice we were climbing up, usually vertical, sometimes slightly overhanging, gradually petered out and left us facing a blank wall of rock and a few cracks, which we had to ascend often without the aid of gear placements. We could not have cared less. It looked all right, so it would be all right—simple!

Luke led off, and after 50 feet or so of ascent he began traversing before ascending some more and going round a fairly awkward, not to mention thin, line around a bulge, which led in turn to the face proper. In this case, "thin" meant there was very little ice to place crampon or ice axe, and he ended up rock climbing on insanely slippery surfaces, sticking his ice axe points into cracks in the rock. The technical term for this is "torquing"; the layman's term, "stuff of nightmares." Afterwards it became clear that this was the most difficult section of the climb. Luke danced up it and called on me to follow him.

It was a tremendous route, steep and physically strenuous, but I was more than up to that part of the challenge. As I approached the bulge, I could see how thin the route was. Crampon points were edging along blank rock, resting on flakes no more than one quarter of an inch wide, sometimes less. The slightest raising or lowering of my heel would result in a fall, since the angle of the crampon point changed almost imperceptibly and immediately lost traction on the shiny rock. I actually enjoyed torquing with the ice axes, though, strange as it may seem. It required commitment and great forearm strength. One could not be tentative in thrusting the point into the crack, twisting hard and then heaving up one's body. Movement had to be firm, smooth, and determined. On top of all that, it looked great. I was enjoying myself.

As I looked down I could see the slope of the mountain falling away steeply beneath me. Even though I had only ascended about 50 feet of the route, the exposure effect was spectacular. Looking down, I could see at least a couple of hundred feet of the drab morning air before the steep snow-covered scree appeared, leading back to the path down the mountain. Hooked onto that ice and rock, a tiny speck on the Ben Nevis massif, I nevertheless felt free and so very alive. Every moment was pure exhilaration, and I moved with boldness and confidence higher up the face.

It must have been one of those almost imperceptible movements of my heel as I rounded the bulge and reached to plant my ice axe into solid ice. It must have been the tiniest of movements of perhaps only one of my boots as I tried to negotiate the crux of the pitch, when, without even the slightest warning, both feet were ripped off the wall simultaneously. It was as if someone had put a shepherd's crook around each ankle and given them both a mighty yank all at once.

My heart lurched, exploding out of my chest. Sweat immediately seemed to spurt from my hands, brow, and back in a stinging, electrifying red alert.

My climbing pack was pulling me away from the wall, tugging and riving at me as I lunged forward, desperate to defeat gravity.

With head spinning, I tried desperately to get control of the situation. I thrust my arm forward to plunge the ice axe blade into ice or a crack in the rock, my feet already in midair over an overhang with no chance of finding any placement.

The ice axe bounced off hard granite, sending a jarring pain down my arm.

Suddenly I was free falling.

My eyes bulged as I imagined the hundreds of feet of nothing immediately beneath me, shock waves of adrenaline coursing through my veins, and my neck throbbing in time with the pounding thump of my heart.

The rope pulled tight. Luke asked if I was all right. He had felt the pull, but since he could not see me from his belay ledge, he had no idea I had actually come off.

As second climber I had been completely protected with the rope above me and had fallen no more than a few feet. If I had led the first pitch, I would have been dead, without any doubt. Had the rope not been there, I would have bounced off jagged rocks for well over 100 feet before sliding down a steep snow and rock gully, which led directly to a sheer dropoff of at least another 100 feet. I was aware of all this in an instant, and my only feeling was one of resentment because I had failed to prove myself yet again, even though no one except me even knew I had fallen.

I could barely disguise my fear as I joined my friend on the ledge of the first belay. I was more than shaken by my near miss; I was demoralized. Even though I led part of the rest of the route, I actually declined to take one of the leads immediately after my fall. It was hard to swallow my pride and ask Luke to do this. Perhaps this was a further step in the process of my learning the particularly painful lesson of humility.

We pushed on up the increasingly steep face of the route. I led a few pitches where the ice ran out completely, and I was left looking at a blank wall of rock, equipped with ice axes and crampons to climb it in. At those times, the first step was to overcome all feelings of exposure and to focus merely on the problem at hand; that is, how to move a little higher up the route.

I had started to analyze the way I had to approach ice climbing. It was a deliberate, acquired skill to override all feelings of fear so that my body did not freeze, and I could therefore operate at peak physical performance in such situations. "It's all about the head game" is the phrase often trundled out. This is the world of the ice climber. Imagine competing in a long and strenuous race, carrying a large weight on your back, and having to go around obstacles requiring extremely high levels of gymnastic balance, skill, strength, and poise. Imagine also having to carry out these demanding feats for hours at a time, almost invariably in a highly inhospitable, frequently painful, freezing climate.

Then imagine someone pointing a gun at your head, safety catch slipped forward into the "off" position, ready to fire. The slightest pressure on the trigger is all that would be required to fire the weapon, and this would be applied without the slightest hesitation the instant you made a mistake.

That is extreme ice climbing, and the secret is to totally ignore the gun. That is the head game we play!

When the ice ran out, I stopped to assess what was best to do. I was still shaken from the fall but had forced myself back to the front of the climb. The only feeling that existed was that of solitude, quite an overpowering sense of being totally alone. Only, unlike on a small crag in a friendly Lakeland valley, it was dark, cold, and stank of danger.

I was accustomed to this feeling and had felt a considerably darker version of the same when I had been in Norway, but then the smell had the rank odour of death to it. It was bizarrely comforting to have this albeit rather macabre familiarity with imminent doom. I reached up for a tiny lip on the rock with my ice axe point, and delicately as a ballet dancer, I stood on a ripple of rock with my crampon points. Repeating this ludicrously precarious process a few dozen times led me to the 20 or so feet higher ledge, from where I anchored myself to the ice and called Luke up to join me, relaxed and elated. The worst was done.

I was still thinking about my Scandinavian epic when Luke interrupted my unwelcome musings with a boyish grin and a firm pull of the rope as he took the lead toward the top of the route, taking in a fantastic narrow ridge with almost vertical walls going hundreds of feet into the clouds, which were well beneath us now. This ridge reminded me of the knife-edge ridge I had crossed with Dave all those years ago in Norway, on Bispen. Dave had elected to straddle the ridge and cross *au cheval*. I had mocked this method in my mind and been more daring. As I straddled parts of this ridge on Ben Nevis, I recall eating my own words and smiling to myself. I was rather too frazzled on this day to start posturing for the non-existent camera. I followed Luke gratefully, being physically and mentally drained. This had been quite an experience. I had thoroughly enjoyed it, but I knew I had been to my absolute limit in terms of technical ability and mental strength. It was fair to say I had been jibbering a bit once or twice! We coiled the ropes at the top and walked down to our rucksacks by another route.

Then suddenly, while at the foot of the route we had just scaled, I found myself for the first time that day in true peril. As I jumped forward into the snow slope from where I had stowed my rucksack, my crampon front points stuck into my gaiter and sent me cartwheeling forward. I landed on the hard snow, facing down hill, and I began to slide down the slope.

Not a problem, I thought, and calmly, even casually, I lifted up my feet to stop the crampons sticking into the snow, and then I held out my ice axe, away from my chest and face area, before sticking the blade into the slope and letting it turn my body around so that I was facing uphill again. Once that manoeuvre was completed, I began to lean into the blade with it against my shoulder in the correct self-arresting procedure.

All was going fine until my blade struck a rock and ripped the ice axe out of my grasp. Normally, the axe would be strapped to my hand, but I had removed both axes after the climb while I put my rucksack back on and had not replaced the straps, assuming, *What could possibly go wrong now?*

I watched the axe as I slid away from its point of anchor in the snow at an alarming and increasing speed. Now I had nothing to slow me down except my crampon points, which, having spun myself around again to face downhill, I was thrusting into the packed snow for all I was worth. Excruciatingly slowly, with my drop-off point tantalizingly close, I began to slow down. Finally, I stopped a mere 30 feet from a drop-off of around 100 feet. The landing would not have been a pleasant one!

Luke was sitting only yards from where I had come to rest.

"Cup of tea?" he grinned, offering me the flask.

"Don't mind if I do." We laughed and sat for a long time, basking in the sun and our achievement. I felt great, just like after Zero Gully, perhaps even better.

Later that night, over a beer and a rather pleasant Scotch, Luke began to enthuse about doing something else the next day. He was keen to go back onto the mountain or go somewhere else to do a "slime climb." This meant doing a rock climb in the rain, basically, or at least to go climbing on a route saturated with water and usually full of vegetation as well.

Here I realized something profound: Luke was hard-wired to climbing. All he wanted to do was go out on the crags and on the snow and ice. He could never get enough of the mountains, and it was possibly a source of ultimate joy and contentment to him. Some of the others with us were of the same mindset.

I was not. For the first time, I realized absolutely and for certain that I was not a mountaineer. Not that I could not climb, not that I did not want to climb, but that I was not defined as a mountaineer. Moreover, I did not *want* to be!

I now knew for a fact the thing that I had suspected but did not want to admit to for years: the drive shaft had been disconnected. I no longer lived to be a mountaineer. I did not want to have my life revolve around the next, more serious route, and I definitely did not want to be driven to greater feats of anything, just because I felt I had to! I had tried to keep this image going. I had tried to force the drive shaft back together again by reconnecting it with baling twine and duct tape, but the fact was, it really had been disconnected.

I had climbed a couple of very serious ice routes, and now I was content to sit back, enjoy the achievement, and go home. I had proven to myself that I could do it, and that was enough. I had nothing else to prove.

Now, hold on a minute! What about the drivenness, the need to go harder to prove my worth?

Someone had pulled the plug on that hamster wheel. I no longer needed it. Actually, that plug had been pulled years ago on the belief that I was only worth something if I was better than I was before, whether it was as a climber or anything else. I had simply taken six years to agree to the fact!

I had tried to keep alive a system of living that was inherently destructive because, I suppose, I did not realize there was an alternative.

Looking at Luke I realized that we were different people, and whereas he loved to climb, I liked it. But once I had done it, I wanted to try something else. I did not have to be the best at it, though for years I thought this was so. Indeed, the notion of not pursuing everything I did to the ultimate level had been anathema to me. Not anymore.

My problem now, though, was what was I going to do with my life? What direction do I pursue, and would the real Russell Fralick kindly step forward? If I was not defined as a mountaineer, then what was I?

Shortly after I returned from Ben Nevis, I made a decision. I was leaving the Lake District. I did not say it out loud, but I knew I was also leaving behind all my ambitions as a mountaineer. There were still some scenes to play out, some routes to climb, and even some posturing about climbing harder and better than ever, but I knew it was over. The fat lady was clearing her throat.

The final blow, the deciding factor, came one night shortly after my last trip to Scotland while I was sitting in the pub (yet again) with a few friends. I have no idea how the subject arose, but someone mentioned religion. I refused to deny the fact or stay quiet and mentioned, matter-of-factly, that I was a Christian, without really knowing why I said it or even how I knew that I was.

"You don't believe all that nonsense do you?" A friend burst out. He laughed derisively, almost sneeringly, and began a soliloquy about how irrational, stupid, and otherwise idiotic Christianity is. I stood my ground but did not make an argument out of it.

Why was it okay to be a tree-hugger, a Buddhist, or an atheist, but being a Christian is worthy of scorn? I thought.

At that point I *knew* it was time to go. Not just to leave the pub, not just to leave the Lake District, but also to leave the whole scene behind, at least until I could be true to what I knew I believed. Despite their laughing protestations, I did not try to fit in with them. I knew He was there—and right and true—and therefore these guys were wrong, and I had to go. It was at once very freeing and very frightening. I had no idea who I really was. I was still torn between wanting to climb and knowing it was not meant to define me, but the alternative was completely uncharted terrain. In addition, admitting that I had spent the last few years of my life pursuing the wrong goal was quite a thing, especially to a young man in his early twenties!

I had run mile after endless mile over steep Lakeland hills, down beautiful bridleways, through bluebell-strewn woodlands, and over tiny stone bridges by the side of chuckling, trout-filled becks—all in the pursuit of mountaineering greatness. All the while I knew I would never arrive at the Nirvana of being "good enough." I only enjoyed all those views when I could look back with clear eyes, several years later. I watched summer end with the last song of the blackbird high in the ancient oaks around Rydal Water. I watched autumn carpet the woodland floor with the brown and green of crunching oak leaves. And I watched the iron-hard freeze of winter claim the same spot that I had squelched through in my fell-running shoes only weeks previously. Finally, I saw the same place leap into life, almost overnight, as spring won through again, and the buds struggled out from inside the bark of the same oak tree, and nuthatches and chaffinches could again chatter about the seeds and grubs that were once more plentiful. Their winter famine was over, but my famine for contentment remained elusive.

All I had seen while I ran through that area was a marker post, an old fence post still carrying some rusty barbed wire with which I could compare my time on my stopwatch to see if I was faster to that point than the day before. Even though my eye had seen and my mind had registered the sights and sounds all around me, I did not enjoy them at all unless the second hand on the stopwatch indicated that I was a better athlete that day. Driven further to dissatisfaction, I robbed myself of the joy of one of the world's most beautiful places on a daily basis. I had now come to understand this and decided it was time to put things right.

With the arrival of spring I left Ambleside—just when I should have been contemplating the summer's rock routes. I still was not sure why I called myself a Christian. What made me one, and why was I sure that I was one? Once I had figured it all out, maybe then I could go for a climbing career, I argued! I still had a long way to go and had to step back to gain some clarity on my life.

Chapter 7

LETTING GO

▲

As I drove away from the climbing mecca of England, all of my worldly goods had fit into a car with a boot no bigger than a suitcase. I knew I was not only changing location but also shifting the whole focal point of my life. I was changing not only my focus but also the very hub on which my life would now turn.

With quite some trepidation and with a large helping of humble pie, I moved back in with my parents for a few months and quietly started going to a local church, accompanied by a couple of my parents' neighbours. It seems they had found God again or something like that. Whatever it was, they were very welcoming and did not ask me any awkward questions. I went along to the services and started mixing with a group of the younger people, mainly late teens and a few early twenties.

One evening as we sat in a circle discussing something very forgettable, I was addressed directly for the first time.

"So Russell, what's *your* testimony?"

What's he on about: testimony? I thought.

"How did you become a Christian? Were you brought up in a Christian home, or did you find the Lord some other way? Perhaps someone led you to Jesus?"

I stared back blankly at the smiling man in the grey flannel trousers and spectacularly middle-aged tie, trying desperately to smile back at him in the same, fun-filled manner.

No idea what he's talking about now; completely lost! All eyes in the group turned on me, and I shifted uncomfortably in my seat (at least it wasn't a pew). The guy in the sharp trousers was one of the church leaders. My brief affair with Sunday school twenty years previously and my occasional, guilt-ridden trips to church while in my first year at university had not prepared me in any way for the church "language" that everyone else seemed perfectly *au fait* with. These questions were almost in a foreign tongue to me. Even the concepts were alien.

I was being asked how was it that I now considered myself to be a Christian. What had happened to make me one?

I had never sat down and considered this. I knew I was a Christian—of that there was nothing more certain. But this certainty in and of itself had made me very uncomfortable for at least four years, maybe more. I felt awkward with this notion because I was acutely aware that I looked anything *but* a Christian. I mean, for goodness sake, I had hardly been to church until very recently. My "church" was the pub (in that the pub is where I went to meet my friends and feel at home), a spirit, to me, still meant Scotch, and I was still noted for my excellent "rollies," my loquaciousness in profanity, and my willingness to comfort almost any available damsel in distress.

The strange thing was that before I had become a Christian, I had always thoroughly enjoyed this lifestyle; indeed, I had craved it every weekend. Over the past few years, however, I had become increasingly dismayed at the lack of satisfaction I had gleaned from my weekly outings. Much more than that, I had become burdened by a gnawing sense of guilt. This cannot have come from any external source since no one around me ever told me what I was doing was wrong. It came from within. The more I tried to kill the feeling with my own pleasure-seeking, the louder the internal alarm bell sounded, and the more aware I became of my guiltiness. I had started to say "sorry" to God after each of my indiscretions, all the while feeling simultaneously silly for saying "sorry" to thin air, truly remorseful for offending Him, and ever more desperate, feeling certain that I was powerless to avoid committing the same crime almost immediately after I had apologized for the latest infraction. This contrast of outward appearance and inner turmoil had become a tiring way of life!

I had left the Lake District a confused and fairly despondent man. I wanted to be a mountaineer. Actually I had wanted to be a *great* mountaineer. Now I knew that I was not going to be one. More importantly, I had even grown to hate the whole image of what my mind and desires had created.

I hated the egomania of mountaineers.

I hated the drivenness and the obsessive nature of rock climbing.

I hated the fact that all I ever talked about was climbing and E-grades and walls of ice in the Alps.

I hated that there was only success to be had in going ever harder, and anything else meant you were a failure, not only as a climber but also infinitely more desperately, as a person.

Most of all, I hated and was ashamed of the fact that all of the above points were about me and did not actually apply to anyone else.

I did not like the person I had become. And I knew full well that this was actually not me, that is, what I would prefer to be. I had loved my time on Ben Nevis because of the day and the people and the feelings and the sights, and, by the way, the climbing was fantastic as well. But it was the whole trip that was amazing, not merely the conquering of a route. I began to see that I loved the outdoors, the countryside, and the hills; but the pressure of going ever harder in an effort to prove myself was getting in the way of that enjoyment.

Most of all, I realized that I was fighting against who I really was, and in so doing, I had robbed myself of any sense of peace and fulfillment. Of course, I had days of excitement, but the underlying feeling was of deep discontentment, a constant awareness of being alienated from everything around me, and the incessant gnawing of being unfulfilled—no matter what I had supposedly achieved in the mountains.

This awareness was not new, of course, but it was gaining momentum. From my first year at university I felt that the drivenness I had earlier enjoyed was now beginning to overtake me, and I understood it could never be sated. Everything had become an unwinnable competition. That knot in my stomach when someone climbed a route next to me that was beyond my capabilities; the slide show in the upstairs room of the Packhorse pub in Leeds, when some lads had done an Alpine expedition that had taken in the Walker Spur on the Grandes Jorasses, and the Matterhorn North Wall, just for kicks, later on in the same trip. I grimaced internally during our own slide show, which depicted our snow plod in the Karakoram, and I felt ashamed. The knot was becoming ever tighter; satisfaction was ever more elusive.

I had returned from Pakistan a different man, and I did not think it was for the better. I was profoundly dissatisfied. My return from the Lakes had left me even more disaffected, since I had done so little climbing compared to my grand plans, which I had shared loudly among climbing companions before I had left university. Now I was reminding myself of these boasts. Instantly the phrase came to mind "the climber who never climbs" as J-P had sneered at me so cuttingly when I had once more declined to go on a climbing trip with the club. I had become tired of the whole race even back then. Even my anger toward him could not mask this truth: I knew that the whole image simply did not fit me.

There were other memories to confirm my predicament. On a trip to North Wales, to the climbing havens of Tremadag and Llanberis, we camped overnight. On the following morning I was to do a fairly well known E1 called The Plum with a guy I hardly knew. All I remember about him was his ungainly walk, awkward appearance, and lack of social graces. He was, however, a better rock climber than me.

I had only recently returned from my Pakistan expedition, and my physical condition was terrible. My muscles had been severely wasted by the effects of exertion at high altitude, and I was simply not up to the strenuous challenge I had set myself. I had effectively set myself up for failure. After a short embarrassing trip, my awkward friend had to lower me off the crux due to my inability to pull myself around it. Six months previously I would have run up it, but on this day I was hopeless. Moreover, others saw my dismal descent. My apologies in the pub afterwards simply made my failure sound all the more pitiful. I was having a very real crisis of confidence. This crisis had started in Pakistan, the first of my failures, but to have a repeat performance on another equally unspectacular stage was psychologically devastating. Now, rather than a mountaineer, I had to consider redefining myself as "useless mountaineer." It did not have the same ring to it!

The strangest thing was the lack of enthusiasm that had overtaken me. Even as I had dragged my slightly hung-over frame out of my sleeping bag prior to The Plum, I knew I simply did not want to go and climb. This was an entirely alien notion from a couple of years before, but I knew it was now true. My quandary was an awful one: here I was, a mountaineer (even a useless one), and I was becoming aware that actually I did not want to climb. It was not about fear, certainly not about physical exertion (I still loved to exercise aggressively), but it was the plain fact that I could not be bothered; I had lost interest.

I had been driving myself on with the whip of blame for my laziness and my inability to stick at something. But since when do you have to convince yourself to stick to a hobby, even a serious one? It is meant to be a pleasure, isn't it? And yet I had started to resent being dragged around the country to another rock face. I did enjoy the countryside and even the physical workout of climbing a good route, but it was the drive to go harder and bigger that was ebbing away.

I toughed it out and kept up the image until university ended. I managed to convince myself, and others, that I would climb mountains and document it all in books and articles, maybe even on film. It all sounded hollow as I had said it, but I had to hold on to my identity.

If all of this went, I ceased to be.

Following this, my year in the Lakes had been designed to make me technically brilliant and rekindle my desire for mountaineering excellence. Despite my few accomplishments, it had been a desperate failure in this respect. It had, in direct contrast, confirmed that incessant niggle that had never gone away: the image I had tried to create for myself simply wasn't me. It was not who I really am. I hated that thought, and yet here I was, a year later, having left the Lake District even more uncomfortable than ever. I had some serious questions to ask myself.

Now, back in the small group in the church, here was this guy asking me a serious question that I ought to have an answer for.

Like a flash, the entire story unfolded in my mind. Of course! How could I not realize, and bizarrely, how come I had not stopped and considered it years ago? I had squashed it out of my conscious mind. It had caused me too much anxiety, too much discomfort to face the facts of what had happened five years previously.

But I knew it was true. Wave after wave of images came flooding back; not only of The Climb but also of the pieces of the jigsaw that followed it, confirming that He had indeed removed the driveshaft of my drivenness and was showing me there was more to life than the next wall of rock, the next challenge to force myself over or die trying. How was I so dull of hearing and blind to see all the signals along the way these past few years?

During my year living in Ambleside, I had been teaching at an outdoor pursuits centre near Keswick as a volunteer. I went there sometimes two days a week, and I usually helped out with the climbing and abseiling activities. I also got involved in sailing, canoeing, and even horseback riding (now that's one activity I could *never* understand). The centre specialized in outdoor pursuits for the disabled, and it taught me vast amounts about mountain safety, teamwork, and, in a paradigm shift for me, about enjoying the outdoors no matter what your technical abilities were! It was also the place where my climbing mentor Dave worked, and we enjoyed days out cragging together after several years apart.

The two of us climbed one memorable route together. It was a beautiful summer's day, and the walk-in to the crag was easy. I had stripped off my climbing vest (a gaudy, luminous, green affair with some equally gaudy logo splashed across it) and enjoyed getting a tan as we selected our route. I chose a steep crack line, graded HVS, which was a good-looking line in an exposed position. A few other climbers were in between routes or had just come along for the day out in the sunshine, so they stopped and watched us as I led off. I enjoyed being "on parade" and set off up the thin crack with boldness and a cocky assurance in my fitness and technique.

It was a bold lead, with little available protection in the higher sections. In fact, I led the last 40 feet or more without placing any gear. It did not matter. I was brimming with confidence, and the route offered me no real difficulties. It was one of those climbs that was purely enjoyable, the exposure and steepness being fun rather than gripping. Someone took a couple of pictures. I looked good: very fit, very lean, very impressive!

Dave followed me and within minutes was blowing quite hard. Repeated phrases like "Watch me on this bit!" "Keep that rope tight!" and "Man, it's thin this, isn't it?" betrayed his increasing disquiet. His characteristic frown of concentration was even more deeply furrowed than usual, and I had forgotten about his talent for sweating, as even I, some 60 feet above him, could make out clearly the rivulets of moisture running down his face and even his arms. I know it was a hot day, but it was self-evident that my friend was having a gripping adventure!

He looked up—I think to check that I was holding the rope still. I smiled down the rock at my old friend.

As he moved toward the crux section, a vertical line with only about half an inch wide to push his fingers into, with tiny incuts to each side and footholds that were little more than smears for his sticky rubber boots, I could see his dismay at the lack of decent holds. He was out of steam and was hanging, straight-armed, constantly shifting his feet around, because he was unsatisfied and unsure of his footholds.

"Watch me, watch me now, I'm coming off! Watch me!"

For the uninitiated, it is important to note, that "Watch me" does not mean, "Have a look; take a photo if you like!" It means, "I'm done for, I'm scared, and I want you to make sure your belay is safe, and that rope will play a C-sharp if it's twanged, because I am about to fall, and by the way, this feels absolutely vile!"

I exhorted Dave to greater heights, literally, and tried to calm him with words of, "No, you're doing fine. You're almost past the worst. It gets a lot easier as you move above there." (What a liar!)

He fell off.

It was not spectacular. The rope was tuned to a G-sharp rather than a C-sharp, but it did the trick. Even with the elasticity of it, he hardly fell a foot. After a rest he managed to get up the remainder of the route, by dubious technique and me pulling hard on the rope to assist as best I could.

"That must be the hardest route I've ever climbed. Good grief, you're climbing well, lad!"

I blinked in astonishment. He repeated the same phrase to me twice more, then again when we came down the crag to meet up with the rest of the gang. I was astonished because he had so freely and so graciously let me know that I was a better climber than he was. More importantly, I was astounded that I did not care! Just being up there was fun enough. There was nothing to prove. I did not want him to fall, nor did I want him to admit I was better than him. I just wanted to climb and spend time with an old friend.

I could not have said the same three years earlier. I was a different person. And it felt great!

At around the same time I was out with a couple of lads at the outdoor centre, taking a group abseiling. This group had various special needs, both physical and mental, but they were all keen on the outdoor activities and were a very determined bunch.

The abseil we used was about 80 feet high and was all overhanging, so much so that the abseil rope would touch the ground some 20 feet or more from the base of the rock. We rigged up a safety rope, and I enjoyed tying all the knots necessary for maximum protection and easy release. We had one individual with cerebral palsy, and it was decided to rig the abseil slightly different for him, in that the figure of eight descending device, or descendeur, would be attached to a sling rather than directly on to his harness. This meant that he would be able to control the flow rate of the rope through this device, and thereby his speed of descent, without having to reach down with his arms or look down at his waist to see what his hands were doing. They could stay as they naturally hung down from shoulder to elbow, necessitating movement only from elbow to palm. Since any movement had to be effectively forced, it meant this way he could potentially abseil "on his own" rather than be simply lowered off on the safety rope. I would abseil next to him, slightly above, in case of difficulty (such as turning upside down, which once happened to a client, fortunately to much mirth from everyone, client included!)

Abseiling is a very simple technique and when done in a controlled environment is both safe and exciting. I have never enjoyed it for two reasons: it is the only time a climber is completely reliant on gear for his survival (at all other times it is simply a safety back-up), and also, my history of abseiling was as a means of escape when the situation was perfectly desperate! It brought back hideous memories of dread and despair rather than a fun day out on a Lakeland crag.

We rigged up our victim (I mean client) in his harness and clipped the descendeur into the rope as he sat in his wheelchair. After a full briefing and ensuring he was ready for the challenge, we swung him out of the chair and basically threw him over the cliff edge! We were always very polite and reassuring about it, though!

That young man did not twitch! He began staring at the figure of eight, and then glancing at his hands. I could see from my hanging stance, a few feet above him that he was willing his hands to move, to release the rope and pay it through the figure of eight, when *he* wanted it to go through. I called up to my colleague to make sure that the safety line was acting as just that: a back-up mechanism and not a means to take any strain off the client. It was clear he was absolutely determined to do it himself, if at all possible.

Inch by inch, then foot by foot he slid down the rope, controlling his rate of descent perfectly and overcoming possibly the greatest physical challenge of his life. I grinned at him all the way down and quietly encouraged him, not that he needed it. As he reached the bottom, his wheelchair was waiting and he landed right into it. I came down next to him, gave him a slap on the back, and untied all his gear, calling up to send the next person down.

But I had realized something. Why did I have to push myself to some mythical "higher level" in my climbing when this guy had fulfilled an ambition on an 80-foot abseil? Whereas I was still a morose, alienated grump, never satisfied with anything I accomplished, this guy looked perfectly at ease with life. What on earth did I have to be grumpy about? It was time I gave myself a good shaking and began to look at what was really important in life, and it certainly was not the next E-grade or even 500-foot frozen waterfall.

I do not suppose that young man will ever know how much he taught me with his example of determination and satisfaction at a job well done and his appreciation of things that I not only took for granted but even poured scorn upon. He was building his character, whereas I had spent the past few years cultivating my increasingly frail ego! He had chosen better, and it did not take an E-grade for him to understand it. After that, I finally began to take in the countryside and the views around me. I began to enjoy myself, and that was a revelation all of its own.

Over the next year, while I was still in the Lake District, and the summer just afterwards, I was asked that same question several times, the one about how I came to be a Christian. Eventually, I sat down and thought about how I was going to answer it completely and truthfully. As I considered my answer, at the same time my ambition in the hills was still being eroded. It had shrivelled further as I taught outdoor pursuits in Devon. On a day off I climbed a fairly impressive extreme route. I knew something was radically different with me because I never recorded the name of the route. I found the whole day fairly nondescript, and in my earlier "rock jock" guise I would not have done that. This contrasted markedly with a day out with my Lakeland outdoor centre earlier the same year, taking a blind group on a walk up Catbells in the Newlands Valley. The weather was pretty awful, and I was disappointed that the views would be diminished by the low cloud. What a twit. They were blind!

As the rain came down and the wind grew to almost gale force, a man walking next to me, who was blind from birth, asked, "What sort of bird is that?"

Is he joking? He must be. I cannot hear anything apart from the wind, I thought. Just as I was looking for a kind reply to his daft question, a tiny Arctic Tern beat its graceful, black-capped lilting flight down past our field of view and then hugged the line of the beck that we were following, keeping itself a constant 15 feet or so above the water, despite the ferocity of the wind.

I was flabbergasted. After a brief interrogation of the man to find out the root of this brilliant trick, I understood that he could hear the wing beats of the tern. He went on to describe in amazing detail all the places he had visited, and the things he had done. His ears, I gleaned from his descriptions, had become his eyes, and they were more acute as an ocular device than I think my real eyes had ever been. He even described how he would like to "see" other places, and I was convinced that he did, indeed, see places in detail that I could not even start to fathom.

I could have wept! What sights, what sounds, and what smells had I missed as I had swept past places of unspeakable beauty on three continents blindly pursuing unattainable greatness? I had stubbornly chased after the gratification of my own ego for a prize I knew would be ever elusive. That walk had been hugely enjoyable, and I started to be glad that this driven-ness was losing its grip on me. I was also becoming increasingly aware that Someone was ensuring it would one day be gone, and I could start to live for what really mattered, not for things that are as fleeting as a burning match.

I finally knew it had gone when I went to do some voluntary work in Colorado, USA. This was real climbing country. I was amazed at the number of 14,000-foot peaks in full view from the centre of a city. The sky was always deep blue, and this made the spires of the peaks look even more impressive. I had packed my climbing gear out of duty, unlike my attitude when I went out to China. I tried to make myself want to climb, but my climbing battery was almost flat. I wanted to do other things, and I had to wrestle with the guilt I felt over this for a number of months. The bare fact was that despite these outstanding hills all around me all I wanted to do was go trout fishing and learn to ski!

One summer's day I took a ride out with a friend to South Park, crossing some breathtaking passes and parking the car in full view of the Rocky Mountains. It was such a perfect day with a gentle breeze cooling the 80-degree heat from a burning high-altitude sun, and I could see all the way to the distant horizon and the Sierra Madre Mountain range far off to the south. I loved the view but enjoyed the trout fishing within that wonderful landscape more than anything else. I had no urge to strap on a rucksack and go and conquer, no desire to find an ice wall and overcome it. In fact, even though I only caught one four-inch trout all day, I was delighted just to be there, perfectly content and thoroughly satisfied. The fat lady was singing loudly now, and little by little, I was starting to enjoy the song.

So as I sat in front of the smiling man in that small church in my hometown, a little nervous of the intent gazes of the others sitting round about, I began to tell my story in answer to his question. Perhaps twenty minutes later I paused and looked up. His face had changed: wide-eyed, mouth hanging open, almost like a cartoon figure, he suddenly cracked his mouth into a grin, not a smile, and with a twinkle in his eyes, said something like, "Well, that is some story, young man. You need to write that down." So, more than 20 years later, here goes . . .

Chapter 8

THE CLIMB

▲

It was not an early start. After all, we were only doing a "roadside crag." Still, this Norwegian roadside crag was well over 1,000 feet high with a route that was meandering to say the least.

We had emerged lazily from our palatial little hut at around eight, made some breakfast, and cleaned up. Actually, Dave did the cooking while I loafed in bed an extra 15 minutes. It was always a tremendously comforting feeling to awaken to the smell of burning stove fluid: methylated spirits to be exact. We used a Trangia stove for cooking everything, and I enjoyed enormously the sight of one in use—especially when it was making my first brew of the day and more especially when the view was from my sleeping bag.

My first task each morning was trying to negotiate the vast mug of scalding tea while trying to remain almost completely horizontal. This was the pattern throughout our trip—my first climbing expedition to Norway—and it earned me the name of Lazarus, since getting me out of my sleeping bag was a feat akin to raising the dead. It did mean, however, that I was always chief dishwasher. I could live with the nickname so long as it meant a brew in bed every morning.

We casually tossed our gear into our rucksacks, throwing in a couple of Mars bars and a sandwich. There was no need for loads of food or extra kit since the walk-in was only a few minutes, and the guidebook assured us the route was climbable in around four hours, perhaps five at most. We strode purposefully across the meadow, past a huge bouldering stone liberally marked with chalk from the fingers of practicing local mountaineers. Then we negotiated a small section of boulders, hardly enough to be called a scree slope, to the base of the climb itself, just by the side of a prominent tree. Already the sun was shining and had burned off the cold, autumnal dampness from the air and ground around us. It was just like the Lakes but bigger, and I felt very much at home.

I smiled as I uncoiled my new climbing rope, enjoying the feel of its softness and pliability to the touch. Dave and I had selected it carefully from the extensive choice in our local climbing shop only weeks before. He told me it was important to buy a rope that you enjoyed the feel of, since you would be spending so much time with it, and it had to be soft enough to tie all the knots you might require, quickly and easily. This one was exceptional.

As I arranged my climbing hardware around my harness, I also took pleasure in noting that we each now had a full rack of gear. I no longer had to borrow some of Dave's in order to be fully kitted out before a lead. I had spent every penny I earned over the previous few months on more kit, and although my runners were all rather too shiny and clearly unused, a mark of a beginner, I nevertheless enjoyed the fact that I had a harness full of my own gear. From a practical point of view this would speed up our climbing, as we would no longer have to stop at each belay stance to exchange all the gear from the second climber to the leader; a brief moment to hand back the gear that had just been used on that pitch would now suffice. This made me less of a hindrance and elevated my status to a co-climber rather than merely the guy accompanying the real climber.

We looked at the guidebook one more time, and Dave led off the first pitch. I was excited that there was frequent mention of "for a rope length" as opposed to most English descriptions of 20 feet here and maybe 60 feet there. I mean, a rope length was at least 150 feet! The sheer scale of climbing out here was completely different from what I had been used to, and I was already riveted. According to what we read about this route, the grade never went above the Norwegian equivalent of Hard Severe, with possibly the occasional bit of Very Severe, so it was all well within our capabilities. As I watched Dave pull himself up the first chimney and round a fairly steep corner, I knew this was going to be a really pleasant, fun day out.

As I passed Dave on the first belay stance, we were already well above the tops of the last remaining trees, and the views across Romsdal Valley really started to open out. The majestic, 5,000-foot-high Romsdalhorn stood away to our right in the distance, and far off directly opposite us was the top of the Troll Wall massif: an imposing array of jagged teeth; the troll himself snarling his defiance at anyone foolish enough to set foot on his battlements! Beneath us was the warm, gentle meadow we had just crossed, and from there the road that drew a line across the boundary of our campsite. I imagined my sleeping bag spread out across my comfortable pine bunk, food stacked in the corner of the room, and a few cans of lager sitting patiently, always beckoning us home after a hard day on the hill. It could not get much better than this!

My first leading pitch was steep and easy, following an obvious crack up a ramp from left to right. The footholds were almost too good, and I wanted something more technical to get my teeth into. However, the easy ramp attracted debris in the form of fallen rocks and in the formation of grasses and other vegetation. I disliked this vegetation; it made me uneasy, as rock boots do not go well with anything but good, clean rock. It is rather like trying to use racing slicks for your sports car on a rainy summer's day. I stepped over any looseness and soil as best I could, pausing occasionally to wipe off the soles of my boots on my trousers. Fortunately, it was only a short distance before the rock became clean again, and I progressed higher on solid granite.

As the wall stretched out above us, Dave once more took the lead and for the first time we found ourselves going off route a little. It was not too serious, but with a multitude of cracks to choose from, it was easy to take the wrong one, and he found it petering out after 50 feet or so. I saw Dave slow down, then stop, looking upwards then from side to side as he realized that he was no longer where he ought to be. Sometimes it is just a feeling that tells you that you are in the wrong place; at others, it is made more obvious by the fact that the route becomes either very difficult, far beyond the grade of the guidebook description, or absolutely impossible with great overhangs and blank walls blocking your ascent. These are the really scary ones, but fortunately for Dave, on this first occasion it was merely a feeling coupled with a rather difficult section that was not indicated in the guidebook.

I grew impatient as he stood on the tiny ledge, pondering what to do. I wanted to get climbing again. It did not matter, I figured, that he was not exactly where he ought to be. He should simply carry on and work his way back to the correct line. It was obvious.

Dave climbed back down the way he had come. Down-climbing is a hairy business, not to be recommended except in cases of absolute necessity. Your balance is completely off and you cannot see where your foot placements are. Each time you remove the gear you have placed, you become exposed to a fall in the same instant as your balance is at its worst—especially if the gear requires some tugging and pulling to remove, which it frequently does! This may not seem too arduous to the uninformed, but if you ever try climbing down a vertical wall, you will instantly understand the fragility of this situation. As soon as Dave called down to tell me of his decision to reverse his steps, I had to concentrate hard to make sure I took in the rope as soon as he moved while never pulling the rope tight in case it interfered with his balance. The process was tiring for both of us.

Finally, he came back almost to the start of the pitch and looked up again to find the correct path. The route description was typically vague, so he took a guess at which line to follow. I began to feel uneasy. Dave had years of experience as a climber, and he was struggling to go the right way. How was I meant to negotiate huge routes like this in my first year? This was a brand-new idea for me—that I was somehow vulnerable—and I had to force the unease to the back of my mind. Just for a moment, I was not enjoying myself. I wished I had thought of this before I found myself a few hundred feet above the ground with a lot more than that to go!

The second time around, Dave led a wonderful pitch to an obvious belay stance. It was a memorable section, taking in crack lines and smooth walls of delicate holds at the top end of the technical grade, which made for exciting climbing. I commented as I followed him what a good lead it was, and I stopped once or twice to take in the view and to imagine my position high above the valley floor, all but invisible to the few passing motorists less than a mile from us. The wind was gentle, and though there were hardly any trees to confirm its presence with the clapping of their leaves, somehow the rock itself hissed peacefully to me as the breeze washed across the crag and down the valley. It was very comforting in that it sounded familiar, identical in sound and pitch to the lilting sighs of a July afternoon climbing the second pitch of Botterill's Slab on Scafell Crag back in the Lake District.

I stopped at the belay stance with Dave and we had our Mars bars together, but I was keen to press on because the delay caused by our detour had cost us probably as much as an hour. With our late start and now this delay, it was well past noon, and we were not even half-way up the route. I wanted to get back in time to welcome our climbing partners Pete and Steve from their day out on a different mountain and sit and exchange stories over dinner and a few beers. Stuffing down the rest of my food, I passed the rope just a few feet from my harness to Dave for him to fix into his stich plate (the device used to pay out rope to the leader, which will lock if put under sudden tension, thereby arresting any fall) and then headed straight up the steep wall to our left. The guidebook just mentioned "a rope length," so I thought I would head out and stop when I ran out of rope. After all, how hard could it be to find a belay among all this good rock?

The first 50 feet was easy climbing. I placed a few runners just to be safe, since we were now around 500 feet up the wall. A few minutes later I came to a bulge in the rock. One way, to my left, went around the steep bulge by big holds and around a corner out of sight. The other way was a delicate wall with what looked like tiny holds, traversing a way before, I assumed, going back straight up the crag. There were no clear cracks in which to place protection, and it looked very bold indeed. I decided that this way was not the route, as it looked very difficult for the grade of climb we were on. I chose the steep bulge with the big holds, and swung around it boldly, like a gorilla. It was not pretty, but I imagined it looked impressive to Dave beneath me.

As soon as I rounded the bulge, I looked up and immediately began to feel uncertain about my decision. The rock above me, now in plain view with the mask of the bulge removed, was a blank wall progressively steeper the higher I looked up it. For perhaps 70 or 80 feet it spread across the crag, and although it was not vertical, I could see absolutely no place to thread protection. It was going to be a run-out of approaching 100 feet, and even after that, I did not know where the route would go. My mouth was suddenly dry, and my fingers were at once wet with perspiration. I was off route—no doubt about it.

Steeling myself for the challenge ahead and forcing myself to focus even harder on the task at hand, I assumed that there would be a way to regain the correct line as soon as I had done this wall. It was not that steep, I argued, and so I would be fine to run up it, and in all probability I would see a place to fix some gear as I moved higher. In fact, it would be fun to be climbing on rock that *possibly may never have been climbed before!* Apart from that, I did not fancy down-climbing the bulge. That decided it: I set off with relish. *Anyway,* I thought, *this route was not technical enough for me; I fancied a bit of an adventure!*

By about the 70- or 80-feet mark, I was getting worried. It was not as steep as I had thought, but there were very few large holds. It was all very delicate climbing that required immense concentration, and I wanted a rest from the strain of it. Compared to the climbs I had done back at home, it ranked almost as hard as any of them that I had led, probably good VS standard. The problem was that I had placed no gear for over 70 feet, and the feeling of exposure of this alone was enough to make me nervous. A glance over my shoulder confirmed the staggering fact that I was also around 600 feet above the valley floor, and this grabbed my attention like a hand around my throat. In addition, I was becoming increasingly aware that the clock was ticking. I did not know why this was bothering me, but it was. I wanted to finish the climb and go home. I felt very alone and very exposed. With Dave so far below me, my source of experience and climbing knowledge, I felt suddenly unprepared for what might lie ahead. I was keen to stop and bring him up to my belay—that is, if I could find one.

At the top of the delicate wall I found a ramp that took me a little to the right. This looked like an obvious line that would take me back into the correct position, since I knew there was no way our route would be as hard as this last section had been. I followed the ramp around a corner and was stopped dead in my tracks by the sight just 10 feet above me. A huge inverted V looked back at me. It was a massive overhanging wall with a crack down the middle along the apex of the V. I could not believe it! A wave of dismay swept over me. Perhaps as I approached it there would be an obvious way around it. I still rejected the thought of climbing back down, as I was aware of how much time would be wasted doing that. So I started up toward this awful sight.

A muffled cry from far below me only served to increase my nervousness. It was Dave.

Not now, Dave; I'm just a tad busy, I thought to myself rather impatiently.

"Russ, can you hear me?" he persisted.

"What?" I yelled as loud as I could back down the mountain, half to make myself heard and half to let him know I was not in the mood to be chatted to.

His answer froze me to the spot.

"You've got less than 20 feet of rope left. Find a belay!"

In an instant I did my calculations. It would take a few feet of rope to make the belay, what with tying knots and the like, and if I actually had less than 20 feet left, say as little as 15 feet, then my end point would be exactly at the point of going round that horrendous V!

I stood for a while. Dave repeated his instruction to me and I called back down, asking him to give me a minute—that I was looking for somewhere to belay.

I ventured tentatively upwards to the inverted V, hoping against hope that I would find another way around it and that I had more rope than Dave had said. Almost as soon as I started I heard the cry, "Ten feet!" and I knew I was in trouble. I put a runner in the crack in the apex of the V and contemplated launching myself around the formidable overhang, guessing there was a place to rest immediately beyond it. I blew in and out, shallow breaths, like a weight lifter preparing for his world record clean-and-jerk. Here we go, chaps, blow the whistle, and over the top!

My feet were as high as my hands, head craning to see over the crest of the overhang, arms pulling with every ounce of strength I had as I shifted my point of balance in a desperate effort to move over the great block of granite that prevented my progress. Six more inches, one foot higher…

The rope tightened around my waist. I cried out in sheer fright. It was pulling me off!

"That's it! You're out of rope!" I knew that fact long before I heard it.

I rolled backwards, first snatching at the air, then at any lip of rock my eye caught sight of. All the while my feet scrambled beneath the overhang out of sight, blindly wheeling in an attempt to find an edge to stand on. I was losing my balance; I was coming off.

All at once I felt a surge of anger burst out of me. I was not having this. Aggression, nasty aggression, yet completely focussed on the singular job of keeping me alive, suddenly ripped through me and fuelled a desperate attempt to keep me attached to the mountain.

In a twinkling I saw an edge for my fingers and gripped it. I squeezed hard and grimaced, forcing more pressure on my fingers. That hold, no matter how painful it was (and it was!), was going to be enough for me to hang on to, no matter what. My feet found a ripple of rock, and I used this to hop down a few more feet onto a good stance. I was safe. I unclipped the runner I had placed and moved down a few feet to a stance just at the top of the steep wall I had climbed moments earlier, panting like a thirsty dog after a chase on a hot summer's day.

I blew out hard and felt the sweat running down my forehead. I called down to Dave.

"There's nowhere to go. I'm going to have to down-climb it to get back on route." I could not believe what I was saying, but I knew there was no other option. After a few minutes waiting, hoping an alternative plan would present itself, I set out, back down the little ramp and onto that blank wall of rock. My heart was in my mouth with each precarious movement, as I shifted my weight from hands to feet, but in reverse order of what is natural to do. I felt for footholds that were invisible and frequently cursed as my eyes revealed, too late, the ample ledge that I had just missed, settling for tiny, painful smears—anything that would hold part of my weight for a few seconds. It was exhausting work and terribly fraying on the nerves. Anger had given way to fear, and I had to force myself to concentrate and slow down when my body and emotions wanted to charge down there quickly and get it over with.

Dave was brilliant in taking the rope in, keeping it reasonably tight so as to minimize any fall, but never once pulling it so tight as to affect my balance nor neglecting to keep taking it in, which would have created dangerous bows in the rope. And he did it all while he could not see me. Superlative stuff.

Physically tired, emotionally drained, and mentally depleted, I arrived back above the bulge from where I had started. I immediately saw a delicate move above this bulge that would access the point just above the move I had originally rejected at the start of the pitch. I could see an obvious ramp up and around the miserable section I had chosen. This was clearly the correct route, and within minutes I was scampering up some very easy rock to an obvious belay stance, almost a full rope length above Dave, just as the guidebook had told me. By now I was most grateful for the ease of climbing; I did not want any further adventures, at least not for the moment.

As soon as Dave joined me, we had a short debriefing session as we gulped some water and what remained of our food. We conceded we had set off too late for a route of this length, and now our poor navigation had cost us a lot of time. We still had a few pitches to climb to the top, so we had to get a move on if we were going to get back down the mountain in the daylight. As we still had a while before sunset, and the sun was still reasonably high in the sky, I did not take this as a real issue but was still eager to bash on and get this thing ticked off before heading back to the hut with another heroic conquest under our belts. As usual, image figured highly in my thinking!

We continued up the crag with purpose, even urgency, as the sun threatened to dip behind the top of the tree-bristled summit of our route. The gentle friendliness of the day that I had felt earlier in the morning was increasingly shrouded in a foreboding cloak of concealed menace, and I fought hard to imagine myself enjoying the climb. This was a losing battle. I longed to be at the top, coiling my rope in readiness for the walk down the other side. My impatience was gradually becoming more of a fretfulness, and I resented having to spend time placing or removing runners, tying knots, and paying out or taking in rope, the things that are basic necessities of climbing. Now they were just delays in reaching the top.

A chill wind suddenly struck up and blew through my shirt, forcing me to dig into my rucksack and put on my fleece jacket just prior to going up the pitch Dave had just led, which I hoped would see us at the top. The fleece was not windproof, however, and the sweat on my back, evaporating with the brisk wind, soon chilled me as much as the heat of the day had baked me only an hour earlier. After the initial surge of cold, however, the extra layer did help to insulate my arms and back. Curiously, Dave had not announced his arrival at the top, and as I set off to join him, I was hoping it was simply too obvious a fact for him to feel he had to mention. We had been expecting to end the climb for the past couple of pitches. Surely he was there by now.

I arrived at the belay stance, a fairly comfortable sitting ledge sur-rounded by small but sturdy-looking trees, at around the same time as the dark grey clouds began drifting, then loitering ominously around the entire crag. They masked much of the remaining daylight, and I felt the first of their drizzle nestle on my face and hands as I made myself secure with slings tied to a couple of the nearby trunks. Looking up, I saw that the summit was still elusive, though I could make out the line of the ridge through a series of broken trees amongst the dullness of the damp, autumnal, late afternoon. Even the sight of it all seemed to chill me.

The two of us sat for a couple of minutes staring blankly out into the fading gloom of the rapidly disappearing day. It cannot have been more than two or three minutes, but in that brief interlude, I watched as the view down the mountain, all the way to the road and our campsite beyond, faded and disappeared before my eyes. It must have been partly due to the cloud, as it descended around us until, enveloping us in its hazy blanket of fine moisture, it cut off our link with the rest of the world. I turned my eyes toward Dave, sitting just a few feet away, and I suddenly realized that it was not just the cloud that had obscured our view. His face was hazy, even so close to me. The trees and his body had become monochromatic, and the outline of everything more than 20 feet or so behind him was decidedly fuzzy.

It was almost dark! The sun had gone behind the mountains, and within minutes it was practically night. It had not occurred to either of us that, at this latitude, similar to the far north of Scotland, the sun sets awfully quickly, and daylight becomes night in a matter of minutes rather than gradually, over an hour or so. I suggested we move quickly up through the trees and the remaining sections of broken crag to find the exit route before we lost the light completely. Dave disagreed.

"The best way is to abseil the whole way down. We do not know the route off the other side, and it may well be a difficult descent. This way, we just head straight back the way we came."

I felt a great knot fill my stomach. This was one thing I had not signed up for. It was over 1,000 feet down the mountain. It was pretty much a vertical drop all the way, and I had never done a multi-pitch abseil before. I knew the drill: simply tie both of your ropes together, loop them around a secure point (usually a tree) and then tie a ball of knot in the loose ends to prevent anyone from sliding off the rope if they inadvertently arrived at the end of the rope without finding a belay point. Next, abseil down the doubled rope until you found another good anchor point. Once both of you had abseiled down to the next belay, it was a simple case of untying the ball of knot and pulling one side of the doubled rope (remembering which side of the tree the knot was on to avoid it getting jammed around a root or a branch) until the rope came loose and fell down to you. Repeat this process all the way down the mountain—simple really.

I strained my eyes searching for any obvious anchor points down the mountain. I could not see more than 50 feet by now, and the rain was beginning to intensify. I asked the obvious:

"How do we know where the next tree is?" I did not try to mask my trepidation.

"There's usually plenty. We'll be fine," came the totally unconvincing reply. Just as I was about to look for an alternative, Dave forced us to start our epic descent by standing up and saying, "Well, we'd better get on with it. We'll need our head torches. Strap it onto your helmet, and I'll start to look around for a good anchor. Can you see a tree down there for us to aim at?"

As I took off my rucksack and began to fumble inside it for my torch, I managed to make out what looked like a good tree, sticking out from the rock, silhouetting itself against the last vestiges of light reflecting off the cloud beneath us. It was probably around 100 feet from us, in a direct line, but off quite a way to our left as we looked down the face. I dismissed this at first, as a diagonal abseil at the best of times is hard work, but on wet rock it is downright dangerous. The possibility of our boots slipping on the rain-soaked rock was high, and the resulting pendulum-swing could quite effectively render us smashed to a pulp on the mountainside as we swung into one of the many jutting flakes on the vast wall of rock.

My fumbling hands had not yet felt my torch in any corner of my pack, but I did not yet look inside, as I was too intent on finding an alternative tree for us to aim toward. Each moment that passed brought us ever closer to pitch blackness, and I could start to feel my pulse quicken. An overwhelming sense of solitude began to constrict my ability to stay focussed on the job at hand. Eventually, I admitted defeat and told Dave that I could only see the one tree to go for. He was also unable to find an alternative and seemed happy with my offering, which calmed my nerves somewhat. If he did not seem concerned at a diagonal abseil, then obviously my concerns were unfounded. I clung to his confidence as mine had deserted me, but I still had not found my torch. Half-embarrassed and half-angry, I spilled the contents of my rucksack onto the ledge around me to finally lay my hands on the stupid thing.

There was no torch in my rucksack. I had not expected we would need it, and subconsciously I had not bothered to pack it. Speechless, I looked over at Dave, and at that moment I could feel the colour drain from my cheeks and a raw blast of dread course through my marrow as he stood empty-handed, gazing back at me wide-eyed, as if *I* could help *him*.

His subconscious had done the same thing. He had forgotten his head torch as well. We were 1,000 feet up a rock wall, in the rain and cold of an autumnal night, and we were as good as blind!

I had absolutely no idea what to do. A sense of complete helplessness threatened to overwhelm me, as I could see no way of progressing in either direction, up or down. All of my self-reliance, my self-belief, and my downright cockiness were all instantly eroded away to nothing, and I stood looking at my friend, desperate for him to provide a miraculous solution to our unspeakably serious situation. His following decision gave my nerves little, if any, respite.

"We can head down anyway. There are bound to be plenty of trees to ab from, and we can just stop when we reach a decent one."

What? That's it? That's all he has to offer me? A few hours of nerve-jangling, brain-frying terror as we abseil down a dirty great crag in the dark, "believing" we will find anchor points on the way! If I had had any fight left in me, I would have protested. But the only alternative was to wait all night, and I was already painfully cold, trying hard to stop myself from shivering.

Despite severe misgivings, I did not offer any objections, not even a suggestion that we try to reach the top of the crag and look for a walk-off on the other side. I simply concurred silently and began almost mechanically to prepare the ropes for the first abseil. Between us we selected a sturdy pine close to our belay ledge. This one, at least, was robust and well rooted.

Dave leaned back over the edge first and swung out over the cliff at an awkward traversing angle just as the final few rays of autumn warmth briefly revealed themselves in a gap in the blackened clouds. The rays clung to the purpled edges of the Troll's jagged teeth opposite us and then suddenly dipped beneath the horizon, relinquishing their grip on the granite, falling back over the distant hills, and leaving us in the dusky solitude of twilight. As he walked and half-bounced across the blank wall beneath me, I imagined my last link with help and human warmth also disappearing with him. Within a few moments he was out of sight, and I could no longer even hear the familiar clinking of climbing hardware jangling cheerfully from his harness.

I was alone. Very alone.

Twilight seemed to last for no more than a couple of minutes, and soon I found myself staring out into a night sky that was darker than a magpie's cape. Visibility was no more than a few feet at times, and I was grateful for the occasional break in the clouds to alleviate the intensity of the inky night. The trees around me and the ever-encroaching cloud and drizzle made for a stifling environment, which, had it not been for the knowledge that I was clipped onto a small ledge high up a mountain with miles of open crag stretching away on both sides of me, could have easily made me feel claustrophobic!

The drizzle stopped briefly, ending the fizzing buzz of rain on leaves and rendering my surroundings silent. Despite the drop in the wind, though, the temperature was falling rapidly, and I kept hunching my shoulders and flexing my legs in an attempt to keep warm and arrest the shivers, which were becoming increasingly frequent and more intense. Making fists with my hands only partially alleviated the horrible pain of hot aches. I could feel my strength waning, and I wanted someone to come and take me off this vile place. I grimaced at the thought of what lay ahead; several abseils in pitch black, desperately searching for belay points without a torch, down-climbing wet rock. We had been off route several times in broad daylight. What if we went the wrong way now, at night, and found ourselves dangling at the end of the rope in mid air, a huge overhang preventing progress up or down?

I was starting to fret. It felt like I was a schoolboy again and had forgotten to do my homework, and now my mind was racing to find a way to escape the inevitable punishment. But this was a completely new situation for me, and though the feeling was similar, it had an intensity that was completely off the chart. I forced myself to think of nothing and to simply listen for Dave's instruction to come down to join him. A bit of company, especially the company of a man of Dave's experience, would make it all right. He knew what to do and would lead me safely down. I had complete faith in him.

A faint noise in the distance, carried on the night air, interrupted my distressed thoughts. Though only a hundred feet away, most of the sound had been absorbed by the rock. Then there it was again—definitely an audible cry off to my left. It had to be Dave calling me down. I pulled on the rope and felt it loose, confirming he had finished abseiling. I could at last go down to meet him and finally begin to make progress down this repulsive crag.

The diagonal abseil passed by without event. In fact, on occasion I allowed myself to feel invigorated at the thought of bouncing sideways down a rock face in the black of night. It felt like the kind of thing the Commandos get up to, and I grinned once or twice at how it must have looked. Every boy would like the idea of doing this, I thought. It was a shame it necessitated such fear and dread in order to be in a position to experience it! I found Dave almost by touch rather than by sight, as my feet found a ledge and then my ears heard the sound of his voice welcoming me aboard his little platform.

But, oh my goodness, was it little: no more than eight inches wide and perhaps a yard long, as far as I could figure. I looked for the anchor point, the sturdy, solid tree from which we were going to carry on down the mountain. As I stepped over Dave and sat down, still looking, my leg hit a branch and I assumed this would be attached to the tree I had somehow missed in the gloom of the night.

That "branch" *was* the tree. It was no thicker than a Coke can and seemed to be sticking out of the rock itself rather than from any soil. Dave assured me he had checked it, and it was sound. I could not be bothered to contend that it actually looked anything but secure. All I wanted to do was pull the rope down and get on with it. The solace I had felt at not being alone again soon evaporated as I pondered our next jump into the dark, reliant on an ash tree of far too few years, if indeed it had had a birthday at all!

Dave pulled on the rope. He pulled again. On the third time he cursed loudly and gave the rope a huge yank, almost lifting himself off his seat on the ledge. I was pleased we were both anchored to the main wall with runners, as he seemed intent on pulling the mountain down to get the thing to move.

"Are you pulling the correct side of the rope? I asked. "The knot is on the right. Are you pulling the right side, the pink rope?"

"Course I am. It's jammed. It won't move at all. It doesn't even start to move. It must be wedged under a root or something."

The rain had started again. I barely noticed as I stared out into nothingness. I did not reply to Dave, nor did I try to pull the rope myself, not that I could reach it anyway. I had nothing left to give. The rain ran down my hair inside my helmet, plastering it to my head, and I could feel my trousers beginning to stick to my legs. I usually hated that feeling, but now I was beyond caring.

"We are going to have to stay the night here," Dave began, "and when it comes light we will be able to see what's happening with the rope. Maybe we can climb back up and free it then."

His words made me hang my chin on to my chest. I was not pouting or complaining; I did not doubt Dave's judgment. I simply could not cope with the thought of a further twelve hours of freezing anxiety and raw fear before maybe, perhaps, being able to jibber and claw my way down nearly a thousand feet of nightmare. My physical strength could not help me, my mental abilities did not know enough to get me out of this, and my emotions were shot to pieces. A night in the bitter cold rain, on a ledge barely big enough to hold both buttocks was not what I wanted to hear.

"Dave! Dave!"

A voice below us carried up the crag by the rock itself! It was Steve.

"Where are you, Dave? Are you okay?"

Pete and Steve were running alongside the base of the crag, calling for their friend. My heart leapt. Here was our hope restored again. These guys could help us out. They were excellent mountaineers.

"We're over here!" Dave yelled back. "Our ab rope's stuck. We're okay!"

Okay? Okay? How exactly does he define okay? I thought. Just how I hoped Pete and Steve were going to help us from the foot of the crag, I am not sure, but as silence reigned again and I understood that they had both wandered off to their warm hut, I knew there was nothing they could do. I felt reassured that they had come to look for us, but I was somehow sad that only Dave got a mention in their calls! I fought off a bout of self-pity and soon forgot all about feeling sorry for myself as the wind made its presence felt—using the rain running down my back to avert my attention. I shivered as Dave instructed me to put on all my spare clothing in my rucksack. Climbers always carry something warm, a couple of extra layers for use in cases of emergency. If we were going to be here all night, we had to avoid the very real danger of exposure setting in, especially in such wet conditions.

The problem was, I was already wearing all my spare clothing—my fleece jacket. It had been a hot day. It was a simple roadside crag. We should have finished the whole route by mid-afternoon. What was the need for a load of extra clothing?

I was in deep trouble. I had no spare clothes, and we had eaten all the spare food as well. How could we possibly spend the night out here? More-over, amazingly, and totally out of character for him to be so disorganised, Dave had no spare kit either. He, with years of alpine experience, had done exactly the same thing as I had! As we both began to shiver, our situation was now becoming extremely serious. Daylight and any hope for warmth were still many hours away.

A few minutes passed in silence before Dave chirped up with a forced cheeriness, his cloaked fear making me even more uneasy, "Tell you what; I'll go further down the rope. There's still fifty feet of rope left, and there's bound to be a better anchor point down there. It might also free up the rope and we'll be able to get all the way down."

Great idea, I thought. *Why wouldn't that work?* Any straw to grasp was fantastic to me, though why he decided to do that, I will never know. In a moment, after promising to give me a yell as soon as he found something, Dave had unclipped from the face and stepped off the ledge, launching himself in a straight line down the wall beneath us, disappearing almost immediately into the night.

It may have been seconds or possibly as much as a minute later that my blank mind, trying not to focus on the pain in my fingers and the aching in my neck caused by the uncontrollable shivering, was suddenly shocked to life by a noise far below me. It was like a rumble mixed with a dull crack, repeated every second or two. I immediately felt deeply troubled. Something was wrong. I stared down into the dark, past my feet as they dangled over the ledge into space, to see if anything became obvious out of the night air beneath me.

Sparks spat out of the wall several hundreds of feet down the crag, fol-lowed by that crack sound again. A moment later more sparks, and more cracks, a deep grumble of rock, and a final splutter of sparks at what I assumed was the base of the mountain.

What was going on? What was this new twist to our horrendous tale? Yet again the adrenaline pumped freely around my body, and my already addled mind fought to retain control of my ragged emotions.

A rock fall! The rumbling was the falling rock. But the cracking sounds and the flurries of sparks, what were they?

"Dave! Dave! Are you all right? Are you okay?"

"Dave!"

My stomach lurched into my mouth in a way I thought was impossible. The wave of nausea coupled with the stinging sweat on my scalp and the involuntary gasp of sheer horror made my head spin. My mind was in disarray, but the conclusion I reached was an obvious one.

In our desperation to start abseiling, we had failed to tie a ball of knot in the end of the rope. In the pitch black of the descent Dave had not seen the ends of the rope dangling in mid-air, and he had simply slid off the end of it. His fall as a result of this had ended in his slamming repeatedly into the sides of the crag, and the metal climbing hardware attached to his harness had caused all the sparks I had seen as they struck the granite.

He could not answer me because he was smashed to pieces nearly 1,000 feet beneath me.

I did not feel grief in that moment. I felt dread; a vicious, hard dread mixed in equal amounts with a quite overwhelming sense of solitude. It was an aloneness that I can only imagine happens to the lone survivor of a particularly brutal battle. A sense that you are alive but you should not be, that somehow you do not deserve to be, and you wished more than anything, in your shame and despair, that you had not survived at all because all you have left is a whole pile of memories that you never want to remember.

My closest friend was dead, and now, as my mind could no longer cope with what was happening, and as my body began to succumb to the cold and the wet, I knew I too was a dead man. It was only a matter of time. A heart-shot deer can still run 200 yards on adrenaline alone but that does not alter the fact that the moment the bullet passed through its body, it was already dead. I was still breathing, but I was a dead man.

I sat there for a minute or two, perhaps a lot longer, thinking of my situation: nineteen years old and utterly spent. All reserves of physical and mental strength had been sapped. I had to use every ounce of my inner strength just to keep control of my mind and prevent total shutdown. I felt embarrassed and ashamed.

In the film *Gladiator*, Maximus quoted his mentor, Marcus Aurelius, as saying, "Death smiles at us all. All we can do is smile back." Perhaps this is true if it comes in a second, but not if it circles you for minutes or even an hour or more. It is more like a nature documentary I once saw, where a deer calf becomes separated from its mother and the rest of the herd in the snow. A lone wolf stalks it, and after a long pursuit the terrified deer stops—unable to continue despite knowing it is being pursued—exhausted and alone in the snow. The wolf takes up position not 20 yards from the calf and promptly lies down: why risk a struggle when the end is inevitable? The desperate calf has no more energy, and after a period of more than an hour or two, it begins to succumb to exhaustion from the freezing cold and the falling snow. As the calf kneels then lies down, so the wolf, as a mirror image, rises on its haunches and begins to walk, not run, to its prey. The jaws of death open almost in a resigned, fatalistic manner. The calf can see its end, indeed it had seen it for some considerable time, and yet is powerless to do anything about it. Completely spent, having tried everything in its strength and abilities to survive, it is now totally bereft of hope. The end is then mercifully quick. The prelude to the end was truly pitiful and utterly horrifying in its cold, calculating inevitability.

That is how Death approached me. I will not accept for one moment all that glib nonsense pedalled out by Hollywood that death is just a part of life, and all we can do is smile and accept it. Death was so close to me I could smell his breath, and it stank.

To have failed so miserably so early in life was not what I had expected. To die alone on a wet mountain, having survived just long enough to hear the death of my closest friend was not what I had thought would happen to me.

Dying alone was no longer a happy thought as it had been when I imagined myself on the road to mountaineering greatness. It certainly had none of the grandeur I had expected, and it certainly was not in the least bit heroic. "Courageous mountaineer dies on a cliff, plunging 1,000 feet to his death. He died doing what he loved," the eulogy would read.

What rot. When death breathed in my face, there was no feeling of heroism or sublime finality. None at all. It was sheer terror. I was totally unprepared to die, and believing my end had come, I felt naked, exposed, desperately alone, and absolutely petrified.

But here I was at the end of myself. My strength had failed me. My mind was spinning out of control, and I was trying hard not to cry—how desperately embarrassing.

Yet again, my innermost being was disturbed by something that I did not at first recognize. There it was again: a movement. Adrenaline coursed through me for the umpteenth time that night. I could hear my heart pounding; I could feel it in my throat. What was it? The third time confirmed my nightmare was deepening: the rock ledge was moving, only slightly, hardly perceptible at first, but definitely moving.

It seemed that I was anchored to a flake of granite that was not part of the wall proper. More importantly, it was rotten, and my weight was starting to make it collapse. Dave and I had disturbed it, and now it was beginning to split away from the crag.

My pitiful and brutal end was imminent. I reckoned that I was in the last minute of my life. I had abandoned any hope of surviving. This was it; what a total waste.

"I don't believe You're out there," I suddenly blurted out loud. "You know that."

"But if You get me out of here alive, I'm Yours. I'm Yours forever. Do with me what You will."

"I know that there is no other way to survive this night. I am about to die, and if I do not there is no other explanation except that You saved me, because only You can. If You let me survive, I will serve You all my life because You have earned me, You will have paid for me, and You deserve my obedience."

I sat for a few moments longer, waiting perhaps for an answer. No audible voice rang in my ears, no great hand from heaven picked me up and brushed me down, but all at once I knew what to do. It was immaterial if it saved my life or if it hastened my death, but I *knew* what to do and I stood up.

The movement of the ledge meant that at least one of my runners simply fell into my hand, the crack having expanded and relinquished its grip on the piece of metal. Seconds later I started to climb across the blank wall of rock to my left, unable to see any holds, as the shroud of darkness and the persistent drizzle made visibility as low as two or three feet.

It was only as I set off, with footholds often as small as one or two inches, and finger holds as small as less than half an inch, that I realized I had no rope! Dave, of course, had abseiled over the edge, and rather than carrying on the diagonal slant of our initial course, had gone straight down the mountain, thereby taking the rope an unknown distance to the left and far beyond my vision.

I was free climbing on tiny holds in the pitch black over a drop of nearly 1,000 feet in the rain just because I knew it was the right thing to do. As I climbed across that blank wall, I saw in my mind's eye how I must have looked to someone looking down from above. What an insignificant speck, alone on a huge black expanse, and yet that speck still had the flicker of light in it, the glimmer of life, and for the first time I knew that that tiny glow of life, *my* life, was important to someone. My tiny light on that great wall of darkness was somehow significant.

I have no idea how far I climbed or for how long. It may have been two minutes or perhaps twenty, but I stopped when I reached a ledge that was big enough to place my whole foot flat. I was extremely tired but was no longer shivering from the cold. All was quiet around me, and the stillness was comforting rather than fear inducing.

I knew fully what to do, and in a ludicrous way, I felt mildly nervous for a moment. It was a simple thing really; I turned and faced outwards, looking yet again into the emptiness of the night air, knowing that the Romsdal Valley slept peacefully far below my now outstretched left foot. I reached out with my right hand, unable to see beyond my fingertips, and I slowly but purposefully leaned forward. As I lost my balance, I think I let out a little gasp and the sweat of adrenaline stung my scalp. I did not expect to live; neither, though, did I think about dying. It was simply doing what I knew was the right thing to do; perhaps it was obedience. I was certainly at peace as I lost my balance off the edge of that crag.

The rope was at once in the palm of my hand, perfectly resting in the V between my thumb and forefinger. I had not reached around in the air, nor had I strained my eyes to find it. It was just there, in the perfect place! By grabbing the rope and holding it, I could pull myself back onto the ledge. I fastened it into my descending device and began to abseil down the wall, wondering, in a rather bemused state, what was going to happen next.

Within 30 feet or so I had to go over an enormous overhang, and directly beneath that I came to a ledge, some 20 feet further down. As I put my feet on it, a voice called out to me:

"How are you doing?" Dave smiled warmly from just a few feet away, and despite his broad grin I could see he was a tired and emotionally drained man. I confirmed I was fine, and the elation I wanted to express at finding him alive was stifled by the knowledge that the two of us still had work to do.

We were both alive. Finding out how Dave had survived would have to wait. For now we had to concentrate on how to tackle the remainder of our worst nightmare.

Chapter 9

SECOND CHANCES

▲

The rain had stopped. Or more likely, the shelter offered by the overhang above us was keeping us dry. Without moonlight we could see very little, certainly not enough to see a route down the mountain to another belay stance. I could, however, see my friend, and his being alive was relief enough. But the fact that I could make out some of his features in the gloom suggested that the weather had improved a little. It could be, though, that we had abseiled beneath the clouds. I suspected that the summit above us was still cloaked in a dense, soaking mist.

"So why didn't you answer me when I was calling out to you?" I asked, half-laughing and half-accusing.

"You see that overhang above us?" Dave asked, pointing at the massive roof of rock we had just come past on the way down the rope.

"Well, while you were calling my name, I was watching the ball of knot at the end of the rope dangling in mid-air just a couple of feet beneath my boots. I had to pull myself back up the rope, hand over hand, until I managed to get to this ledge. I was in no fit state to be shouting anything. Once I had secured myself, I couldn't hear you anyway—probably because of the overhang."

Bearing in mind that Dave weighed over 180 pounds and was carrying a rucksack full of climbing gear, this was quite a considerable feat of athleticism! Moreover, he was gripping a soaking wet climbing rope. I was both impressed and at the same time horrified at what he had been able, or rather, what he had been forced to do in order to survive.

"What about the crashing sounds, and the sparks?" I continued. "That scared me half to death! What was that about?"

"As I came over the lip of the overhang, my feet and, I think, the rope began to dislodge rocks from the underside. Some were the size of telephone boxes, and as I swung under the bulge more fell away and were flying past my head! Any one of them would have killed me. It was these that sparked as they struck the lower sections of the crag. Now do you see why I wasn't in the mood to chat?"

I was filled with admiration for Dave's resolve and his courage. How he kept his nerve under such monumental duress still staggers me. I began to realize that we were both alive by nothing short of miraculous protection. Now, however, was not the time to rejoice. Our situation was very similar to the one we were in barely an hour earlier.

The only major difference was that the ledge was a little smaller, and the "tree"; ah yes, the tree.

The tree, positioned only inches from my right buttock and protruding from bare rock at an angle of around sixty degrees was, I am almost certain, an ash. More specifically, it was an ash sapling. It had the diameter of a baby's arm or thereabouts. Granted, a pudgy baby perhaps, but it was definitely no wider than about two inches across.

It would not have held the weight of a dog.

I glanced around in a cursory manner, as if looking for the real belay anchor but knowing all the while that this was, in fact, our only option. That knot in my stomach, the one that had disappeared for a few moments after I had sat down next to my friend again, was now back with a vengeance.

Dave pulled on the rope. It came down without the least objection, running smoothly around the tree that had only a short time ago so insistently resisted all manner of persuasion to relinquish its grip. I have never understood how the rope came free simply because we had abseiled further down it. Perhaps the downward force as opposed to the diagonal pull we had at first put on it helped. Whatever it was, we both heaved a sigh of relief as coil after coil came tumbling down toward us from out of the night sky.

Looping it around our little broomstick anchor point was a depressing affair. I could hardly believe that we were actually going to trust such a ridiculously frail-looking object, but I was acutely aware that staying put was not practical. It was still very cold, the ledge we were on was extremely uncomfortable, and most ominously, the overhang just above us could have dropped any number of skull-crushing boulders onto us at any moment. We had to keep moving.

"See you in a minute." Dave tried to sound cheerful, but his expression remained sombre. After his last descent I could only imagine what he must have been feeling as he plunged once more into the night. What horrors awaited him this time?

Almost immediately, the tiny glimmer of hope that had dared to rekindle itself after I had arrived unexpectedly alive on the ledge was drenched with the bitterly cold waters of dread. I thought it not only imprudent but wholly unnecessary to shout down the mountain to explain to him what was unfolding just beside me. He could do nothing about it and neither could I—not in time anyway.

The sapling was giving way. It was not snapping, but it was bending dramatically under Dave's weight, and within a few seconds it was almost perpendicular to the rock. If it bent much further, the rope would start to slide down the pitiful little trunk and disappear forever down to the valley below. I tried to grab higher up and somehow pull the tree back into a more upright position. But as I leaned over I could hear, and then see the twanging snap of roots pulling clear of the rock in which they were insecurely clawing a foothold. One by one, tiny flecks of crumbly soil flicked into the air as another fingernail of security ripped out of the rock, and the tree itself, like the hand of a stopwatch on countdown, bent further and further, inexorably down toward the point when the bell would toll, and that, as they say, would be that.

My hands were useless. I could not cheat destiny. Any second now either the tree would bend too far and the rope would disappear, or the last root would detach itself from the crag, and both tree and rope would be gone. I began to despair as I could see that it was the same scenario as earlier. All that had gone before had merely delayed the inevitable. Yet again I was becoming frantic, trying desperately to be more useful than the hopelessly inadequate attempts I knew I was making. It was a matter of seconds now, and I knew all my straining and pulling, as urgent as it was, was achieving nothing more than trying to assuage my guilt; not that I was going to live much longer to feel any guilt. The countdown was nearly over.

"Okay, I'm down! It's a full rope length. Come down when you're ready!"

The voice took me completely by surprise. I had no idea Dave would have covered the distance so quickly, and for a moment I felt an elation that was completely incongruous with my situation.

I examined the tree. The elation vanished and Dread once more returned to take his appropriate place. All I could see before me was a piece of wood of virtually twig-like proportions, dangling, almost teetering on the edge of a precipice, its roots clearly visible, as if recently ravaged by both thunder storm and grizzly bear. It was unmistakably pointing slightly downhill, the rope around it being held on merely by the friction of the ripples in the already distressingly smooth bark. Given a choice, I would have refused to use it either as a tent pole or as a tether for a lamb. It was unsuitable to perform either task.

But I had to abseil 150 feet down a sheer wall—and stake my life on it. It was astounding that it had held for Dave, but the damage done to it by his descent had rendered it useless for me. I threaded the rope through my figure of eight one more time, placed my hand around the scrawny base of that pitiful ash sapling, and prayed,

"You've saved me once tonight, but now I need *Your* hand around here to keep this in place, or else we both know I'm dead."

I suddenly had an idea. More of a revelation, in fact. I was no longer going to live in fear of dying. I had had quite enough of that, and I decided that either He would rescue me or He would not. But I was not going to fret and worry about whether I walked off this hill tonight or was carried off in a few days time. I had given myself over to Him, and so it was His decision. With that in mind, there was no point whatsoever in creeping gingerly down the rock face, trying to make the anchor hold. Either He wanted me to live or He wanted me dead, and it just did not matter. I was going to find out definitely which one it was, and I knew how I could be sure.

Picking up a few coils of the rope and throwing it into the void behind me, and then, bending my knees, I jumped backwards for all I was worth and launched myself into the dark sky. At the same moment I raised my left hand, which held the lower end of the rope, so that it zipped freely through the descender and sped me downward at a speed only marginally slower than free-falling.

As I began to swing back in toward the rock, I pulled the rope around my back to slow down and enable myself to gain a foot purchase on the crag so that I could push off again and carry on my descent. This placed enormous strain on the anchor point above, since my entire body weight plus my considerable downward momentum act together against my belay while I slow down. This is exactly what *not* to do in order to protect an unsatisfactory belay; it was precisely my reason for doing it.

I completed 150 feet of abseiling in three bounds. By the third jump I felt like something out of a James Bond film, and I was grinning, almost swaggering, as I joined my friend. I could not see his face clearly, but he would probably have rolled his eyes at such reckless abandon! The fact that I was still alive was a most unexpected but very welcome bonus to the night's proceedings. However, neither of us was in the mood for levity, and my brief expression of fun evaporated into the cold night air as soon as I had clipped myself to the rock next to Dave. I then simply unclipped my figure of eight, removed the rope, and automatically began to pull it down from above, praying briefly that it did not become wedged in one of those useless little roots on its way down.

The number of abseils we did eludes me, and the direction we took, whether straight down or criss-crossing across the crag is uncertain. Eventually, though, we arrived at a place where the rock was not quite so steep, and the vegetation completely disappeared. We had nothing to use as an anchor point. Even cracks in the rock in which we could thread runners to abseil from were proving impossible to find. Perhaps our very limited vision concealed them, or our high state of anxiety caused us to miss obvious places, or maybe there simply were not any for us to use. Whatever it was, we realized that we had to find a different method of descent, and our options were few.

Actually, our options were one: down-climb the remainder of the mountain.

Down-climbing a route, as I had discovered to my enormous chagrin earlier that afternoon, was indeed a most difficult, gripping, and wholly unsatisfactory means of escape.

Down-climbing in the dead of night without a torch was all that and also spectacularly foolhardy, except in cases of absolute necessity.

Add to this the spices of climbing down *wet* rock *without a rope*, and you have consummate recklessness, a disastrous notion that could have only one possible outcome. I realized I had been kept alive so far, but this latest twist left me unconvinced that I would remain so for more than a little longer. The churn in my stomach and the tom-tom beating of my heart confirmed that I was still very much aboard the roller coaster of hope and terror as it set off once more!

Though hardly the time or place for philosophical reflection, and perhaps in an attempt to counter the free-flowing adrenaline, I found myself trying to look around at our environment in order to gain a deeper understanding of our situation. Straining my eyes to see where we were in relation to the top, or far more importantly the bottom, of the crag left me frustrated and anxious. On occasion, while waiting for Dave to finish the last abseil,

I had been able to examine the rock in the few feet around me. This was a bonus compared to the almost pitch black of night I had experienced at the moment of actually stepping out over the edge of the sheer face, now a few hundred feet above me. This newfound lifting of the night's veil probably had to do with the fact that the cloud was above me, and the clear air had allowed some light from the masked moon above and from the lights of the valley below to permeate through a little. Now, however, we were beginning to descend into a fairly sharp-sided gully with steep rock walls on either side. This once again put a shroud around us, which refused to allow light in from either above or below. Once more I could see only a matter of feet, and this did nothing to alleviate my racing pulse and high state of insecurity.

We undid the ball of knot in our ropes, and having checked mine for tangles, I began to coil it around my neck. Neither of us spoke. Having only just become used to the notion of sliding down a rope at night, I was expecting us to carry on until we reached the valley floor. Actually, I had imagined the feeling of walking down the granite until I finally put one foot down onto soft lush grass. That feeling would have signified the end of our ordeal. How I was longing for that sensation! Over the past hour or two, I had finally begun to convince myself that I might indeed make it down from this hill alive. Now, as I felt coil after coil of wet rope weigh down my shoulders, this hope was taking a severe battering. After all, I simply could not keep sticking my head into the jaws of a lion and not expect him to take a bite at least once. We were playing a game of cat and mouse with Death himself, but I sensed he was becoming bored and was about to cut short his playtime.

As I tied the final knot and secured the rope around me, I felt most awkward. This great mound around my shoulders, heavy and cumbersome, made me decidedly top-heavy and completely off-balance. My fingers were already numb from the cold and the wetness of the rope.

And then, what was that? Ah yes, the drizzle had returned. These numb digits of mine somehow had to feel holds as we began to grapple with the task ahead of us.

It was probably fortunate, for once, that I could not actually see down the crag. I knew that a void of hundreds of feet would be looking back at me, and the rocks at the foot of the mountain that I was so longing to touch would hold only certain destruction for us both if we did not climb with every ounce of skill and patience we could muster. We were now climbing blind in the cold and wet, with absolutely no protection at all. The unavoidable result of a single mistake would be to bounce all the way down to the snaggle-toothed grin of a boulder field—not my first choice for a safety net!

There was no point in trying to look for a route, so we simply headed vertically down, hoping there were holds for hands and feet as we went. The only consolation was that the rock was not as steep as before, and we could rest frequently, which I needed. The stress alone was making me again feel a little nauseous, and I had to keep squeezing my hands in an effort to try to regain some feeling in them. For the most part, it was like trying to rock climb while wearing boxing gloves.

My cheeks must have been flushed, as they felt hot. My face stung when the wind blew against it. As I contemplated our hideously exposed position, clinging precariously to the crag we were on and to life itself, I felt another gust against my cheeks, and a tiny flurry of water blew against my helmet. It was too heavy to be the drizzle, and my mind then began to register something else: the noise of running water above and below me, but different from the constant dripping that had surrounded us for much of our descent. It was much fuller, and more urgent, and it had the mark of danger attached to it. My hands felt it before my head realized what we had stumbled into.

Water was running over my fingers. As I moved across the rock a little and down a few more feet, I could feel my trousers becoming increasingly soaked. All at once, a stream of icy water came running around the rim of my helmet and down my face and neck, sending a jolt of bitter chill down my spine.

I suddenly realized that we were in the middle of a waterfall!

It was not a huge body of water, and whether it was a permanent feature of the mountain or one caused by the rain that night, I cannot say. But it was clear that our only way down this mountain was to try to negotiate this latest obstacle and hope it led to easier ground. After we decided to follow the course of the water, I took a deep breath and stepped into the chilling embrace of this fresh peril.

We tried our best to climb down the edges of the water as far as possible. Frequently, however, there was no option but to step headlong into the flow of the frigid waterfall itself. Sporadic cascades mingled with steady streams to make this new adventure as physically uncomfortable as it was hugely dangerous. I could hardly believe what we were doing, and I fully expected to be wrenched at any moment from the slippery rock by the next torrential surge and dashed onto the base of the crag.

Each downward movement, as difficult as it was, became exponentially more fearsome as the smooth and inhospitably greasy rock refused to allow me to gain a comfortable or convincing foothold on it. At the same time, my hands were so cold that they had long ago ceased to operate in a satisfactory manner. I could not trust them to feel for a hold accurately, nor could I make them grip effectively once a hold of any description had been found. Leaning over as far as I dared, while always off-balance due to the rope lashed around my back being constantly bombarded with water from hundreds of feet above me, I was forced to try to look at my fingers to see if they were holding onto anything at all. Then I gingerly transferred my weight onto that hand and hoped that I was actually gripping properly onto a good hold. The pain was most illuminating!

My helmet protected my hair from becoming too sodden, but it acted as a conduit for the constant streams of liquid ice that flowed freely down my back. I gasped almost incessantly, trying to take a full breath of air rather than the shallow gasps I kept drawing as new areas of my body fell prey to the clawing fingers of Norway's winter chill. Usually the flow was little more than a generous trickle, but on occasions I found a surge of several buckets' worth pouring over the back of my head. The force suddenly placed on my rope, coiled about my neck, pulled me backwards and tried to tear my hands from their feeble hold on the rock wall. This was a desperate clinging for survival.

The noise of the water so close to my ears was deafening, even though, from only a few feet back, it would probably have been a fairly gentle sound. Pouring over my head that night, it had the thunder of wild horses to it, and they were bearing down on me quickly. It was rather like those terrible dreams of trying to escape a monstrous pursuer only to find yourself in a thick swamp with legs that will not move beyond slow motion! I knew I had to climb my way out of this dream. If I found myself "waking up," it would be from a fatal fall. This knowledge remained ever-present in my mind.

Mercifully, after a few terror-filled minutes, the terrain relaxed a little, relatively speaking, of course, as we continued our descent. The angle had softened, indicating perhaps that we were near the bottom of the route. On occasion, we could turn and face away from the crag, shuffling and sliding down the rock and waterslide without having to pick each hand and foot hold carefully. The water then fed into a steeper section of the gully, and we followed it. Taking this route was very committing, and we knew it, as there was no way of retracing our steps if we were to meet a dead end or some insurmountable obstacle. The kind of thing we had to avoid at all costs was this route ending, say, at a black hole in the rock where a chute of water rushed through it into a dropoff of unknown size, but possibly hundreds of feet to the valley floor.

Which, of course, is exactly what it did!

There was no way around it. We were stuck. The two of us stood on a flat section of rock, almost like a pool, our boots submerged in the water, and we stared into the blackness that was swallowing our waterfall. I put my hands on my hips and looked up into the night sky and then down at my boots. All this way to reach a dead end! How unspeakably cruel! We had survived an epic, and now we were completely stuck.

There was nowhere to go at all.

"How far do you think the drop is?" I asked, ludicrously.

"Only one way to find out!" Dave simultaneously spoke and sat down on the edge of the hole, before pushing himself off the rim and into the blackness, almost as if making a parachute jump.

Before I even had time to shut my gaping, incredulous mouth I heard a thud and a groan, then, to my enormous relief, his voice:

"It's about twelve feet. I'll catch you!"

Without any further thought, and almost with relish I sat on the edge, ignoring the water running into the top of my underwear, and pushed myself off into "the abyss." Poor Dave received a pair of soggy boots in his face, and we landed in a crumpled heap amongst a pile of boulders.

Boulders?

Boulders! It was the boulder field, the scree slope at the foot of the mountain.

We were down.

Unbelievable!

The unthinkable had happened. We scampered across the rocks, trying to pick out an easy path, but I did not care if I turned an ankle or scraped a shin as we headed as fast as possible to the meadow that I knew was there. We could now see the lights of the campsite not more than half a mile away, probably much less, in fact. They were almost level with our eyes.

It was over. We were down.

We were down, and we were alive.

Stopping at the meadow, we checked to see if we had all our gear with us. What a stupid thing to do! Was I going to go back up that horrid mountain to retrieve a lost karabiner, for goodness sake? The two of us walked abreast and plodded back to the hut where we both quietly and half-ashamedly stepped into the warmth that just a few minutes earlier I thought I would never feel again.

Pete and Steve both smiled and made fun of us. We did not explain any more than that the rope had been stuck for a while. I silently changed my clothes and wolfed down my beans and lager. I fell asleep feeling strange and uncomfortable. I was very aware that I did not want to explain what had happened to me on that rocky crag. That was for me, and me alone. Almost as if, in explaining it, I would be robbed of the satisfaction and the power of what had undoubtedly happened. It would be more than I could have borne if they did not believe me, or worse, tried to explain it all away as mere "good luck." That would have been too horrible. As terrifying as it all had been, it was also far too precious to me to simply blab the tale around. This was personal just for me; it was all mine.

I have reflected on this feeling many times since that date. It has stood me in good stead for many occasions later when I have talked about something particularly precious or poignant that God has done in my life and have been completely robbed of the joy of it by the blank stares, or worse, the incredulous raise of the eyebrows that I received as a response.

You see, God, I have discovered, works with us as individuals, and He speaks to individuals in a way that only the person He is addressing can fully understand; that is the beauty of it all. What I received that night was far more than a rescue from death. Many have received that; indeed Dave received the same physical deliverance from a dreadful end that I did. The difference was that *I met God,* and I knew I would never be the same again. I have finally learned that it is immaterial if I am believed or not, and I can accept the raised eyebrows without the feelings of rejection and insecurity that I used to suffer so desperately from. That is why I can now write it all down. That process started the very night I returned alive from The Climb.

The next day, as we drove up the pass toward our next climb (what was I thinking? I went climbing the very next day!), I looked back on what I had done. I listed the number of chances I had been given during the course of The Climb and the descent. It was at least five.

"Okay," I said. "You did what I asked. Only You could have done it, and You repeated the same thing more than once, just to drive the point home. I'm Yours for all of my life. Do with me what You will!"

I gazed out of the window as we drove up the pass. The views washed over me and I soaked them in. I felt no elation, no great emotional watershed, and I could not say I had a huge spiritual awakening.

But I felt at peace. I had given my life away, and I was perfectly happy with that, because He had proved that He cared about me and that He was both willing and able to rescue me. That *demanded* a response, not because He paid for me (even though He had) or because I offered myself to Him (even though I did) but because He showed that He was *worthy* because He loved me. He loved me enough to die for me and to rescue me while I still did not acknowledge Him or want to serve Him. This was a remarkable truth, a devastating realization. It still is to this day.

I was aware in that car that the notion that I could offer my future life in exchange for His offering His life for me, and saving mine, was quite the most ridiculous idea possible. It was rather like offering the dung of a backstreet cur in exchange for the Kohinoor diamond, only much more unbalanced! And yet He had agreed to such an idea. It was this Grace, this Love that demanded my response and further demanded my abandonment to Him. Once I had met God, it was impossible to do anything but give my all to Him, irrespective of where that led. He is worthy. Full stop. And now that I knew, there was nowhere else to run.

Unfortunately, I spent the next few years trying to do precisely that. You see, in giving up my rights to my own life, I still believed I could pursue what I wanted and simply get God's blessing along the way. I did not understand the concept of sanctification; the idea of living a life that is pleasing to God each day. This was the beginning of my new life but also the start of some of the greatest struggles that I could have imagined. I knew I had no rights to my life anymore and that I had been bought and paid for—though I only understood the physical aspect of this at first. I did not realize that it was a spiritual and eternal transaction. I certainly had a lot to learn, and just like my very first lesson, I insisted on learning it all the hard way!

As we drove up the mountain pass toward our next little foray on the rock walls of Norway, I knew I had started a whole new adventure of my own. The sun shone hot and bright through the car window, and as I blinked back the tears that this sudden burst of solar power had brought, I knew in my depths, just like Saul knew in the blinding light on the way to Damascus, that I had met One who could not be denied. I had no idea where I was going and certainly no idea what it looked like to "be a Christian," but I knew that I belonged to Him, and the thought of leaving His side, or not going along with His will for my life, was as silly as denying He existed. What I did not expect were the demands made on my own personality and lifestyle, and so the lessons of the following years were often painful ones.

But then, what worthwhile thing ever came to fruition without times of trial and occasional, sometimes substantial pain? Much like coming down a mountain in the dark of night—cold, wet, and scared to death—but at least after that you know the joy of simply being alive!

Chapter 10

OVER THE TOP

▲

I t has been more than 20 years since I stepped off a mountain in Norway
and gained my life.

Trying to keep the flame of ambition in the mountains alight had
become an exhausting and tedious job. Battling the Almighty really did
become a thankless task; even for someone as determined and dogged as I
am! In the end I admitted defeat.

My last few routes from back then have become a blur. There was a
nondescript E1 down south in Devon, a bouldering problem in the Lake
District, and a random training climb in Colorado, USA, all of which were
not recorded—not in any record book, not in any diary, not even in my own
mind. I finally gave up on being called "a climber," and the great mountaineer died before he was really ever born.

Do I have any regrets? I would loved to have climbed the north wall
of the Matterhorn. It's a classic route, filled with tales of adventure, and it
occupies an almost legendary status in my mind. It is also so very beautiful;
the position and the views must be stunning. Norway's Troll Wall lurks in
my mind as the one that got away, but I wanted to climb that just to prove I
was not scared of it. Even today, my hands start to sweat as I read the route
description. Having looked up that wall from the bottom, having heard two

204 ▲ OVER THE TOP

rock falls in the space of a few minutes, and having examined the forbidding, almost insurmountable steepness of the upper sections viewed from the summit, it still scares me. I would have liked to have proven to myself that I could beat that troll. Another one I would like to have ticked off is the Cuillin Ridge on the Isle of Skye in the winter. By all accounts it's a classic expedition, and I have always loved Scotland. Further afield, to have gone above 25,000 feet on any hill, perhaps Kanchen Junga or maybe Nanga Parbat, the hill I saw in Pakistan, would have been a wonderful achievement. Such thoughts are little more than daydreams today, though I am pleased that my desire for adventure remains.

Perhaps it is worthy of note that I felt, and indeed on occasion still feel, a tinge of sadness when I recall a certain phone conversation with my in-laws from Colorado. I was newly married and living in England when they called and told me, with complete indifference, "Oh yeah, someone came and bought the rest of your climbing stuff today. We didn't realize it was worth so much."

I was indignant that they would doubt its "worth," and I was actually angry when they described one person declining to buy my Koflach Ultra ice-climbing boots for some silly, perfunctory reason—probably in search of an offer of a discount!

Do they realize where those boots have been? Climbing on three continents, great walls of ice . . . I ranted to myself for a while before bursting out laughing at my own pomposity. Still, it was clear that the nerve was yet raw.

The old rock boots I gave away still carried the bloodstains on them from when I was caught in the rock fall in Scandinavia. I had given away to my brother-in-law Tim the rope that had arrested my fall on the ice on Ben Nevis. He wanted it to cut into lengths so he could use it as a towrope when he was out four-wheeling in the mountains of Colorado. Had I still been "a climber," I am certain I would not be nearly as sentimental about my kit, and indeed, most days I am entirely unconcerned by such memorabilia. But all these old friends had been a huge part of my life, and my identity had been closely linked with all of them. It was hard to imagine my friend cut in to lengths and covered in engine oil.

Moreover, it was well over a decade before I actually spoke of my experience on the mountainside in Norway to a group of climbers. Anyone else was fine, but to go back into the fraternity and start to relive it all was just too much. There is still a part of me that wants to push the limits, driven by personal ambition and a screaming ego, to go higher and more remote than mind and body can bear, just "because it's there" as Mallory so famously put it. Thankfully, this drive has been harnessed to a large degree, but I can still, on occasion, feel the urge to break out of the harness and go do something reckless. That will always be a part of me, and I am actually pleased to have it—so long as it is never unleashed in polite company!

I am still a very "over the top" person; it is an intrinsic part of me. I enjoy the eccentricity, even the unbridled aspect of this character. Even now there are times when I need to check my exuberance, curb my opinions, and calm my drivenness. But I am no longer held prisoner by my ambitions, nor am I captive to dissatisfaction. I can, inconceivably to the man of twenty years ago, be as completely satisfied with a gentle stroll or a pleasant day fly-fishing as I could winning a mountain marathon or landing a black marlin.

One of the first tangible indicators to me that climbing had run its course in my life and that I was no longer enslaved to the next achievement, was when I went fishing in the South Park area of Colorado on the Platte River. I went with a friend and we stood up to our knees in the crystal clear waters, dabbling a fly into the gentle, gurgling flow as it snaked its way down toward the mountain town of Deckers and beyond. I looked across the high plateau and admired the array of 14,000-foot mountains around us. Their snow-capped peaks shone and sparkled against the brilliant blue Colorado sky, and the hot, burning high-altitude sun, even though it could burn the skin, was still unable to prevent the bite of the occasional gusts of wind sailing across the plain. It was at least a couple of hours before it hit me that I had absolutely no desire to go and climb any of those peaks. In fact, I was amazed that I had not already started to plan a trip to one of them, nor had I imagined myself on an ice wall on one of them either.

I laughed as I returned the four-inch trout I had just caught and went back about my day's fishing, perfectly content, still loving the mountains, but finally able to see them as more than merely another stepping-stone to the ever-elusive goal of "great mountaineer" or the even more nebulous, satisfaction of a goal realized. I had redefined satisfaction as "peace," and I now knew this came in the form of a Person and not an achievement.

There is, of course, absolutely nothing wrong with climbing, or with mountaineers in general. It was a personal issue that I never actually saw, and I was certainly never able to enjoy the beauty of the hills and the countryside to which I was so intimately linked as I pursued the next rock face or wall of ice. It was the drivenness that had to go. I had to recapture the inherent fondness I had for the countryside, long since replaced by the insatiable need to climb and conquer everything I laid my eyes on. There are doubtless multitudes of climbers unaffected by the malaise that gripped me. Likewise, there may be many as driven as I was who have never set foot on a crag. This was about me, not about climbing.

I have always loved hills and mountains, especially the rolling countryside and meandering rivers that had been a constant part of my growing up. I had first been bitten by the bug of fly-fishing as a boy of only ten or eleven, and I spent all of my leisure hours out with rod and fly line on the becks and rivers that proliferated in the quiet countryside I was so privileged to grow up in. This had me outdoors in all weathers, rod in hand, searching for yet another private pool or isolated spot where I could pursue my passion in peace and tranquillity.

One night, having grown impatient catching little brown trout and only occasionally landing one worth taking home for the pot, I decided to go to a nearby pool accompanied by a school friend in search of the fabled sea trout. These monsters of the sea, coming up into fresh water once a year to spawn, were renowned for their formidable fighting abilities. Tales abounded from the older fishermen I knew, tales of screaming reels and snapped lines, all in the dead of night, while the rest of the folk in the surrounding villages slept on, ignorant of the adventures unfolding on the quiet streams nearby. This seemed more like it: a bit of adventure to add to the proceedings!

We arrived at the pool a little after dark. As soon as we started to tackle up, our torch battery failed and left us fumbling in the blackness, unable to tie our flies onto our lines (what is it about me and torches?). A friendly householder from nearby gave us some nightlight candles and thereby saved our expedition from a premature demise. We were casting across the black pool within a few minutes. It was a beautiful place; the pool was deceptively deep for the beck that fed into it, and both sides of the stream were banked by steep, almost cliff-like sides. It was *my* lost valley, hardly visited by anyone. I fished there in delighted solitude on most occasions, the landowner's groundsman having granted me unofficial leave to visit, "so long as I didn't bring all my friends!" I had only brought one, and it was nighttime after all!

The candle offered only a flicker of light around the base of our tackle bags, and the rest of the bank and river were completely dark. Had I been by myself, it would have been altogether too eerie for a young boy to bear; I always disliked being near a river at night for the simple reason that the sound of the water masked any noise made by the approaching footfalls of an assailant! I have always viewed silence as a most welcome guard dog, especially while alone in the hills or forests.

We had fished the pool in the little beck for half an hour, and I was probably dreaming, as was my wont, of the monster that would miraculously surge up the stream, grab my bait, and thrash like a demon for an hour or more before finally succumbing to my masterful technique and dogged determination. Suddenly, my senses were assailed by quite the most spectacular jolt on my line that I had ever experienced. What happened next took no more than ten seconds, but it felt like a lifetime to a little boy who thought he had the white whale itself on the end of his line!

I felt the sting of adrenaline even before I felt the tug on my line, and all at once the water exploded into life with great heaving splashes, made even more dramatic by the echo from the gully walls of shale all around us.

I had no idea what to do at first as leviathan itself launched from out of the depths of our pool and wrenched repeatedly at my line!

My line! I was into a sea trout!

"You've got one!" my friend yelled out and dropped his rod, running over toward me as children are apt to do just to get a better look, or more likely, to better share in the thrill of it all.

But the line suddenly went slack, and the boiling water returned to an oily stillness as quickly as a kettle removed from the hob. He was off and away. I had lost him.

The cheap little rod I used that night has long since been thrown away, and I have not seen or spoken to that friend for over 20 years. The memory of that fish is vibrant in my heart, however, as is that pool of water—now merely a trickle in a vastly altered environment—but still a depth of expectant hope to my mind. It is true to say that that one event makes me a fly-fisherman today, and every time a sea trout grabs my lure in the dead of night, the thrill remains as powerful and the feeling of glee, puerile as it may be, remains as full and wonderful as the first time it happened.

As I began to grow away from climbing, I noticed that this thrill, this beautiful relationship with the outdoors, had very rarely happened while I was out on the crag or even when up an enormous mountain in the winter. I had stopped looking around, and I hardly ever simply drank in the stunning vistas around me. Even in Pakistan, as I passed both the Trango Towers and even Nanga Parbat, all I saw was something else to conquer and add to my CV. In fact, I disliked seeing the bigger peaks because I knew I was not good enough to climb them! This rather sad lesson took a long time to learn, and it only made sense after I went fishing on the Platte River, but it probably only sunk in properly a few years after that.

Again I was on a river, but this time I held a salmon rod in my hand, and I was pursuing the king of game fish on a blustery September morning. I was on my local river, the Lune, where an old friend had invited me as a guest on his private beat. Despite one or two gusting blasts from the east, it was a clear day, and the occasional showers only gave us another opportunity to have another sip from our hot flasks and change our fly to a more lethal looking salmon deceiver.

As I cast the fly across the river with a powerful stroke of the 15-foot fly rod, I took great satisfaction in watching the line stretch out smoothly and gracefully through the air before coming to land in a wonderfully straight line onto the surface of the glassy water. I looked further up the Lune Valley, past the woodland and toward the tabletop hill of Ingleborough in the distance. It is a mere 2,400 feet above sea level, yet imposing in its own right. It is easily recognizable to any local, as if it were Kilimanjaro itself. Perhaps a little too grandiose a comparison, but a beautiful sight nonetheless.

I knew that past the hill were the limestone crags of Twistleton, clearly envisaged in my mind's eye. A March day almost 20 years earlier came to my memory. It was my first experience of the terrible pains of "hot aches" as we climbed a tough route for a beginner in the cold winds of early spring. I had not enjoyed that route, but I knew then that it was good training for future expeditions.

I was glad not to be there on that day; there was no peace on that crag. There was nothing but peace by the side of this river. There was the promise of future fame and glory by overcoming the technical difficulties and cold on that route. I could not have cared less about fame, glory, or who even knew I existed as I cast the fly again, this time messing it up, as a gust of wind tied the fly leader into a knot and forced me to put down the rod and walk over to the tip of the line lying on the grass. It just did not matter. As I patiently untied the knot, I watched a pair of kingfishers flying purposefully upstream, their unmistakeable style of rapid wing beats as they almost skimmed the surface was nearly as distinctive as the electric blue and orange of their plumage. As they passed by, I followed them with my gaze, and the tell-tale blue diamond on their backs emerged, the sun glossing up the picture as it appeared from behind a grey cloud formation—as if to try to impress me even more.

I was immersed in a beauty that few people are able to share, and I knew I was indeed very blessed. The autumnal shades in the forest on the bank opposite were just starting to show, and the emerald of the grass complemented the darker greens of oak leaves and the hues of grey and brown that were beginning to emerge among the tree canopy. It was glorious, and as I recommenced fishing, I did not even mind when the fly line suddenly held still in the water instead of being dragged further downstream by the current, indicating a snag under the water. It was probably a rock or tree root.

Half-heartedly I tugged on the line and was still enjoying the brief arrival of some autumnal sun as I considered moving downstream to try to release the snag by tugging at the line downstream from the snag. I gave one last strong pull from where I was standing in the hope it would release and let me re-cast the fly.

Tap, tap, tap, tap; the noise and the feeling on my thumb were unmistakable but did not register in my mind for at least a couple of seconds. I looked down as I felt the strong, steady pull on my rod and line, and then, for only a flash, the sight of a silver side and a great paddle tail as it plunged deeper into the river's depths. I looked down at my thumb and saw the reel handle spinning round, catching my thumb with each revolution, and then *the scream* made it all make sense!

That unmistakeable, marvellous scream of the reel, that beautifully melodious metallic whine, as yard after yard of line was stripped away from the spool, dragged into the heart of the river by an incredible power of muscular sides fanning a great square-edged paddle of a tail.

I had hooked my first salmon, and my heart pounded as if I was leading my first frozen waterfall!

Unlike a trout, which thrashes and leaps out of the water like a spinning top, the salmon dives deep into the river, and then it shakes its head from side to side in a determined effort to rid itself of the unwelcome metal in its mouth, drawing it upwards and out of its very world. Each dogged shake puts enormous strain on the line and especially the knots, and the power generated by these magnificent creatures is quite extraordinary when felt on the rod and line. It brings a respect for the quarry and a love of the countryside that simply cannot be achieved from reading a book—and certainly not from buying a side of pink flesh from an ice slab in the supermarket.

Some fifteen minutes later I had my first cock salmon lying on the grass, still in the landing net. I shook hands with my friend Fred, and we talked for a while of the fight this fellow had given and the wonderful feel to the whole day. Each time I took a salmon steak from the freezer in the weeks following, I re-lived every moment of those fifteen minutes. In fact, I would re-live the entire day, since catching the salmon was only the icing on a beautiful cake.

Fred caught four salmon that day. He returned all but one of them. Had I been the same man as the obsessive mountaineer of 20 years earlier, my friend's success would have ruined my whole day. I would have tried to be happy for him, but all the while, all I would have felt was a sense of failure because I had only caught one fish to his four. The fact he had been fishing for 50 years would have been irrelevant! I would not have seen the river, the kingfishers, or the hills around me, unless they pertained directly to my "goal" of catching a salmon—a big salmon, a salmon bigger than anyone else's that day!

How I have enjoyed breaking free from that trap! How wonderful it was, and is, to enjoy a day's fishing for all it entails. Any fly fisherman will tell you that fly fishing is not about catching fish. If you want to catch fish, go buy a boat and a big net, or perhaps some dynamite. If you want to enjoy fishing in stunning surroundings, and if you want to learn patience and tranquillity by the side of a river, buy a fly rod!

I do not know if climbing to a high standard actually *requires* such a driven mind-set as I had, but I do know that such an approach to life can be terribly destructive, and its effects go far beyond a rock face or snow gully. There was a darkness and an obsession with self in that man who saw mountaineering as his *raison d'être*, and I would have been robbed of so much if I had not been persuaded, on that cliff edge, to let him die and allow the person I was designed to be start to live. Certainly I could not have enjoyed my days on the river if I was the man I used to be.

In all the countries in which I climbed, and on all the routes I romped, struggled, gasped, or laughed my way up, there were probably only a handful of occasions when I felt truly settled and satisfied with life. The night I bivouacked high above the snowline in Pakistan was wonderful. Staring at the Romsdalhorn as it disappeared into the darkness after sunset, accompanied by Andy, was a special view and a wonderful moment of reflection, even though my thumb was still throbbing from our earlier adventure! Perhaps once or twice after a route in the Lake District I felt a sense of well-being, but it evaporated as soon as I looked at all the harder routes I had yet to climb on the same crag. I was, however, perfectly peaceful the moment I stepped off The Climb, and that is clearly paradoxical, to say the least!

So, what deal was done that night, high on that crag in Norway? I was frequently perplexed and never felt at ease in describing, or even considering in my mind, that I had made a deal with God. It simply did not fit with the events or with the after effects. The notion that I could offer any deal, of "my life for His" as it were, is silly. How completely ludicrous is the notion that I could offer the King of all creation anything at all, especially anything from my own physical frailty!

That He saved me physically is almost secondary to this story. He revealed himself as being able to move the world, an all-powerful God, but He was also, incredibly, willing to do this for a single individual, a self-obsessed, arrogant egomaniac at that, who refused to acknowledge Him. This was a God of infinite love, of ceaseless patience, and the only Author of amazing grace.

My problem arose from a selfish ambition that could never fulfil the plan God had for my life. In addition, it would almost certainly have rendered me dead on a mountain somewhere before the age of thirty-five. Indeed, that was my intention. As I look back (way back!), I am truly thankful to be off that particular train. The fact is that God brought me to the end of all my strengths and abilities to the place of absolutely knowing I could not help myself, and He offered me the choice of allowing Him to save me or carry on dying, my way. I believed my identity could be found on the next mountain summit; in fact, it was found by stepping off the edge.

I knew as I stepped off that mountain, deep down in my heart, that I had met this God, and whether I lived or died, that *demanded* my obedience. He had revealed that He was who He claimed to be, and He was worthy of my life, whether I lived for another sixty years or for less than sixty seconds. This realization of what I had really done with God only struck home years later, and it transformed my life.

I did not put on Christ to get me out of a crisis or to have a better life or to be all that I could be. I gave myself to Jesus because He deserves me; because He bled and died on the cross for me and paid for my life with His. He is an all-powerful God who loves every individual with an amazing passion. I want to scream and shout that wherever I go! I knew back on that cold, wet desperate night that I was without hope, and I offered the rest of my life to Him if He showed me that He was all the Bible claimed He was. Once I arrived at the point of stepping out from the rock, I already knew He had proven himself, so I stepped off without a thought about living or dying. That was irrelevant; I was no longer my own, so He could do as He wished with me.

Knowing the truth, I tried to live in the lie that I could still do as I pleased despite having relinquished the rights to myself. Small wonder I was miserable! But He would not be cheated of His reward. He loved me too much to let me destroy myself and my potential by satisfying my own selfish desires. So for the next few years, as I struggled against what I knew to be true, He never gave up on me and kept drawing me back to himself. The tale of the prodigal son in Luke's gospel strikes a note deep in my heart whenever I read it!

Now as I tread carefully through a bluebell wood in the late spring, the heady perfume of the flowers pouring through my senses and distracting me from my job for a few moments, I can sit down and wander off into my memories as the stillness of the pre-dawn keeps at bay any other interruption to my reminiscences. I am thankful that my mind has been able to store away for future recollection so many of the events and feelings that I totally ignored in my drive of self-obsession. I thank God that He brought them all back to me, even though I missed them the first time around: the smell of the campfires in the mountains of Pakistan; the feel of the hollow granite on the Romsdalhorn; the sight of the unknown, beautiful young woman barely holding back with the bridle a stunning chestnut mare as it pranced full of nervous energy and raw power down a grass lane in Norway. Then, at the slightest squeeze of her legs, it exploded into a breathtaking gallop straight past us and on to the pine forest some three hundred yards away. Doubtless she was trying to impress us: she succeeded.

Countless routes, myriad experiences, phenomenal scenes. These are in my storehouse of memories all available for me to enjoy while sitting on the woodland floor waiting for the weather to change or for the sun to rise, or simply having a rest. The revelation of His presence has let me tap into this wealth of life experience and has helped to round and deepen my character; yet, had He not intervened, I may never have been able to fully enjoy these life-enriching episodes. Standing in a wood, rifle slung over my shoulder, dog at heel, I can drink in the beauty all around me and add it to all the stunning places it has been my great privilege to have seen.

Have I undergone a personality change? Has God forced me to change who I am, to capitulate my true identity and stop being the person I was? Quite the reverse: my personality, my true character was actually stifled for years by my obsessive desire to find my identity in my pursuits. I tried to find who I was in what I did, and all the while I found myself increasingly constrained and unable to be free. The more I attempted to be a climber, the less I was free to be me. It was in complete contrast to the dancing woman in the church service I attended; she did not care who looked at her as she expressed what was in her heart, her true self. I, in contrast, stifled my true self in a vain effort to become the person I clearly was not. God showed me who I really was and enabled me to enjoy that person. It was an unexpected and enormous relief to allow myself to be me!

I have always been a passionate person, and as a climber this was a fuel for the next ambitious project. Now, however, the object of my passion, rather than the gratification of my own ego and the advancing of self, is the glorifying of God and the lifting up of who He is and what He has done. Rather than living life for myself, I intend to live it for the only One who really deserves recognition. I can best explain what I want to be with a story I heard only recently.

It is the true story of two young Moravians who lived over two hundred years ago. They heard of a British plantation owner in the West Indies who kept three thousand slaves on an island to work in his fields. The owner was an atheist, determined to have nothing to do with religion and dismissing it as utter nonsense. So formidable was his hatred of Christianity that he forbade anyone to come to the island to preach. Even if a minister was to be shipwrecked there, he swore to keep them separate from his slaves on a different part of the island until a rescue ship arrived to take him away.

Having heard of this place and of the slaves condemned to a life of servitude without ever hearing of the gospel of salvation, the two young men decided that they would take the message out there themselves. However, they were also aware that there was only one way to accomplish this, so they sold themselves to the plantation owner. They became his property so they could minister to the other slaves. They even used the money gained from their sale to pay for their own passage to the island, since the owner would not pay for the tickets himself!

As these two young men, probably in their early twenties, boarded the ship in Hamburg bound for the West Indies never to return, their families and friends lined the dock, embracing their boys and weeping as they said farewell. This was no four-year "mission trip." It would be for their entire lives. They would never see their families again. They faced a life of unspeakable hardship and probable persecution, completely at odds with the life of promise and ease they would have enjoyed had they remained at home.

The ship weighed anchor, the ropes were unfastened from the pier, and these young men waved to their loved ones for the last time. As the ship moved further from the port the two men linked arms and with one hand raised in farewell they let out a cry, the last words heard from the bank. It was a cry that became the banner of the Moravian missionaries, and when I first heard it I wept as I understood it is the cry of my own heart as well:

"May the Lamb that was slain receive the reward of His suffering!"

No thought for themselves, no self-pity, no despair, no desire for praise, no personal ambition, nothing except that Jesus be glorified for the price He paid for all mankind. This rang in my heart with a resonance that I have never known before, and I suddenly knew in words what I had felt in my heart for years. This is why I was made, and this is my real goal in life. Everything else is vacuous nonsense in comparison; it is the only thing worth being driven about.

I have been lost in my thoughts of this adventure many times, often when sitting in a high seat overlooking a wood or crouching by the side of a bracken bed waiting to see what would come toward me through the forest. Now, as I stand up slowly and deliberately from the woodland floor, careful not to disturb any wildlife and constantly looking for the telltale flick of an ear behind the bracken shoots that would betray the couching Roebuck I was pursuing, I begin to weave my way through the bluebell carpet. Occasionally I step on the lush broad green leaves of the plant, and the crunch they make underfoot, even though revealing my presence, is nevertheless a beautiful sound: a thick, satisfying gravelly chomp, juicy and full like a horse crunching into a fresh carrot.

I smile as I hear the result of the bluebell's betrayal of me: a young buck sets off at the gallop, his gruff barking alerting all in the woods that the hunter is here again, and his intentions are not honourable. Time to head back to the car. The dog looks up wistfully, knowing he will not be called upon to follow the trail any more today.

"What are you looking at?" I smile and rub his chin. It's good to be here. I am thankful for a life truly blessed, for the freedom I enjoy compared to the life of those two Moravians, and for the fact that I was arrested all those years ago by the only One who brings true freedom.

As I look back 20-plus years to the moment I met God, I can see that, in all probability, someone *did* fall down that mountain to his death. It was the old me; the one who would have carried on growing had he not met God and somehow survived that night. The only outcome, however, would have been that an even more driven, morose, and dissatisfied young man would have died on a nondescript hill somewhere else, having wasted most of the rest of his life. Distracted by the fool's gold of ambition and false fulfilment for the part of life that he had experienced, he would have undoubtedly been found, or not, as cold as ice while his soul was beginning eternity in the heat of hell.

Today God uses the man He formed, complete with my own personality, in order to bring glory to His great name. I do not put on Jesus to save my life, nor to make life good, nor even to save me from hell. I put on Jesus, or rather I am identified with Christ, that He may be glorified through me, because He is worthy, even if I do not gain anything at all at the end of it. I am His because He deserves me, not because I deserve Him. I am one of His medals of honour that He won on the cross and so richly deserves, for a valour that we cannot possibly comprehend.

My life is now to serve Him, and it has so far been as exciting and thrilling a ride as I could ever imagine. I see no point in pursuing the things of the world when this is only a brief stopping off point on the way to eternity. How I live now defines how I will live with Him then. I am now driven, not by the whip, but by love, to this end alone: to live a life in pursuit of holiness, completely abandoned to the One who set me free, so that the Lamb who was slain receives the reward of His suffering. And in His strength I will go wherever He leads in order to satisfy that calling.

That is what I want—to be completely abandoned to that end. This excites me beyond all measure, and I intend to pursue it with vigour for the rest of my life. I want never to be satisfied, always at peace and full of joy; perfectly fulfilled yet never sated! This is the marvellous paradox of the Christian life. It is the recipe for true adventure. To be a Christian, a real Christian, is to be completely over the top, at least in the eyes of the world. The Bible puts it simply: "For the word of the cross is foolishness to those who are perishing, but to us who are being saved it is the power of God" (1 Corinthians 1:18).

Are you on the real adventure?

EPILOGUE

Just in case you were wondering, the sound it makes is, *Ping* (brief pause), *ping, thud*. The pings are preceded and followed by an odd fizzing hiss and the thud is deep, resonant, and has the air of a crunch to it. The fizzing hiss is the noise of the rope sliding through the karabiner as it tightens under the load of a falling climber, and yes, the pings are the sounds of gear ripping out of the rock.

The thud was the sound of me hitting the floor, or "decking out" as we like to call it. Just in case you were wondering.

It was only twenty-something feet, and the rope did tighten a little before the gear ripped, so the impact was not quite from a free fall. I did land feet together and then bounced into a crumpled heap on the next ledge down, a few feet away. Only after doing a mental body check and concluding that I was indeed alive and relatively unharmed did I notice the boulder less than a foot to the side of my head. I had avoided head-butting it by a matter of inches, and only now did I realize I was not wearing my helmet. It was safely stowed in my rucksack, no more than a few yards away at the foot of the crag. That could have been nasty.

Chris asked if I was all right. I shrugged off the incident and went back up the route, but Chris insisted on leading it, and even he avoided the crux move. We had been climbing for quite a while, and this route was a bit of a swine: small holds, a delicate move, and it was already late in the day. I followed up and then winced gingerly back down the side of the crag. Things were already stiffening up at the end of my legs.

I would love to say that this incident happened in my exuberant youth when my zeal exceeded my abilities. However, my first experience of decking out came just a couple of years ago when, it seems, my zeal still exceeded my abilities! At least I was on *extreme rock*, if only just, and I comforted myself with that fact (and made sure I let everyone else know that fact) for months afterwards.

So, I am back into climbing. How did that happen, after God went to such lengths to get me out of it? In a very matter-of-fact sort of way, actually. I had become the pastor of a small church in the Lake District, something I would never have envisaged even on the remotest edges of the radar screen of my life (my wife's phrase rings loudly in my ears: "Russell, you are not a pastor, and I am most certainly NOT a pastor's wife!" Amen, sister!).

However, having convinced us both by many and varied ways, God finally landed us miraculously in a little house in the woods with a small faithful body of believers and a whole National Park to look upon as our mission field! I was enjoying just being there when I became reacquainted with someone I had met years before at an evening "do" where I had shared my story for perhaps the first time with a bunch of mountaineers. I had found it quite nerve-wracking, but they had been very gracious.

The two of us soon became friends, and I began to realize that his job as an international Mountain Guide meant he was a *serious* mountaineer, the kind of guy I would have previously been scared to death of and simultaneously both resentful of and worshipful toward. He had heard my story, so he asked me if I wanted to go climbing one day.

I went. It was great. I have never looked back. I have been out on the crags, on the indoor walls, and on the frozen waterfalls and snow gullies that have abounded in the Lakes these past few winters. I have bought new gear and been given a whole lot more. In short, I am back in the world of outdoor pursuits.

Does God approve? Like I have already said, He made me the way I am, so He wants me to live my life for Him using the personality He has given me. What I had to learn was that this personality could never run my life nor could I use my own ambitions and abilities for my own selfish ends. Once that was learned and the "bug" no longer gripped me, I was free to express myself in the mountains again. The beautiful thing is that God is such a redeeming God: I am climbing now almost as hard as I ever have, and my technique is certainly better than it has ever been before (Chris has seen to that!) I go out on the hills and enjoy the whole day. The drive to conquer the next harder route has gone. I still enjoy pushing myself, but the whip across my shoulders no longer exists. I simply enjoy the personal challenges that come about quite naturally with my personality.

Am I still over-exuberant and a bit over the top sometimes? Do I still go beyond what I ought, or what is "the norm" (whatever that is)? Going back to my stiffening feet, I went home and rested for a day. The swelling was not too inflationary, and I decided on not attending the emergency room. Ten days later I was to complete my assessment to become a Mountain Leader (whereby, if I passed I would be qualified to take groups mountain walking anywhere in the UK). This involved 5 days of mountaineering, including crossing rivers, going up and down quite a few thousand feet of ascent as well as steep ground work and various rope techniques. The following week I was being assessed on technical climbing, and if I passed that I would be qualified to teach rock climbing, at least on a small scale. This involved two days of pretty intensive technical rock work. I completed and passed both assessments. My feet hurt all the time, so much so that I was having to elevate my feet each evening and spend most of each day with gritted teeth. Three weeks later, I noticed a hard lump on the side of one foot. I decided to go along to see a doctor.

I was sent on for an x-ray. Torn ligaments were confirmed by the doctor. Broken feet were confirmed by the x-ray. Apparently, a fall of that distance usually results in multiple fracture of the ankles, so when I complained to my physiotherapist about the length of time my recovery was taking, he gave me a cutting glance and informed me that had I gone to the hospital the day after my fall, I would have still been in a plaster cast. I stopped complaining.

My point is not to boast about any heroism of mine. It is simply to say that the overzealous personality that was so close to destroying me in my earlier days, once harnessed, is still very much who I am. Even though it is not great to lob off a rock route nor to wince my way over the mountains with broken feet, doggedly refusing to give in, I *love* that God made me this way. I *love* that He uses this personality in all aspects of my ministry for Him, and I *love* most of all that He smiles when He sees me going over the top again and again. I find it almost impossible to stop charging forward at the sound of the whistle, be it leading a group beyond where *they think* they can go, pushing my own body when my feet are cracked, preaching a very challenging message to people who are already scowling at me, or simply being available to go anywhere and drop anything at His behest, irrespective of the consequences. I think He enjoys tugging gently on the bridle, whispering, "Easy, Tiger" every time I begin to get carried away with a thought or plan. Making myself His bond slave has made me a freer man than I ever thought possible.

In addition to all this, from a very practical point of view, my climbing has opened all kinds of doors for ministry. One of the funniest was when, as a church, we had been praying how to reach the young people in the villages near us. I had addressed them in the local high school on a number of occasions in their morning assemblies (as a visiting minister). They are very anti-Christian and have no time for "religion." They would point at me in the street afterwards sneering and joking, being sure to let me hear their profanity and blasphemy. A little later, however, as I was training at the local climbing wall, who should walk in but a bunch of the older lads, accompanied by a teacher. In God's perfect timing they looked up and saw me completing a route on an overhanging section, and I could immediately see from the look in their eyes two things: they knew who I was, and I was climbing harder than any of them could even dream of! Suddenly, I had a whole new set of friends. They wave across the street to me now and we share a smile and a hello. One day, God willing, I will be sharing much more meaningful conversations with them.

God sent His Son so that we can all have the chance for salvation. I can bring this message in the manner that best suits my God-given character, both from a pulpit, and while on a rock face, on a mountainside, or in the woodland. He truly satisfies our deepest desires if we abandon all to Him. So let me leave you with this challenge: get on with it, and step off *your* cliff. Nothing else will satisfy. Nothing.

GLOSSARY OF BRITISH EXPRESSIONS

bank holiday: a national holiday in the United Kingdom.

beat: a section of a river allocated to a specific person or specific angling club. The rights for the fishing on many rivers are allocated according to "beats."

beck: a small brook or creek.

biro: a ballpoint pen, named for Laszlo Biro, a Hungarian newspaper editor, who patented the first ballpoint pen in 1938.

"Bloody" and "Bloody Nora": mild British expressions that denote surprise, contempt, or outrage.

boot: trunk of a car.

bonnet: hood of a car.

Capstan Full Strength: a brand of filterless, very strong cigarettes. Smoked by old, salty sea dogs and Irish road diggers.

Caravan: small travel trailer.

Chinese takeaway: Chinese take-out food.

Chris Bonington: British mountaineer and Jim Henson look-alike. Climbed Mount Everest.

CIC hut: Scottish mountaineering hut. Named for Charles Ingis Clark, a soldier who was killed in action during World War I.

gap year: the year between the end of secondary school and the beginning of university training. It is common for British students to take this year off between the two schooling situations.

guarana: a berry-based drink from South America that has an effect similar to a caffeine drink.

hob: shelf or projection on a fireplace meant to keep food warm.

jibbering: very afraid.

John Smith and Joshua Tetley: British beers.

Kohinoor diamond: a 186 1/16 carat diamond that is set in the crown of Queen Elizabeth. Its value may surpass a billion dollars.

knackered: exhausted. Stock animals are sent to the knacker's yard (or slaughterhouse) when they are too old to work or bear offspring.

Mallory: George Mallory, British climber who said he wanted to climb Mt. Everest "because it's there." He died after possibly reaching the summit in 1924.

National Trust: British equivalent of the US National Park Service.

petrol: gasoline.

poxy: stupid or dumb.

press-ups: the exercise Americans call push-ups.

physiotherapist: British term for physical therapist.

Silk Cut: a very mild, low-tar brand of cigarette.

Shandy: a drink made of half British lemonade and half English "bitter" beer. Low alcohol content.

sledging: sledding in snow.

student grant: an old system whereby those from low-income families got government aid to attend university. At one time, it paid for all tuition and most living expenses. Vacation jobs were needed to make up any shortfall. Some students spent their entire grant in the first few weeks.

RAC: Insurance in the United Kingdom for car repairs. RAC stands for the Royal Automobile Club. Now called RAC Limited.

Telephone box: British term for telephone booth.

GLOSSARY OF CLIMBING TERMS

abseiling: a German term, commonly used in the UK for the process of descending a rope using a descending device. Also known as rappelling, which comes from the French.

anchor point: the place to which one anchors the rope, or person. Usually with "gear" like camming devices or metal wedges (known as "runners," short for running belays). These runners come in many forms, according to manufacturers' individual names, but they have names like, Hexes, nuts, wires, friends, chocks (old), and rocks.

ascent: going up the crag or mountain.

au cheval: French term. Literally "in the style of a horse." Straddling the rock, one leg on each side, like you are riding a horse. It's effective but not impressive to look at.

bandolier: a strap that goes over the shoulder and under the opposite arm pit, to which you clip all your protective gear. A climber takes off piece by piece to place it in the rock as he ascends. It means there is less weight attached to the harness (the other place on which to clip your gear). This is the best way to carry gear, especially on winter routes—though many use it for rock climbing as well.

belay: the point at which you anchor yourself to the rock or ice and then bring up your second. A running belay is the point where you place protection on your way up to the belay point. This is used in multipitch climbs.

bivvy gear: Equipment used to make a temporary shelter, or bivouac. It usually consists of a waterproof cover, which will contain the mat, sleeping bag, and if possible a rucksack at the open end. Bivvy gear may also include a stove and food, though usually it only refers to the stuff needed to get a warm, dry night's sleep.

bouldering: rock climbing on short, usually technically challenging places, typically a large rock, and where ropes are not needed. It is gymnastic training involving solving climbing puzzles, and it usually involves very little if any risk of injury since height is not the purpose of the exercise. It has become a sport of its own in the last 20-plus years.

climbing harness: the thing that goes around your waist and is then tied to the ropes you use. It has a waist belt and loops for your legs. There are also loops on which to clip your gear should you prefer that method to using a bandolier.

cowbell: a very large piece of gear, usually hexagonal or thereabouts in section, used to wedge into large cracks. When positioned properly, its size makes it an excellent anchor. Named because it resembles the bells put around cows' necks in the Swiss Alps areas.

crag: a rock face on a mountain side.

crampons: metal spikes attached to your winter boots for walking and climbing up ice and snow. Technical crampons also have two front points on each crampon so vertical ice walls can be climbed by sticking these points into the ice or snow. The boots made to accommodate these must be absolutely rigid to enable such progress.

crevasse: a big crack in a glacier, often forming a cavernous hole. These must be circumnavigated or crossed very carefully to avoid falling in. Once in one, the fallen climber is in huge trouble, with plunging temperatures, steep falls, and no easy way out.

crux: the hardest point on a climb.

descendeur: a device used to go down a rope in abseiling fashion. Used to be a figure of eight descender; now other devices are used. These double as belay plates and descendeurs combined, thereby reducing the overall weight and bulk of the kit.

Eve and Adam: names of two classic routes adjacent to each other on Shepherd's Crag, Borrowdale, Lake District. Though graded the same (VS 4c) Adam is more strenuous than Eve and requires some bolder climbing.

glissade: sliding down a snow slope. Either standing or seated.

Gore-Tex bivvy bags: covers for you and your sleeping bag made from Gore-Tex (breathable) material. This means you have a very light, very small shelter available as simply a cover to sleep in, and your sweat will be wicked away by the Gore-Tex fabric.

gripped: terrified!

guidebook: books containing detailed route descriptions of all the routes in a particular area, showing how to access the crag, where exactly the routes are, and the grade of each one.

holds, handholds: places to place feet and hands. These are either small edges, cracks, ripples on the rock, or almost imaginary smears of "grippiness" on the rock!

hot aches: the pain that comes on your fingers and sometimes toes when blood begins to course through your frozen digits again. The pain really is quite spectacular, and this occurs usually several times on a decent ice climb. I have since learned that having a large stock of gloves in one's pack is essential to reduce this drama. Not to wear them all at once, but to change them when they become too wet ("waterproof" gloves simply are not, forever! They ALL leak eventually). One climber grades the difficulty of his winter days on a "number of pairs of gloves" scale: one pair in the day is a doddle, up to a four pairs day (the maximum he carries, as do I) is a real epic that ended with quite a degree of discomfort!

ice axe: also called simply an "axe," it is a metal pick used to climb steep ice and snow. On technical routes two are used, one in each hand, and these pick their way up the route, replacing using hands to find holds.

In the old days climbers used one axe to cut a hole in the ice to then insert their hand and climb. Today two axes are used and these simply stick into the ice and snow, and along with the front points of the crampons, enable progress up the wall.

ice-climbing boots: winter boots that are very stiff and thermally insulated.

ice screws: gear used to literally screw into ice walls or very solid snow. They have an eye at one end that is used to clip in a karabiner, which in turn has the rope clipped into it. It is used as a running belay device or as an anchor for the person belaying his second. In some instances it is used as an anchor for an abseil rope but this is recommended for emergencies only.

jug hold: a big hold on a rock—a hold that a climber can get his whole hand around or into. If the route is full of jugs, it is a relatively easy one.

karabiner (sometimes spelled *caribiner*): a trapezium-shaped metal device with the smaller of the parallel sides having a gate opening. Used to clip the rope for running belays and for all kinds of anchoring needs. The staple piece of kit. Most climbers have at the very least twenty of these in different shapes and sizes.

    straight gate: a karabiner with the opening parallel side being straight. This is the standard shape.

    bent gate: the opening side is curved, making it easier to slide the rope into, and this is useful when you are leading a climb, getting tired, and want to clip the rope in fast.

    screw-locking gate: there is a separate piece on the closing gate that has a screw thread, and this is tightened over the gate once it is closed so that it cannot open unless it is deliberately unscrewed. This is useful for making belays, and it is a safety device used especially when attaching the karabiner to devices like belay plates and descending devices. It would be rather unpleasant if a climber were belaying someone and accidentally removed the belay device from the harness!

kit: all the stuff you use for climbing, from rope and harness to helmet, goggles, ice axes and camming devices. And torches.

lead climber: the guy who goes first, taking all the risk. The one "who doesn't fall" (see chapter 1).

loop a sling: used as a verb, "looping a sling" over a spike of rock, for instance, means simply throwing a sling (which is a loop of varying sizes) over a piece of rock and then clipping a karabiner into it and then the rope, in turn, into the karabiner. It is used to form a belay.

overhang: rock or ice that is more than vertical.

pitch: a section of a climb between belay points. If the whole of a route cannot be completed in one go (if there are obstacles that would impede smooth running of the rope, if there was a significant change in direction, or if the route was simply too long to be done on one rope length), then it is split into multiple pitches.

plastic boots: winter boots not made of leather, so they do not freeze. Not sure it is actually plastic, but that's what they're called. Very stiff to walk in and quite uncomfortable, but superb on steep ice and snow.

rock boots: technical boots for steep rock climbing. Rubber soles grip the rock well. Boots are meant to be very tight fitting so you can feel the rock on your feet and so your feet do not move at all inside them. It's like some kind of sadist made up that idea, though, as they hurt after a day climbing. The relief taking them off is almost euphoric!

rope: 9m, 11m: An 11mm rope could be used as a single rope, because it is so strong. The 9mm is used together with another 9mm and is useful especially if the routes are not straight; a single rope would snake up the rock and cause the rope to drag, thereby pulling at the lead climber. Two 9mm could be clipped in a way so that both run pretty straight even if the route meanders. It also means that both climbers would carry a lighter (9mm) rope each, rather than one of them having to carry a huge 11mm up to the crag. It avoids any arguments to use two!

rucksack: a backpack.

runners: running belays. A piece of metal, or a camming device, or a sling over a rock spike, into which the rope is clipped by the lead climber with a karabiner (also called a krab). This would then arrest a fall should the climber come off (he would only fall the same distance beneath the runner as he had ascended past it; therefore, he would just swing in the air rather than hitting the floor). He might bounce on the way, though, so it was not a completely desirable occurrence!

salopettes: basically, bib and brace overalls, usually with thermal properties. They covered the legs and go up the base of the back and up the chest at the front.

scree: a steep slope at the bottom of a mountain or crag comprised of loose rock ranging in size from pebbles to boulders.

"slack" and "tight": climbing commands. Slack means "give up some rope." Tight means "take in rope" (usually because things are getting tough and you don't want to fall very far).

squash shoes: just as it sounds—shoes for playing squash in. Worn by climbers who cannot afford to buy proper rock boots!

stichplate: a belay device used to pay out rope to a climber from the second. It will lock if put under a load (for instance, if the leader falls off).

top-roping: climbing a route by having the rope go through an anchor at the top of the route then back down to you at the bottom. The climber then always has rope above him for full protection—as if he were climbing second.

torch: flashlight.

Trangia stoves: brand name of a famous stove system. It is powered by methylated spirits.

traverse: going across the rock face/wall as opposed to an ascent or descent.

trekking route: a walking route as opposed to a climbing route.

walk-ins: the walk toward the climb itself. Sometimes a little hike is involved in getting to the desired climbing spot. Sometimes it's a long hike!

wedge (or wire): pieces of protection for slipping into cracks in the rock while lead climbing. These come in myriad shapes and brands.

PAKISTAN

★ Islamabad
◫ Magnified Region
▲ Climbing Locations
A Rawalpindi
B Gilgit
C Nanga Parbat
D Skardu
E Trango Towers
F Gondokoro Glacier
G Gondoro Peak

CHINA

AFGHANISTAN

Indus River

PAKISTAN

IRAN

INDIA

Arabian Sea

N
W E
S

PAKISTAN

CHINA

B

E
F
G

C

D

AFGHANISTAN

Indus River

★
A

INDIA

NORWAY

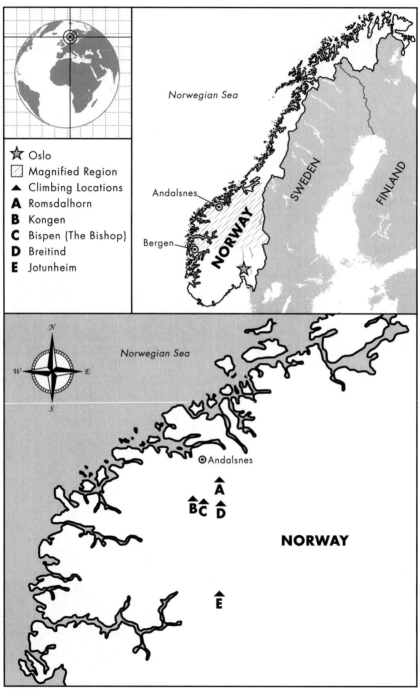

Oslo
Magnified Region
Climbing Locations
A Romsdalhorn
B Kongen
C Bispen (The Bishop)
D Breitind
E Jotunheim

Norwegian Sea

Andalsnes

Bergen

NORWAY

SWEDEN

FINLAND

N
W   E
S

Norwegian Sea

⊙ Andalsnes

A
B C D

NORWAY

E

═ UNITED KINGDOM ═

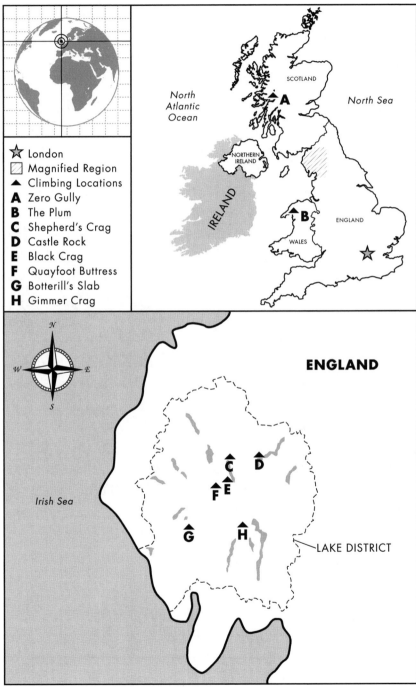

London

Magnified Region

▲ Climbing Locations

A Zero Gully
B The Plum
C Shepherd's Crag
D Castle Rock
E Black Crag
F Quayfoot Buttress
G Botterill's Slab
H Gimmer Crag

North Atlantic Ocean

SCOTLAND

North Sea

NORTHERN IRELAND

IRELAND

WALES

ENGLAND

N
W   E
S

Irish Sea

ENGLAND

LAKE DISTRICT

ACKNOWLEDGMENTS

When I first felt the urge and the prompting to write my story, several key people encouraged me. Pivotal among these was Lissa Smith, who diligently proofread my first efforts, correcting me and always encouraging me to keep pursuing the goal. I am so grateful to her and to Jeremy, her husband, for spurring me on with kind affirmation and real, rare friendship.

Along with them are Mike Derry, and Rob and Jane Guinney, all of whom offered solid criticism, never massaging my frail ego but never crushing it either; they got the balance right, and I am very thankful for them.

For the staff at Discovery House Publishers, especially Dave Branon, who made the editorial process not only bearable but great fun. They were all very gracious with this first-time author.

Finally, to my wife, Debbi, who knows more about me than even I do, and loves me all the same: Thank you for everything. You have stuck with me, put up with me, offered the tough advice and the difficult counsel; you have watched and waited as I skulked, sulked, ranted, and despaired my way through the trials of life that coincided with the time of writing this book. And at the end of it all you are still here: steadfast, patient . . . and mine. I thank God for you, all the time.

NOTE TO THE READER

The publisher invites you to share your response to the message of this book by writing Discovery House Publishers, P.O. Box 3566, Grand Rapids, MI 49501, U.S.A. For information about other Discovery House books, music, videos, or DVDs, contact us at the same address or call 1-800-653-8333. Find us on the Internet at www.dhp.org or send e-mail to books@dhp.org.

ABOUT THE AUTHOR

Russell Fralick is a pastor, writer, outdoorsman, climber, and deer stalker. Aside from these professional titles, he is a husband and father. His diverse roles have given him insight into a relevant, real, and exciting God. He leads a rural congregation in the Lake District, England's largest national park, and preaches and teaches throughout the U.K. He has a special ministry to young people, especially young adults who find his willingness to tackle hard questions refreshing and challenging. Russell has written articles for RBC Ministries, including devotions aimed at military personnel for a special edition of *Our Daily Bread*.

Russell is a qualified mountain leader and rock climbing instructor and takes individuals and groups hiking, canyonning, and rock climbing. He is responsible for managing the deer population on two English estates, and he teaches young people and adults about bushcraft and survival, all within the framework of celebrating God's creation, His provision, and His message of salvation.

Prior to going into ministry, Russell was the managing director of a chemical trading company and later head of marketing in the U.K. for a chemical producer. He is fluent in Mandarin Chinese and has played his trumpet for the Queen.

Russell has been married to Debbi for nearly eighteen years and they have two teenage daughters, Sophie and Hannah. They live in a forest in the hills of the Lake District, along with chickens, ducks, and their two hunting dogs. When he is not engaged in any of the above occupations, Russell can often be found swimming the length of one of the Lake District's many lakes.

Russell sees all of his pursuits as ministry and he lives his life like life should count for something; more than that, he inspires others to do what it takes to find meaning and to live for something great.